Chomsky's Politics

Chomsky's Politics

MILAN RAI

VERSO

First published by Verso 1995
© Milan Rai 1995
All rights reserved

Reprinted 1995, 1996

Verso
UK: 6 Meard Street, London W1V 3HR
USA: 180 Varick Street, New York, NY 10014–4606

Verso is the imprint of New Left Books

ISBN 1 85984 916 4
ISBN 1 85984 011 6 (pbk)

British Library Cataloguing in Publication Data
A catalogue record for this book is available from the British Library

Library of Congress Cataloging-in-Publication Data
Rai, Milan.
Chomsky's politics/Milan Rai.
p.   cm.
Includes bibliographical references and index.
ISBN 1–85984–916–4. — ISBN 1–85984–011–6 (pbk.)
1. Chomsky, Noam – Political and social views.
2. Language and languages – Political aspects.   3. World politics – 1945–   I. Title.
P85.C47R35   1995
327.73—dc20   94–48859
                                                                        CIP

Typeset by Type Study, Scarborough
Printed and bound in Great Britain by
Biddles Ltd, Guildford and King's Lynn

Grateful acknowledgement is made to the following for permission to reprint extracts from the following works by Noam Chomsky.

Black Rose Books: *Language and Politics, Pirates and Emperors* and *Manufacturing Consent: Noam Chomsky and the Media,* edited by Mark Achbar. Reprinted by permission of Black Rose Books, C.P. 1258, Succ. Place du Parc, Montréal, Québec H2W 2R3, Canada.

Common Courage Press: *Chronicles of Dissent.* Reprinted by permission of Common Courage Press, Box 702, Monroe, ME 04951, USA.

Pantheon Books, a division of Random House, Inc: *American Power and the New Mandarins, At War with Asia, The Chomsky Reader, For Reasons of State, Language and Responsibility, Manufacturing Consent, Problems of Knowledge and Freedom* and *Towards a New Cold War.* Reprinted by permission of Pantheon Books, a division of Random House, Inc.

South End Press: *Necessary Illusions* and *Turning the Tide.* Reprinted by permission of South End Press, 116 St Botolph Street, Boston, Mass. 02115, USA.

Contents

Introduction

By any standards, Noam Chomsky is a remarkable figure. As a linguist, Chomsky is recognized as the defining figure in his field. He is also one of the most famous, or notorious, critics of US foreign policy, and is known to have devoted much of his life to dissident politics. This is a very rare mixture of qualities and commitments. The reaction to Chomsky's work has also been mixed, to say the least. His achievements in both fields have won him great acclaim as well as fierce criticism. In a sympathetic profile in 1968, Israel Shenker wrote in the *New York Times*, 'In his twenties, Noam Chomsky revolutionized linguistics. In his thirties, he has been trying to revolutionize society. By his forties – which begin two months from now – there will be few worlds left for him to change.'[1] Shenker was writing during a brief period of cultural opening in the mainstream media. Since then, when they have mentioned Chomsky, the major journals and newspapers in the United States (and across the Atlantic) have been hostile and often vicious. Twenty years after Shenker, Auberon Waugh wrote of Chomsky in the *Independent* newspaper: 'It is plainly right that anyone engaged in such a fatuous area of research should be allowed a hobby. Just as Tom Lehrer took time off from theoretical mathematics to write rude songs, Chomsky writes rude remarks about American society, thereby hoping to change its entire character and course.'[2]

Despite a rearguard action in certain quarters and the ignorant reaction of a few commentators such as Waugh, Chomsky's work in linguistics and philosophy has earned him worldwide recognition and a place in the history of ideas. A standard biographical entry observes that Chomsky 'has been widely accepted as having revolutionized the discipline [of linguistics] in its goals, boundaries, epistemology, theory, and methodology'.[3] When we turn to Chomsky's social criticism, the picture is quite different. The reaction has been described as 'a weird mixture of neglect and abuse' in the major journals.[4] His writings are 'read by nearly everyone with an ounce of intellectual curiosity, yet ignored in the traffic of normal critical debate', the literary critic Jim Merod has noted. Merod adds, 'This duality is startling for its ability to reveal the academic decorum scholarship thrives on, as if even those who admire Chomsky's work are embarrassed by the scope of his observations.'[5] The sharply different responses in the US cultural mainstream to Chomsky's two bodies of work are well captured in a famous passage in the *New York Times*. Paul Robinson writes, 'Judged in terms of the power, range, novelty, and influence of his thought, Noam Chomsky is arguably the most important intellectual alive.'[6] However, Robinson continues, Chomsky is also a 'disturbingly divided' intellectual: 'On the one hand there is a large body of revolutionary and highly technical linguistic scholarship much of it too difficult for anyone but the professional linguist or philosopher, on the other, an equally substantial body of political writings, accessible to any literate person but often maddeningly simple-minded. The "Chomsky problem" is to explain how these two fit together.'[7] Robinson claims that the discrepancy in quality between the two bodies of work is more extreme than for any other major intellectual.

There are two issues here: influence and quality. Chomsky's influence can to some extent be quantified, and the results confirm Robinson's judgement. 'Social science citation counts show Chomsky to be the most influential psychologist of the 20th century – well beyond Sigmund Freud.'[8] Chomsky's work in linguistics has been cited in more academic papers than the work of any other living writer, although citation may not mean approval.[9] Judgements of quality are inevitably more complex, especially comparisons between Chomsky's two areas of concern. Chomsky's own response to this question is to point to the very different reception his political writings receive in the United States compared to other Western societies. For example, consider the reaction to Chomsky's examination in *The Fateful Triangle* of US foreign policy in the Middle East. Barely mentioned in the US press, the book was reviewed in every major journal in Canada, and in many minor journals, including the *Financial Post*, Canada's equivalent of the *Wall Street Journal*. The book was also reviewed in the Canadian equivalents of *Time* and *Newsweek*. Chomsky comments, 'If the judgement is one of quality, then it's striking that the judgement is so different across the border.'[10] Christopher Hitchens investigated the treatment of *The Fateful Triangle* in some depth:

Consider: One of America's best-known Jewish scholars, internationally respected, writes a lengthy, dense, highly documented book about United States policy in the Levant. The book is acidly critical of Israeli policy and of the apparently limitless American self-deception as to its true character. It quotes sources in Hebrew and French as well as in English. It is published at a time when hundreds of United States marines have been killed in Beirut and when the President is wavering in his commitment, which itself threatens to become a major election issue. It is the only book of its scope (we need make no judgement as to depth) to appear in the continental United States. The screens and the headlines are full of approximations and guesses on the subject. Yet, at this unusually fortunate juncture for publication, the following newspapers review it: (1) the *Los Angeles Herald-Examiner*; (2) the *Boston Globe*.[11]

Hitchens adds, 'Many months later, after its foal, the *London Review of Books*, has devoted many respectful columns to the book, and after almost every major newspaper and magazine in England, Canada and Australia has done the same, the *New York Review of Books* publishes a "mixed review".' Note that the Canadian reviews of *The Fateful Triangle* were generally hostile. What is significant is that in Canada, Chomsky's position is regarded as part of the debate, to be taken seriously. In the United States, he is excluded from the discussion completely.

The only exception to the policy of exclusion in the United States, and a temporary one at that, was the *New York Review of Books*, an elite journal which brought Chomsky's political writings to a national audience between 1967 and 1972. In 1972, Chomsky and other dissident writers were shut out.[12] Brian Morton observed in 1988, 'It's strange, isn't it, that [Chomsky has] never been invited to write for the *New York Times* Op-Ed page or its *Book Review*, or for *Harper's*, or the *Atlantic*, or the *Village Voice*.' Morton asked, 'Why is he so isolated?'[13] As the *New Statesman* once commented: 'Since the end of the Vietnam War, American liberal publications have collectively and successfully ensured that one of America's brightest and most interesting left-wing writers is denied a wider audience.'[14] There are a number of possible explanations for this phenomenon. But it would be wrong to accept the question as it is framed by Morton. It would be wrong to assume that a cultural quarantine operated by elite journals such as the *New York Times* and the *Atlantic* by itself signifies 'political isolation'. Chomsky is one of the most sought-after speakers in the United States, apparently unable to accept more than a fraction of the invitations that he receives. His books are selling in larger numbers than ever.[15]

Chomsky may be excluded by the elite journals and mass media, but he is far from being 'isolated'. He describes the amusing experience of being handed a leaflet claiming that even his colleagues on the Left are deserting him, as he was leaving an auditorium in Michigan where he had addressed an audience of over one thousand people, on his way to Detroit to speak to yet another capacity audience.[16]

One of the perennial fascinations of the debate around Chomsky, described by Paul Robinson as the 'Chomsky problem', is the conjunction of Chomsky's work on linguistics and his political ideas. Many have suspected a connection. Geoffrey Sampson, a British academic who has made something of a career out of attacking Chomsky, alleges that Chomsky himself claims that 'the revolutionary political ideals he advocates follow as a natural corollary of the new view of human nature suggested by his academic research on syntactic structure in human language'.[17] Sampson continues, 'Chomsky claims that syntax refutes liberalism, but the claim fails; Chomsky ignores semantics, and semantics strongly supports liberalism.'[18] Sampson does not produce any evidence that these are Chomsky's views. There is a simple reason for this: there is no such evidence. Chomsky has never made any such claims. He once dismissed Sampson's work as 'an extraordinarily silly book that tries to argue that I deduce anarchism from syntax, or some such manic idea'.[19]

It may be worthwhile to untangle some of the issues which Sampson successfully confuses. Chomsky's work on language broke with the prevailing assumptions in the field, with tremendous implications for the study of human intelligence and the conception of 'human nature'. Chomsky argued that rather than being born with a homogeneous, featureless mind which painstakingly builds up knowledge of the rules of language from observations of the environment, human beings are born with a genetically determined capacity to learn, or rather 'acquire', language. This 'mental organ' he termed the 'language faculty'. Chomsky argued that

consideration of the character of the grammar that is acquired, the degenerate quality and narrowly limited extent of the available data, the striking uniformity of the resulting grammars, and their independence of intelligence, motivation and emotional state, over wide ranges of variation, leave little hope that much of the structure of the language can be learned by an organism initially uninformed as to its general character.[20]

Consider a Martian scientist investigating humans who observed that some individual knows both English and modern physics. From his [sic] point of view, there would be little reason to expect, on general grounds, that the learning of physics was an intellectual achievement of an incomparably higher order which required generations of genius, while the normal child discovers the structure of English with no difficulty. Observing this, he would conclude that one system is fitted to the human mind in a way in which the other is not.[21]

This is not to say that the particular grammar of a particular language is genetically transmitted: 'It is the *mechanism* of language acquisition that is innate.'[22]

In this view, the ability to acquire language is part of the genetic inheritance of the species, and therefore part of 'human nature'. Chomsky has been very careful to distinguish between his work on 'human nature' in this sense and his political activities, based as they are on an idea of 'human nature' in the broader sense. His one essay devoted to the possible connections between 'Language and Freedom' ends with these words: 'In these speculative and sketchy remarks there are gaps so vast that one might question what would remain, when metaphor and unsubstantiated guess are removed.'[23] In another passage, also available to Sampson and which he in fact quotes, Chomsky cautions, 'It is, to be sure, a great intellectual leap from observations on the basis of cognitive development to particular conclusions on the laws of our nature and the conditions for their fulfilment.'[24] As Chomsky points out, he has only offered his speculations on the subject in response to questions or, in the case of his essay 'Language and Freedom', to a request. Sampson's bizarre distortions may be due to simple incomprehension, although there are other possibilities.[25]

There is, then, no 'Chomsky problem' in the sense in which Sampson has posed the question, although there are undoubtedly some interesting connections to be drawn between Chomsky's work in psychology and philosophy and his political writings, a topic to which we shall return.

It is no doubt irrational, but, as Charles Glass comments, 'one longs in reading Chomsky to know more about him, what made him the inflexible guardian of the American conscience'.[26] Chomsky is reluctant to discuss his personal life, and for good reason. There can only be a tenuous and ambiguous relationship between the personal experiences and the political commitments of any individual. Chomsky once wrote, 'I am not writing about myself, and these matters don't seem particularly pertinent to the topics I am addressing.'[27] Despite this, Chomsky has occasionally, usually reluctantly, responded to questions about his childhood. His answers give some insight into his early development. Chomsky himself is unwilling to draw any strong conclusions. David Barsamian elicited the following story:

> I remember when I was about six, first grade. There was the standard fat kid everybody made fun of. I remember in this schoolyard he was standing outside the school classroom and a bunch of kids outside were taunting him. One of them brought over his older brother from third grade, a big kid, and we thought he was going to beat him up. I remember going up to stand next to him feeling somebody ought to help him, and I did for a while, then I got scared and ran away. I was very much ashamed of it. I felt, I'll never do that again. That's a feeling that's stuck with me: You should stick with the underdog ... I think everybody must have personal experiences of this kind that sort of stick with you and colour your choices later on.[28]

Chomsky comments that it 'was a personal thing for me, I don't know why it should interest anyone else'. Such stories are of very limited significance in understanding the development of a particular person. Chomsky might have drawn any number of conclusions from such a confrontation. He might have decided that it would be wiser in future to align himself with power rather than risk the fate of the underdog. What is, I think, interesting is the characteristic honesty with which Chomsky describes his role in the affair.

Rather more significant than such anecdotes is the cultural milieu within which Chomsky grew up and developed his political understanding. This is particularly so as, by his own account, Chomsky's political ideas have remained essentially the same since the age of twelve. Many have wondered how Chomsky manages to perceive his own culture from such a detached point of view. He suggests that part of the reason may be that 'in a certain sense, I grew up in an alien culture, in the Jewish-Zionist cultural tradition, in an immigrant community in a sense, though of course others reacted to the same conditions quite differently'.[29] Chomsky's parents had come to the United States from Eastern Europe. William Chomsky fled from Russia in 1913 to escape conscription into the Czarist army.[30] Elsie Simonofsky was already in the United States, her family having left Lithuania when she was a year old.[31] The Eastern European Jewish community was, in Chomsky's view, a 'very backward society' with a deeply authoritarian strain running through it:

You weren't supposed to read, to know anything, no books. This *Fiddler on the Roof* version has not very much to do with it. . . . In the European Jewish ghettos I don't think they had any history or geography books until the nineteenth century, because the Bible didn't say it so it wasn't true. There was no America. The Bible didn't say anything about America.

In this traditional society, Chomsky's father was an unusual figure, sufficiently independent to learn Hebrew and even some Russian. Self-taught, he became a noted scholar.[32]

Born on 7 December 1928 in Philadelphia, Pennsylvania, Chomsky was a child of the Depression: 'Some of my earliest memories, which are very vivid, are of people selling rags at our door, of violent police strikebreaking, and other Depression scenes.'[33] Chomsky recalled one of these scenes, a textile workers' strike, in an interview with David Barsamian:

It was mostly women, and they were getting pretty brutally beaten up by the cops. I could see that much. Some of them were tearing off their clothes. I didn't understand that. The idea was to try to cut back the violence. It made quite an impression. I can't claim that I understood what was happening, but I sort of got the general idea. What I didn't understand was explained to me. Also this was not that far out of the general understanding. My family had plenty of unemployed workers and union activists and political activists and so on. So you knew what a picket line was and what it meant for the forces of the employers to come in there swinging clubs and breaking it up.[34]

Between the ages of two and twelve, Chomsky was sent to an experimental progressive school, Oak Lane Country Day School, connected with the local university, which he describes as a 'bit of personal good fortune'. The school was 'Deweyan, not libertarian in [an anarchist] sense, but [it] did encourage independent thought and self-realization in the best sense. It wasn't till I entered a city high school, for example, that I discovered, to my surprise, that I was a good student. It was assumed in my earlier school experience that everyone was.'[35] At Oak Lane, there was 'no sense of competition, no ranking of students', and there was 'a tremendous premium on individual creativity, not in the sense of slapping paints on paper, but doing the kind of work and thinking that you were interested in'. 'It was a lively atmosphere and the sense was that everybody was doing something important'; 'I can remember a lot about elementary school, the work I did, what I studied and so on. I remember virtually nothing about high school. It's almost an absolute blank in my memory apart from the emotional tone, which was quite negative.'[36] In contrast to his own experiences, Chomsky notes that his own children 'as far back as the second grade knew who was "smart" and who was "dumb," who was high-tracked and who was low-tracked. This was a big issue.'[37] Chomsky's first political article was an editorial in the school newspaper about the fall of Barcelona 'a few weeks after my tenth birthday'.[38] 'The Spanish Civil War, of course, was a major experience from childhood which stuck.'

According to Chomsky, his political views, while now 'more sophisticated', have not changed fundamentally since he was twelve. 'I can't really say how I came to be influenced by anarchist ideas; I can't remember a time when I was not so influenced.'[39] While his parents were in the political mainstream, both 'normal Roosevelt Democrats',[40] Chomsky's aunts and uncles were often more radical – members of the Communist Party or part of the anti-Bolshevik Left. Chomsky says of the Communist Party, 'by the time I was 12 or 13 I had worked out of that phase'.[41] 'I was just a little too young to have ever faced the temptation of being a committed Leninist, so I never had a faith to renounce, or any feeling of guilt or betrayal. I was always on the side of the losers – the Spanish anarchists, for example.'[42] Chomsky grew up in what he describes as a 'very lively intellectual culture', dominated by the radical Jewish intelligentsia of New York. It was a

> working-class culture with working-class values, solidarity, socialist values, etc. Within that it varied from communist party to radical semi-anarchist critique of Bolshevism. That whole range was there. That was not untypical. But that was only a part of it. People were having intensive debates about Stekel's version of Freudian theory, a lot of discussions about literature and music, what did you think of the latest Budapest String Quartet concert, or Schnabel's version of a Beethoven sonata vs. somebody else's version.[43]

Chomsky has often declared that it was a much more lively intellectual culture than he later found in such elite institutions as Harvard and the Massachusetts Institute of Technology (MIT).

As he has often testified, the most significant figure of Chomsky's youth was his aunt's husband, who did not finish fourth grade at school, became a 'street person', and then, because of a disability, was granted a licence to run a newsstand in New York. His uncle had had a chequered political career: 'First he was a follower of Trotsky, then an anti-Trotskyite', according to Chomsky. 'He also taught himself so much of Freud he wound up as a lay psychoanalyst with a penthouse apartment.'[44] The newsstand functioned as a meeting point for émigrés and dissidents, and attending late-night discussions was one of the highlights of Chomsky's youth. 'That's where I got my political education.'[45] 'The great moments of my life in those years were when I could work at the newsstand at night and listen to all this.'[46] 'They were the most lively intellectuals I've ever met. On the other hand, there are plenty of people who teach in elite universities whose work could be done by a well-trained clerk.'[47]

While a high school student in the early 1940s, Chomsky 'used to spend some time hanging around the Fourth Avenue second-hand bookstores in New York where there were some anarchist offices'.[48] Chomsky mentions the office of *Freie Arbeiter Stimme*, the Jewish anarchist newspaper, in particular. 'I would hang around left-wing bookshops and the offices of offbeat groups and periodicals, talking to people – often very perceptive and interesting people who were thinking hard about the problems of social change – and seeing what I could pick up.'[49] 'I was connected loosely with various types of groups, searching for something that was within the Marxist or at least revolutionary tradition, but which did not have the elitist aspects which seemed to me then and seem to me today to be disfiguring and destructive.'[50] Chomsky never formally joined any of these groups. 'Partly it was that I am not much of a "joiner", I guess. Furthermore, every organization that I knew of, on the left at least, was Leninist, either Stalinist or Trotskyite.' Chomsky saw no significant differences between the Trotskyites and the Stalinists, except that the Trotskyites had lost. The differences that did exist were, he felt, 'exaggerated'; 'That's what I felt at the time, and I still feel that essentially.'[51]

Chomsky was aware of anti-Semitism from an early age. 'We happened to be the only Jewish family in a largely German and Irish-Catholic neighborhood which was passionately anti-Semitic and actually rather pro-Nazi in fact.' During the war, the Jewish children sometimes had to have police escorts on their way to Hebrew school. 'The police would hang around the school to keep it from being broken into. When you made it to the subway you were on your own.'[52] 'There were certain paths I could take to walk to the store without getting beaten up. It was the late 1930s and the area was openly pro-Nazi.' 'It's not like living under Hitler, but it's a very unpleasant thing, there was a really rabid anti-Semitism in that neighborhood where I grew up as a kid.'[53] Despite his anti-fascist beliefs, Chomsky remembers being 'appalled by the treatment of German POWs. For some reason, there were some in a camp right next to my high school, and it was considered the red-blooded "thing to do" to taunt them across the barbed wire. That struck me as a disgrace at the time, though I was more of a committed anti-Nazi than the kids engaging in this sport. I recall bitter arguments about it.'[54]

During the Second World War, Chomsky was untouched by the war fever. 'I was rather skeptical about the Second World War. I didn't know anybody who shared that skepticism, literally not a single person.' The end of the war saw him feeling even more alienated. 'I remember on the day of the Hiroshima bombing, for example, I remember that I literally couldn't talk to anybody. There was nobody. I just walked off by myself. I was at a summer camp at the time, and I walked off into the woods and stayed alone for a couple of hours when I heard about it. I could never talk to anyone about it and never understood anyone's reaction. I felt completely isolated.' Chomsky reflects, 'Ever since I had any political awareness, I've felt either alone or part of a tiny minority.'[55] 'I always felt completely out of tune with almost everything around me.'[56]

This feeling of isolation extended even to one of Chomsky's passions, Zionism, the main political concern of his youth. He had been raised as a 'practicing Jewish atheist', 'not as much of a contradiction as it sounds'.[57] William and Elsie Chomsky were Hebrew teachers, and deeply involved in the cultural Zionism of Ahad Ha'am. 'Their life was basically Jewish. Hebrew scholarship, Hebrew teaching, Jewish life, etc.'[58] They were very involved in the revival of Hebrew, and Chomsky grew up 'deeply immersed' in these issues. He remarks that he 'probably did more reading in that area than any other' until he was fifteen or sixteen.[59] 'Then I was very much interested in a Jewish organization which was opposed to the Jewish state in Palestine and worked for Arab–Jewish cooperation on a socialist basis.'[60] Chomsky was 'enormously attracted, emotionally and intellectually', by what he saw as 'a dramatic effort to create, out of the wreckage of European civilization, some form of libertarian socialism in the Middle East'.[61] He was 'strongly opposed to the idea of a Jewish state back in 1947–48', in part, because he felt sure that the 'socialist institutions of the Yishuv – the pre-state Jewish settlement in Palestine' – would not survive the state system. Integration into a system of state management would destroy the aspects of the Yishuv that he found most attractive.[62] 'As I mentioned, I never joined any organized group because of sharp disagreement and skepticism about them, though emotionally I was drawn to such youth groups as Hashomer Hartzair, which in those days professed a commitment to socialist binationalism in Palestine and kibbutz values, as well as the Hebraic culture that I was very much part of.'[63] 'I was influenced by the kibbutz movement, and in fact lived for a while on a kibbutz and almost stayed on. I think there is much of value in the kibbutz experience, but we must also not forget (as I have sometimes tended to do) that the historical particularity of the kibbutz movement in Israel embodies many serious flaws, sometimes crimes.'[64]

Chomsky entered the University of Pennsylvania 'with a good deal of enthusiasm and expectations that all sorts of fascinating prospects would open up, but these did not survive long, except in a few cases. . . . At the end of two years, I was planning to drop out to pursue my own interests, which were then largely political.'[65] Through his interest in Arab–Jewish cooperation in Palestine, Chomsky met Zellig Harris, 'a really extraordinary person who had a great influence on many young people in those days. He had a coherent understanding of this whole range of issues, which I lacked, and I was immensely attracted by it, and by him personally as well, also by others who I met through him.'[66] Harris, who had 'a kind of semianarchist strain to his thought',[67] happened to be one of the leading figures in modern linguistics, teaching at the University of Pennsylvania. At the time Chomsky was, by his own account, 'really a kind of college dropout, having no interest in college at all because my interest in a particular subject was generally killed as soon as I took a course in it. And that includes psychology, incidentally.' Nevertheless, Chomsky began to take Harris's graduate courses 'just to have something to do'. Gradually, 'I got interested in the field and sort of put it into the center of my concerns.'[68] This was not Chomsky's first encounter with linguistics. His father had produced an edition of the thirteenth-century work *David Kimhi's Hebrew Grammar*, and Chomsky had proof-read this for his father at a very early age.

Under Harris's influence, Chomsky also began to take graduate courses in philosophy and mathematics, 'fields in which I had no background at all, but which I found fascinating, in part, no doubt, thanks to unusually stimulating teachers. I suppose Harris had in mind to influence me to return to college, though I don't recall talking about it particularly, and it all seemed to happen without much planning. Anyway, it worked.'[69] 'So the problem in my case was not how the linguist became a radical, but rather the opposite. It was how the radical student became the linguist sort of by accident.'[70]

Although Chomsky did obtain a degree, he only went through the first two years of college; after that he 'did not really attend college in the normal manner'.[71]

11

The linguistics department consisted of a small number of graduate students, and, in Harris' close circle, a very small group who shared political and other interests apart from linguistics, and was quite alienated from the general college atmosphere. In fact, our 'classes' were generally held either in the Horn & Hardart restaurant across the street or in Harris' apartment in Princeton or New York, all-day sessions that ranged widely over quite a variety of topics and were intellectually exciting as well as personally very meaningful experiences. I had almost no contact with the university, apart from these connections ... and received [highly unconventional] B.A. and M.A. degrees.[72]

His master's thesis was based on an undergraduate thesis on 'Morphophonemics of Modern Hebrew', a precursor of Chomsky's later work on generative grammar. During his time at university Chomsky lived at home and worked part-time at Mikve Israel School 'teaching Hebrew school afternoons and Sundays, sometimes evenings as well'.[73]

During 1950, Chomsky was an assistant instructor of linguistics at Pennsylvania University, and the following year was selected for the prestigious Society of Fellows at Harvard, where he stayed until 1955. The Fellow's stipend for the first time freed Chomsky to concentrate on linguistics without having to work to support himself. 'With the resources of Harvard available and no formal requirements, it was a wonderful opportunity.'[74] According to an account in the *Listener*, 'It is said that several attempts to obtain a permanent position for him at Harvard were vetoed by the university administration because of his family's politics.'[75] Chomsky technically received his doctorate from Pennsylvania University in 1955, by submitting a chapter of a book that he was then working on (*The Logical Structure of Linguistic Theory*), but he had had no contact with the university since 1951, apart from with Harris and Nelson Goodman. Chomsky's request to Pennsylvania for a PhD was made, he revealed in 1989, in order to delay being drafted for the Korean War. Curiously, he was never subsequently contacted by the draft board, a fact he ascribes to military sexism. At that time, 'strange names' were taken to be women's names, and Chomsky suspects that the forces failed to pursue him because he was called 'Avram Noam Chomsky'; 'in fact, on my birth certificate, my two names are crossed off in a clerk's hand, and "Noam" is changed to "Naomi" and "Avram" is changed to "Avrane".'[76]

'So my college experience was unusual to say the least.'[77] So were his qualifications. 'I didn't have any real professional credentials in the field. I'm the first to admit that. And, therefore, I ended up in an electronics laboratory ... largely because there were no vested

12

interests there and the director, Jerome Wiesner, was willing to take a chance on some odd ideas that looked as if they might be intriguing.'[78] According to Dixon, 'For a while he was forced to teach German at the Massachusetts Institute of Technology.'[79] For Chomsky, 'The research climate at MIT was close to ideal. I could not possibly have obtained a position in linguistics anywhere – I really was not professionally qualified by the standards of the field.'[80]

It was during 1953 that Chomsky had visited a Buberite kibbutz in Israel for six weeks, 'planning to come back, maybe to stay, in a few years',[81] as his wife very much wanted to do at the time.[82] Chomsky had married Carol Schatz on 24 December 1949. She went back to the kibbutz for a longer stay in 1955, but 'For one reason or another, without any particular conscious decision at any point, we never did return.'[83] Chomsky had obtained his position at MIT, and, once there, he became engrossed in developing the ideas which have since revolutionized the study of linguistics.

After many frustrating efforts to introduce his ideas to the linguistics community, his book *Syntactic Structures* was published in Holland in 1957, and an influential review helped to break Chomsky's isolation. Together with his colleagues, Chomsky began developing a graduate programme, which they were able to do largely because, 'in a sense, MIT was outside the American university system. There were no large departments of humanities or the related social sciences at MIT. Consequently, we could build up a linguistics department without coming up against problems of rivalry and academic bureaucracy.'[84] 'Within a few years, a rather new field had emerged.'[85]

Chomsky notes, 'I withdrew during the fifties from political involvements, though of course I retained my intellectual interest. I signed petitions, over the Rosenberg case, for instance, and went on occasional demonstrations but it did not amount to much.'[86] 'I was not an activist. I was, until the early 1960s, working in my own garden, basically, doing the kind of work I liked, intellectually exciting, rewarding, satisfying, you make progress. I would have been very happy to stick to it. It would have been from a narrow personal point of view much better for me in every imaginable respect.'[87] In the 1960s, Chomsky became more active. 'Like most people, I had something to do with the civil rights movement. But in retrospect I think I was very slow in getting involved. It was only when the Vietnam war began escalating that I began to take any really active political role. Much to [sic] late, I am afraid.'[88] There is a brief mention of Chomsky's experiences in the civil rights movement in his book *Radical Priorities*. In February 1969, he said,

13

everyone who is involved (I can tell you stories from my minimal involvement) can give examples of cases in which the federal authorities, far from using this power [to protect people's civil rights], stood by and took notes while people were being beaten and, on occasion, murdered. I myself have seen cases where federal marshals threw protestors fleeing from the police into the hands of state policemen who then carried them off to what can only be called concentration camps. Others who are more deeply involved can speak about it in much greater detail.[89]

Chomsky's feelings about his late involvement in the opposition to the Vietnam War were spelled out in his introduction to the first collection of his political writings. He explained that because of the book's critical tone, 'I want to make it clear at the outset that if any note of self-righteousness creeps in, it is unintended and, more important, unjustified. No one who involved himself in anti-war activities as late as 1965, as I did, has any reason for pride or satisfaction. This opposition was ten or fifteen years too late. This is one lesson we should have learned from the tragedy of Vietnam.'[90] He added, 'As for those of us who stood by in silence and apathy as this catastrophe slowly took shape over the past dozen years, on what page of history do we find our proper place? Only the most insensible can escape these questions.'[91]

I faced a serious and uncomfortable decision about this in 1964 – much too late, I think. I was deeply immersed in the work I was doing. It was intellectually exciting, and all sorts of fascinating avenues of research were opening up. Furthermore, I was pretty well settled then into a comfortable academic life, with very satisfying work, security, young kids growing up, everything that one could ask from a personal standpoint [sic]. The question I had to face was whether to become actively engaged in protest against the war, that is, engaged beyond signing petitions, sending money, and other peripheral contributions. I knew very well that once I set forth along that path, there would be no end. For better or worse, that is what I decided to do, with considerable reluctance. In those days, protest against the war meant speaking several nights a week at a church to an audience of half a dozen people, mostly bored or hostile, or at someone's home where a few people might be gathered, or at a meeting at a college that included the topics of Vietnam, Iran, Central America, and nuclear arms, in the hope that maybe the participants would outnumber the organizers. Soon after, it meant participation in demonstrations, lobbying, organizing resistance, civil disobedience and arrests, endless speaking and travel, and the expected concomitants: threats of a fairly serious nature that were quite real by the late 1960s, which I don't particularly want to enter into, and so on.[92]

Chomsky's decision was precipitated in part at least by his responsibilities as a teacher. He said in 1968, 'I don't think it's going to be possible to restrict myself to professional work. How can I, when my students are refusing military service? How can any professor be indifferent when his students are faced with prison?'[93] By 1968, Chomsky was well established as one of the leading critics of the US war effort and of US foreign policy in general. A year later, his first book of political writings was published.

A review of *American Power and the New Mandarins* in the *New Republic* in 1969 opened with Martin Duberman's confession that he had anticipated 'little surprise' in Chomsky's first collection of political essays. 'I could not have been more wrong,' he continued. 'Even those essays which might be familiar, turn out, on a second reading and in juxtaposition with the others, to yield unusual rewards.'[94] Robert Sklar, writing in the *Nation*, agreed:

> Noam Chomsky's historical and political essays in collected form make a different impact from when they were read singly in the columns of magazines ... brought together, they are perhaps inevitably both more ambitious and more limited – more depressing in that concentrated evidence of governmental and intellectual perfidy, and more exhilarating, in the clarity and unity of their focus on the task ahead.[95]

One of the effects of collecting Chomsky's essays on some readers is apparently an increased sense of difficulty in understanding and digesting his work. There are real difficulties for the reader first encountering Chomsky's political writings; they are both intellectually and morally demanding. At the simplest level, Chomsky's books are packed with information. A sympathetic reviewer complained of *American Power and the New Mandarins* that

> One small trouble with the book is Chomsky's tendency to tackle everything at once within a single essay: not only the war, the intellectuals, and the social problem of scientists, but also the parallels with the elitism of the Bolsheviks (showing Old Left homework well done), and long diversions on the conduct of the British government during the Spanish Civil War. All that diminishes the force of the main attack.[96]

The essay Wilks is referring to, 'Objectivity and Liberal Scholarship', Duberman describes as 'at once the most rewarding, and the least readable in the collection'.[97] This combination of reward and difficulty is perhaps characteristic of Chomsky's work. Chomsky takes giant strides in his argument, perhaps out of a wish not to, in his view, insult the intelligence of his readers. He generally deploys large masses of information which can often obscure the strand of argument around which the blocks of data are organized. Following the thread of Chomsky's arguments can require a very high degree of concentration, certainly much higher than in the general run of commentary. That much of the information he presents is shocking and excites scepticism compounds the problem.

Chomsky's work is intellectually demanding on another level. As we shall see, his work is directed at precisely those assumptions and beliefs that are so deeply held that they have become as invisible as the air we breathe. He comments, 'An independent mind must seek to separate itself from official doctrine, and from the criticism advanced by its alleged opponents; not just from the assertions of the propaganda system, but from its tacit presuppositions as well, expressed by critic and defender. This is a far more difficult task.'[98] It is because Chomsky's political writings have to a very large degree the 'power to free our minds from old perspectives'[99] that his work is in such demand. The fact that his interpretation of events is based on a political and moral perspective which is radically different from the political mainstream and from many on the Left means that one has difficulty in adapting to this new perspective.

Chomsky's work is marked by a strain of irony which can also be shocking and sometimes confusing. For example, during the Vietnam War, the US economist Richard Lindholm commented on the failure of economic development in South Vietnam in the following terms: 'The fact that a large portion of the Vietnamese imports financed with American aid are either consumer goods or raw materials used rather directly to meet consumer demands is an indication that the Vietnamese people desire these goods, for they have shown their desire by their willingness to use their piastres to purchase them.' Chomsky remarked bitingly,

> In short, the Vietnamese *people* desire Buicks and air conditioners, rather than sugar-refining equipment or road-building machinery, as they have shown by their behaviour in a free market.... Of course, there are also those two-legged beasts of burden that one stumbles on in the countryside, but as any graduate student of political science can explain, they are not part of a responsible modernizing elite, and therefore have only a superficial biological resemblance to the human race.[100]

Chomsky told the *Boston Globe* in 1989, 'My natural style is irony. Irony is a way to deflate pomposity. Irony, if it is spontaneous, is a way of revealing things. It's hard to be pretentious in the face of irony. I like to mock the pretence of benevolence and the pretence of profundity.'[101]

The density of information, the horrifying nature of much of that information, the recurrent use of irony and Chomsky's 'unsettling' perspective fuse to create an intellectually and morally challenging atmosphere. They also create some difficulties for readers. Chomsky has been much criticized for his prose. Robert Sklar, in one of the gentler criticisms, described Chomsky's style as 'rarely felicitous'.[102] I am not sure this is completely justified. The major difficulty in reading Chomsky, in my opinion, arises from the difficulty most people find in digesting his ideas. However, apart from this, and problems caused by his use of irony, there are sometimes difficulties caused by Chomsky's style and the way he organizes his material. Some of the complexity of his work may derive from his working habits: 'Most of the time I work directly at the typewriter. You know, I don't work it out and then write it up, but I sort of work it into the first draft. Even in my technical work I do that.'[103] Furthermore, he told an interviewer, 'I'm very lucky. I'm able to work in 20-minute spurts. I can turn my attention from one topic to another without any start-up time. I almost never work from an outline or follow a plan. The books simply grow by accretion.'[104] Another factor in Chomsky's complex prose style and the sometimes labyrinthine structures of his work may be the residual influence of his cultural heritage. He observes, 'My idea of the ideal text is still the Talmud. I love the idea of parallel texts, with long, discursive footnotes and marginal commentary, texts commenting on texts.'[105] This seems like a perfect description of many of Chomsky's essays, with their layers of analysis and what amounts to marginal commentary built into the fabric of the main passage and placed in footnotes.

Chomsky once remarked, in connection with modern literature, that sometimes a great writer may use such economy of means that the reader will be forced to determine the meaning for herself on the basis of her own intellectual ability: 'I think that one of the major techniques of writers who may seem abstruse or obscure is to force the reader to become a kind of creator.'[106] I doubt that Chomsky wishes to appear obscure,[107] and he certainly would deny any pretensions to being a 'great writer'. Nevertheless, I think it is true that Chomsky's political writings do force the reader to become 'a kind of creator'.

Incidentally, Chomsky is not entirely happy with the widespread use of his interviews and talks as educational tools. He wrote to Mark Achbar questioning the ability of transcriptions of the spoken word to clarify issues: 'The more considered and careful versions that reach print in the normal course of affairs are far preferable.'[108] Friends of Chomsky have often suggested that he put his ideas across in a simplified and concise form.[109] He notes that 'if you're constrained to producing two sentences between commercials, or 700 words in an op-ed piece, you can do nothing but express conventional thoughts'. Conventional thoughts do not require arguments or evidence to support them. 'If you try to express something that's somewhat unconventional, people will rightly ask why you're saying that.... If I refer to the United States' invasion of South Vietnam, people will ask, "What are you talking about? I never heard of that." And they're right.... Then you have to explain. You have to given some background.' Chomsky remarks, 'I could say what I think in three sentences, too, it would just sound as if it was off the wall, because there's no basis laid for it.'[110] According to Chomsky, it is this need to document every statement he makes that results in his turgid prose style.[111]

The chapters that follow are an attempt to provide a critical introduction to the string of books and articles which have followed Chomsky's decision to become engaged beyond signing petitions and other peripheral contributions.[112] I should make it clear that nothing that follows should be taken, or is intended, as a summary or an assessment of Chomsky's political work as a whole. Delivering the first Bertrand Russell Memorial Lecture in 1971, Chomsky said of Russell, 'I would not presume to assess or even to try to record his achievements in interpreting or changing the world. To several generations, mine among them, Russell has been an inspiring figure, in the problems he posed and the causes he championed, in his insights as well as what is left unfinished.'[113] I have borne these words very much in mind.

1

The Propaganda Model

Noam Chomsky's career as a political commentator has been dogged by controversy and confusion. This is understandable. It is only natural that there should be some turbulence in the wake of novel and disturbing ideas. Jim Peck, a veteran US radical, observes, 'To confront a mind that radically alters our perception of the world is one of life's most unsettling and yet liberating experiences.' He adds, 'In all American history, no one's writings are more unsettling than Noam Chomsky's.'[1] Chomsky's writings are all the more unsettling for their ability to defy easy pigeon-holing. He is, as the conservative columnist Joseph Sobran comments, 'a man without a sect'. Sobran observes that Chomsky has 'a deeply original view of the way the world works', and at the same time, 'a kind of innocence', which is reflected in his gentle, rational manner, 'so different from the inflammatory quotations his enemies manage to cull from his writings'. Chomsky's 'innocence', writes Sobran, 'comes of his refusal to join any of the major sects of political opinion – what Orwell called "the smelly little orthodoxies"'. This kind of innocence is the opposite of naïvety, Sobran suggests: 'The naïve man [sic] believes everything he hears. The innocent man believes everything he sees.' For Sobran, Chomsky remains 'the most interesting phenomenon of the '60s', whose 'austere integrity commands respect'.[2]

Chomsky's work has given rise to much controversy. In addition to the normal disagreements and misunderstandings, there has also been a stream of misrepresentation and vilification of his views. It is this tide of denunciation which has dominated mainstream discussion of Chomsky's work, to the extent that in the 'respectable' literature, it is difficult to find serious attempts to deal with his arguments. In such a situation those who wish to understand (or to represent) Chomsky's political ideas should proceed with some caution. There are, however, many incentives for proceeding and exploring the work of this extraordinary critic and activist. Chomsky is widely recognized as one of the most powerful minds of our time, and this is reflected, I think, in his political no less than in his professional writings.

Whether in the end one agrees with him or not, struggling to understand the way in which Chomsky sees the world is itself an enlarging experience. Sobran comments,

> Education is largely a matter of internalizing as many voices as possible. Being able to hold an internal conversation is more important than simply taking sides. And when someone as original as Chomsky comes along, he deserves to be included in your inner conversation, whether or not you wind up in full agreement with him.... At the very least, you'll encounter a man with an almost disturbingly deep sense of intellectual honour.[3]

The first step in understanding Chomsky's political writings lies in understanding the two poles around which the bulk of his work revolves. To use the title of one of his books, these twin concerns are 'power' and 'ideology'. Chomsky is perhaps best known as a critic of US foreign policy – the exercise of US power abroad. However, he is equally concerned with the domestic moral and intellectual culture of the United States, and the narrow set of beliefs which, in his view, govern the thinking of much of the population. Chomsky argues that this system of ideas, or 'ideology', creates a social framework which permits and facilitates the illegitimate use of US power abroad. The successful indoctrination of much of the US population in violent anti-communism, for example, was a major factor in the US assault on Vietnam, by inducing popular apathy and at times even enthusiasm for the use of force. Another ideological underpinning of the war effort was the carefully cultivated idea that the United States, alone among world powers, should be permitted to use force unilaterally and without regard to law, in pursuit of its objectives. Anti-communism may now be a dying force, but belief in the United States' uniqueness and benevolence appears to be an enduring feature of the cultural scene, and not only in the United States.

Given the interlocking nature of these two social spheres, it is only natural that Chomsky has constructed a cultural critique in parallel with his critique of US foreign policy. He is constantly shuttling between an analysis of the ideology of mainstream intellectuals and often detailed studies of the circumstances surrounding particular acts of US foreign policy. The juxtaposition of these two kinds of analysis, and the speed of transition between them, can pose difficulties for readers. The difficulty is increased by the startling nature of the facts put forward, the charges made and by the extremely compressed fashion in which Chomsky presents his material. For the sceptical reader, constantly referring to Chomsky's detailed footnotes, and trying to digest new information and untangle puzzling analogies, it can become extremely difficult to follow Chomsky's argument. The fact that there are generally at least two lines of argument, addressing questions of culture in parallel with questions of policy, tends to make the task even more challenging. Chomsky often subordinates the story of state crimes to his analysis of media behaviour, which can be difficult to follow. It can sometimes seem as if Chomsky is doing little more than knitting together a mass of fascinating but unrelated insights and facts about US policy. If nothing else, learning to follow Chomsky's arguments develops one's mental agility.

Of the two areas of major concern, it could be argued that Chomsky's writings on US culture are more significant than his exposure of particular US policies in Vietnam or Central America. It seems plausible without detailed investigation that the actions of any state will be constrained to some extent by the attitudes and values of its citizens. If so, the moral level of a society in some sense generates or constrains the moral level of state policy. Whether or not Chomsky's work on ideology is in any useful sense 'primary', it is this area of his political writings that we shall examine first.

The conventional picture of the Western mass media, in the United States in particular, is one of independence, devotion to the truth and service to the public. The press is seen as a countervailing power, restraining the government by exposing the failings and misdemeanours of officials and politicians. Judge Gurfein, deciding in favour of press freedom during the Pentagon Papers case in the 1970s,[4] declared that while the United States had 'a cantankerous press, an obstinate press, a ubiquitous press', this troublesome crew 'must be suffered by those in authority in order to preserve the even greater values of freedom of expression and the right of the people to know'. Anthony Lewis, a well-known liberal commentator, responded to the Gurfein decision by observing that while the media had not always been as independent, vigilant and defiant of authority as they had become, in the Vietnam and Watergate eras they learned to exercise 'the power to root about in our national life, exposing what they deem right for exposure', without regard to external pressures or the demands of state or private power. Lewis cited Supreme Court Justice Powell, who had argued that as 'no individual can obtain for himself [sic] the information needed for the intelligent discharge of his political responsibilities ... the press performs a crucial function in effecting the societal purpose of the First Amendment', by enabling the public to assert meaningful control over the political process.[5]

Chomsky responds to such claims with scepticism. He notes that the debate in respectable circles is whether the media have gone too far and now endanger the fabric of democracy with their challenges. There are those who ask, 'Must free institutions be overthrown because of the very freedom they sustain?'[6] Others argue that such risks must be taken to preserve the freedom of the press. It is accepted on both sides that the mass media are indeed independent and defiant. It is this common assumption which Chomsky seeks to challenge. Chomsky and his colleagues have argued that the mass media in the United States, far from being defiant of ruling circles, are in fact supportive and compliant towards those who hold power. Chomsky's presentation of this argument has varied somewhat over the years, but the core elements of his analysis have remained constant. Chomsky and his co-author Edward Herman developed what was initially described as a 'general theory of the Free Press',[7] and then grew into a 'Propaganda Model' of the mass media, presented in its final form in *Manufacturing Consent*, written primarily by Herman.[8]

According to the Propaganda Model, the media do indeed serve a 'societal purpose', but one quite different from that imagined by Justice Powell: 'It is the societal purpose served by state education as conceived by James Mill in the early days of the establishment of this system: to "train the minds of the people to a virtuous attachment to their government," and to the arrangements of the social, economic, and political order more generally.'[9] It is the societal purpose of 'protecting privilege from the threat of public understanding and participation'.[10] In other words, the purpose of the media is to cultivate public stupidity and conformity, in order to protect the powerful from interference by the lower orders. This is an 'unsettling' interpretation of the media, no doubt, but argument and evidence are offered in support, and there is a case to answer.

One interesting feature of the Propaganda Model is that it is not part of the debate over the media. There are no reasons, a priori, why the Propaganda Model should not be discussed. There are, Chomsky suggests, three good reasons why the model should be part of the debate. In the first place, elite intellectuals have actually advocated that the media take up a propaganda function. For example, the US liberal, Walter Lippmann, welcomed the 'revolution' in 'the practice of democracy' in the early years of the century, as the 'manufacture of consent' became 'a self-conscious art and a regular organ of popular government'. According to Lippmann, 'the common interests very largely elude public opinion entirely, and can be managed only by a specialized class whose personal interests reach beyond the locality'. The public should remain merely 'interested spectators of action'.[11] Chomsky's name has now become associated with the phrase 'manufacturing consent' – it is interesting to note that he adopted it from Lippmann.[12]

A second reason why the Propaganda Model might be expected to be part of the debate about the media is that it is intuitively plausible: 'If you simply look at the institutional structures of the media and the pressures that act on them and so on and so forth, you would tend on relatively uncontroversial assumptions to expect that the media would serve this function.'[13] Media corporations are still corporations. It would be surprising if they worked to undermine corporate interests.

Finally, Chomsky points out, there is considerable public support for the Propaganda Model view of the media. In 1981, a poll for the *Washington Post* found that the complaints aired by the public were at variance with complaints repeatedly voiced by what was described as 'the growing corps of professional media critics'. Forty per cent of those polled, the largest group, felt that the media were 'not critical enough of the government'.[14] A Gallup poll carried out for the *New York Times* in 1986 also found that 53 per cent of respondents considered the press to be too often 'influenced by powerful people and organizations', including the federal government, big business, trade unions and the military.[15]

'Well, from those three observations, elite advocacy, prior plausibility and kind of general acceptance of the view, you would draw one conclusion at least,' Chomsky argues. 'You would draw the conclusion that the Propaganda Model ought to be part of the debate, part of the discussion over how the media functions.'[16] The fact that it is not part of the debate is revealing.

These are side issues, to some extent. The crucial issue must be 'descriptive adequacy': to what extent is the Propaganda Model an accurate description of social reality? According to Chomsky, 'There are, by now, thousands of pages of documentation supporting the conclusions of the propaganda model. By the standards of the social sciences, it is very well confirmed and its predictions are often considerably surpassed. If there is a serious challenge to this conclusion, I am unaware of it.'[17] He goes further: 'I would hazard a guess that it is one of the best-confirmed theories in the social sciences.'[18]

This confirmation has been provided by dozens of different tests, all of which seem to have validated the proposal that the media systematically distort the news in favour of ruling elites. Chomsky employs three main techniques to test the model. The strongest possible test is to select those cases put forward as examples of the independence of the media, and to see if the Propaganda Model holds up. The results of this kind of test could not be dismissed on the grounds that the example was an aberration. Another test is to study paired examples of historical events, and to see if disparities in media behaviour can be found. This is Chomsky's most common method of analysis. A third approach to testing the model, and the first actually used by Chomsky, is to explore 'the range of permitted opinion' on important topics: establishing the boundaries of acceptable discourse in the mainstream media. In practice it is difficult to separate the different kinds of approach. Chomsky intermingles these techniques seamlessly in his writings.

In the case of the Watergate affair, probably the strongest test of the Propaganda Model, Chomsky uses paired examples to test the conventional interpretation of the scandal. The Watergate affair is seen throughout the world as a high point in investigative journalism, demonstrating the power of the independent press to challenge the political establishment, even to depose a president. Chomsky's interpretation is quite different. The major scandal of Watergate, as portrayed in the mainstream press, was that the Nixon administration sent a band of petty criminals to break into the Democratic Party headquarters, for reasons that remain obscure. It is interesting that there was no scandal when, 'just as passions over Watergate reached their zenith', it was revealed that the FBI had been disrupting the activities of the Socialist Workers Party, a legal political party, by illegal break-ins and other measures for a decade, 'a violation of democratic principle far more extensive and serious than anything charged during the Watergate hearings',[19] Chomsky commented. Documents that the government was forced to release at this time under Freedom of Information legislation exposed a systematic and extensive programme of terror, disruption, intimidation and the instigation of violence, 'initiated under the most liberal Democratic administrations and carried further under Nixon'.[20] The targets of FBI harassment and terror included the US Socialist Workers Party, the Young Socialist Alliance and the Black Panthers.

Another major charge against Nixon was the so-called 'enemies list'. This list, as well as containing the names of dissidents such as Chomsky himself, contained the names of powerful and influential people such as

Tom Watson of IBM. Chomsky comments, 'I know perfectly well from my own experience that absolutely nothing happened to anybody on the enemies list. They didn't even audit our income tax returns, and that was particularly striking in my case because I was publicly organizing tax resistance.' Nixon's crime was not that of persecuting those named on the list, but simply to have drawn up a list at all. Chomsky gives his interpretation: 'In other words, it's a scandal to call powerful people bad names in private.'[21] At the same time as the enemies list was uncovered, it was publicly revealed that the FBI had directed the assassination of a Black political organizer, Fred Hampton. Hampton, an influential member of the Black Panthers, had been involved in the politicization of gangs such as the Blackstone Rangers in Chicago. The FBI had first attempted to disrupt the relationship between the Rangers and the Panthers, and then turned to the destruction of the Panthers themselves. Chomsky notes that Hampton was regarded as particularly dangerous because of his opposition to violent acts or rhetoric and because of his success in community organizing. In a pre-dawn raid in December 1969, the Chicago police raided the flat where Hampton was staying, and fired approximately a hundred shots, killing Hampton and another Panther, Mark Clark. At first the police claimed that they had responded to the fire of the Panthers, but it was quickly established by the local press that this was false. All the gunfire had been directed at the inside corners of the flat rather than towards the entrances, and it transpired later that the police had been supplied with a floorplan by the chief of Panther security and Hampton's personal bodyguard, William O'Neal, who was an FBI infiltrator. Hampton had been killed while he lay in bed. There is some evidence that he had been drugged.[22] Chomsky comments, 'This event can fairly be described as a Gestapo-style political assassination.'[23] He points out that this incident alone 'completely overshadows the entire Watergate episode in significance by a substantial margin'.[24]

The pattern is difficult to avoid. The media defend the rich and the powerful, not the poor and marginalized. 'The lesson of Watergate is stark and clear,' Chomsky concludes: 'the powerful are capable of defending themselves.'[25] For the media, he writes, Watergate was 'yet another cynical exercise in the service of power'.[26] The evidence does seem to support this interpretation.

In *Manufacturing Consent*, Herman and Chomsky compare the media's treatment of victims of state power in foreign parts: in Poland – then an official enemy state – and in Latin America. They study media reactions to the deaths of religious figures at the hands of the security forces in these two regions. In particular, they compare the coverage of the killing of the Polish priest, Jerzy Popieluszko, in October 1984, with the killing of one hundred religious figures in Latin America between 1964 and 1980. According to the Propaganda Model, the killing of a priest in an enemy state, especially a communist one, would be given greater prominence than the killing of a priest in a client state, because the former would tend to increase popular support for US foreign policy, while public awareness of the latter might interfere with US support for client regimes. A priest in Eastern Europe would, in a Propaganda Model media system, be a 'worthy victim', one of several macabre terms invented by Chomsky and Herman to capture the realities of media behaviour. Latin American martyrs, on the other hand, would be 'unworthy victims'.

When Herman and Chomsky examined the coverage of these different deaths, they found that the quality of coverage was markedly different. Reporting the murder of Popieluszko, the US media attempted to create an intense emotional impact on readers, quite rightly, Herman and Chomsky suggest. Reporting the murders of the Latin American religious figures, on the other hand, there was a distinct lack of indignation in the coverage. A comparison in terms of quantity was even more striking. Judged both in terms of numbers of newspaper articles and in terms of total column inches, Popieluszko received more attention in the *New York Times*, *Newsweek* and *Time* than the entire one hundred religious victims studied by Herman and Chomsky. In the *New York Times*, the hundred martyrs were accorded 604.5 column inches, just over half the total for Popieluszko.[27] Herman and Chomsky comment, 'we can calculate the relative worthiness of the world's victims, as measured by the weight given them by the U.S. mass media'. By such calculations we find that 'a priest murdered in Latin America is worth less than a hundredth of a priest murdered in Poland'[28] in the mainstream value system.

This test of the Propaganda Model was the subject of a rare critique within the mainstream media.[29] Rare in the sense that the critique actually addressed the issues rather than simply condemning the argument out of hand. Nicolas Lemann, a national correspondent of the US journal *Atlantic Monthly*, suggested an alternative explanation for the discrepancy in treatment. According to Lemann, the 'big-time press' concentrates intensely 'on a small number of subjects at a time', shifting attention 'unpredictably' from country to country. Thus Popieluszko 'was killed when the U.S. press was most focused on Poland. Archbishop Romero was killed before the press had really focused on El Salvador.' Therefore, no lessons can be drawn as to which death was regarded as more important by the press; 'the discrepancy can be explained by saying the press tends to focus on only a few things at a time'.[30] (Note that the ninety-nine Latin American victims other than Romero have somehow disappeared.) Chomsky responds, 'Let us ask only the simplest question: how much coverage were the media giving to El Salvador and to Poland when Archbishop Romero and Father Popieluszko were murdered? We find that the coverage was almost identical, eliminating this proposed explanation without any further consideration of its quite obvious flaws.'[31] The problem is actually more severe. If we exclude the Popieluszko and Romero cases themselves, and compare the attention given to El Salvador in 1980 and Poland from August 1984 to July 1985, there was slightly more coverage of El Salvador in the period under review, according to Chomsky.[32] By Lemann's standard, then, Herman and Chomsky understated the bias of the media.

It is interesting that Lemann's response is so patently inadequate. As Chomsky pointed out, it is the work of a few moments to check the *New York Times* index for the relevant years and to compare the levels of attention given to El Salvador and to Poland. What makes this exchange particularly interesting is that Lemann's may well be the most coherent critique of the Propaganda Model to have come out of the mainstream press. In the case we are about to consider, this level of rationality was not attained.

Just as one can compare media responses to individual victims, one can compare media behaviour in the case of large-scale atrocities. According to the Propaganda Model, the mass media should treat atrocities differently according to how useful they are in propaganda terms. Chomsky and Herman in their two-volume study *The Political Economy of Human Rights* (*PEHR*) defined three categories of atrocities: 'constructive', 'benign' and 'nefarious'. 'Constructive' bloodbaths serve the interests of US power; 'benign' bloodbaths are irrelevant to these concerns; and 'nefarious' bloodbaths are those that can be blamed on official enemies. The first-order predictions[33] of the Propaganda Model are that constructive bloodbaths will be welcomed in the media, benign bloodbaths ignored and nefarious bloodbaths passionately condemned. For example, Chomsky and Herman point out, the constructive bloodbath in Indonesia in 1965, when the Indonesian government massacred hundreds of thousands of people to defeat nationalist forces and eradicate the Indonesian Communist Party, was welcomed enthusiastically by Western observers.[34] The 'benign bloodbath' caused by the ethnic massacres in Burundi in 1972 neither advanced nor undermined US interests, and therefore evoked little interest.

The most famous nefarious bloodbath of the postwar era took place in Cambodia under the Khmer Rouge, between 1975 and 1978. It was met with a flow of outraged condemnation in the Western media in what Chomsky describes as 'a barrage with few historical parallels, apart from wartime propaganda'.[35] In December 1975, not that far away, Indonesia invaded East Timor, a neighbouring country formally in the process of decolonization from Portugal, but which had declared its independence shortly before the invasion. It soon became clear that the Indonesian occupation was exacting a fearful toll on the East Timorese people. The reaction to the Indonesian massacres in the Western media was almost total silence. The contrast in media responses to these two bloodbaths was one of the central cases in *PEHR* and remains one of the most important tests of the Propaganda Model. Chomsky and Herman commented,

> In the case of Cambodia reported atrocities have not only been eagerly seized upon by the Western media but also embellished by substantial fabrications – which, interestingly, persist even long after they are exposed. The case of Timor is radically different. The media have shown no interest in examining the atrocities of the Indonesian invaders, though even in absolute numbers these are on the same scale as those reported by sources of comparable credibility concerning Cambodia, and relative to the population, are many times as great.[36]

It is important to bear in mind that the focus in *PEHR* is on assessing the performance of the media – its handling of the evidence available at the time. The focus is not on judging the situation in Cambodia itself. Chomsky and Herman made it clear in *After the Cataclysm* – the second volume of *PEHR* – that 'our primary concern here is not to try to establish the facts with regard to postwar Indochina, but rather to investigate their refraction through the prism of Western ideology, a very different task'.[37] If Western propagandists had later proved to be accidentally correct in their estimates of Khmer Rouge killings, this would not mean that they had been honest. Chomsky once illustrated this point by noting that if he were to claim that Harvard's Widener library was burning – without any evidence to that effect – he would not have been proved 'honest' in retrospect if by some accident the library had indeed been in flames at the time of his remark.[38] Accidental accuracy based on conscious lying is not the same as honesty.

Despite Chomsky and Herman's repeated statements that they were not disputing the available evidence, only the way in which it was being handled, they were harshly attacked for allegedly doubting the facts of the Khmer Rouge massacres.[39] The vilification and distortion of Chomsky's alleged views reached across the political spectrum. Even the *New Statesman*, a left-liberal periodical, criticized Chomsky's attempts to 'challenge the evidence of atrocities committed by Cambodian Communists before the Vietnamese takeover'.[40] At quite a different position on the British political spectrum, the columnist Leopold Labedz wrote substantial essays in *Encounter* attempting to prove that Chomsky dealt 'in the same way with Pol Pot's Kampuchea as do other cranky characters with Hitler's Germany and Stalin's Russia when, even now, they deny or minimise the extent of these historic cases of genocide'.[41] These and many other attacks were devoted to condemning precisely two pieces of writing by Chomsky and Herman: a review article in the *Nation*, and a single chapter in *After the Cataclysm*.[42]

There was a high level of dishonesty in the attacks on Chomsky. Critics charged that Chomsky 'disbelieved' refugees' reports of atrocities in Cambodia, despite the fact that in both their essays on the subject Chomsky and Herman stated that Cambodian refugee reports should be 'considered seriously'.[43] As, they noted, should the reports of East Timorese refugees. The point of lying about Chomsky's attitude towards Cambodian refugees is that this was a necessary component of the bigger lie that he denied the scale of the Khmer Rouge atrocities in Cambodia.

There are various formulations of this allegation. Labedz claimed that in his 1977 *Nation* article (Herman having disappeared), Chomsky concluded that,

> the Cambodian 'executions have numbered at most in thousands.' [sic] He presented his conclusion as based on 'analysis by highly qualified specialists who have studied the full range of available evidence', dismissing such first-hand studies as the book by Father François Ponchaud.[44]

The phrase 'numbered at most in the thousands' appears in the following sentence in the original: 'such journals as the *Far Eastern Economic Review*, the London *Economist*, the *Melbourne Journal of Politics*, and others elsewhere, have provided analyses by highly qualified specialists who have studied the full range of evidence available, and who concluded that executions have numbered at most in the thousands...' Chomsky was not presenting *his* conclusion 'as based on analysis by highly qualified specialists'; he was presenting the conclusions of the specialists themselves, without comment. As for Ponchaud's *Année Zéro*, whatever its merits, his book is based on interviews with refugees, and by definition cannot possibly be a 'first-hand study'. Furthermore, far from dismissing Ponchaud's book, Chomsky and Herman described it in their review article as 'serious and worth reading', and distinguished it from much of the commentary it elicited. This tiny portion of Labedz's article, though a small sample, gives, I believe, an accurate indication of the intellectual and moral standards of the vilification campaign directed against Chomsky.

We have taken something of a detour from our discussion of the Propaganda Model. This is only to be expected, if the Propaganda Model is an accurate depiction of reality. Those who challenge the 'Right to Lie', as Chomsky describes it, can expect to be met with vilification and distortion. Such vilification campaigns succeed by making the accusations against the critics the topic of debate. By forcing critics into an endless defence of their positions, the propaganda system distracts attention from the substantive issues.

The anger of Western intellectuals against Chomsky derived in part from Chomsky and Herman's painstaking exposé of the extravagant lies told about Cambodia. It may be worthwhile to examine the background to the controversy briefly. François Ponchaud's book came to the attention of the English-speaking world through a review by Jean Lacouture in the *New York Review of Books*,[45] in which Lacouture misread Ponchaud in a number of instances. In particular he inflated Ponchaud's estimate of the number of Khmer Rouge killings to two million. Despite this and other errors, Lacouture's review was highly influential and was cited as authoritative by many commentators in the US press. When Chomsky obtained Ponchaud's book from France and discovered errors in the review, he wrote to Lacouture and to other journalists who had used the review as the basis for their own comments on Cambodia, pointing out the mistakes. Pressed by Chomsky, Lacouture issued 'Cambodia: Corrections' which withdrew the two million claim.[46] Lacouture wrote that he 'should have checked more accurately the figures on victims, figures deriving from sources that are, moreover, questionable'. What is interesting is that the two million figure passed into official history, despite Lacouture's correction.

A detailed analysis of Lacouture's errors, or those of other commentators, is not required for the purposes of the present test. It is simply necessary to demonstrate that the reaction of the US mass media to the two sets of atrocities was sharply different. This was illustrated graphically in the film *Manufacturing Consent*, when the film-makers unrolled two paper strips pasted with entries for Cambodia and East Timor respectively from the *New York Times* index, for the period 1975–79. East Timor accounted for 70 column inches of index entries, Cambodia for over 97 feet.[47]

In evaluating media performance in the case of East Timor or Latin America, or indeed in the case of the FBI programmes, it is important to bear in mind the moral significance of media silence. In 1975, the United States supplied diplomatic, military and economic aid to Indonesia in order to facilitate the invasion and the massacres in East Timor. Daniel Moynihan, US ambassador to the UN at the time of the invasion, boasted about his accomplishments in his memoirs:

> The United States wished things to turn out as they did, and worked to bring this about. The Department of State desired that the United Nations prove utterly ineffective in whatever measures it undertook. This task was given to me, and I carried it forward with no inconsiderable success.[48]

Moynihan followed this by noting that within a few weeks of the invasion some 60,000 people had been killed, '10 percent of the population, almost the proportion of casualties experienced by the Soviet Union during the Second World War'. It seems clear that domestic criticism in the United States could have reduced US military, economic and diplomatic support for the invasion, and might even have led to an end to the killings. The lack of such criticism led directly to the deaths of hundreds of thousands of people in one of the true genocides of the postwar era.[49] Those who turned away carry a heavy burden. Similar observations apply to media silence over the killing of religious figures in Latin America or Black political organizers in the United States. When we turn to the Khmer Rouge atrocities, we find that those who fuelled the storm of condemnation against the Khmer Rouge had no suggestions as to how to help the people of Cambodia. Perhaps it is worth stressing once again that Chomsky never denied the existence of Khmer Rouge brutality; he simply pointed out that there was no need to lie about what was going on, and there was an appalling double standard regarding Cambodia and East Timor.

Before we consider other aspects of the Propaganda Model, it is worth noting an important procedural point. Chomsky points out that some care has to be taken when comparing paired examples. It could be argued, for example, that the *Boston Globe* operates a double standard against the City of Boston, subjecting it to unfair criticism. This might be 'proved' by taking as paired examples treatment in the *Globe* of corruption in the city government in Boston and in Seattle, or a murder traceable to the police in Boston and in Karachi. Clearly in each case the Boston news would be given incomparably greater exposure, 'proving' that the editors and staff of the *Globe* are 'self-hating Bostonians'. Chomsky comments, 'The argument is plainly absurd. Obviously, comparison must begin by setting as a baseline the ordinary level of coverage of affairs in Boston, Seattle, and Karachi in the *Globe*, and the reasons for the general selection.'[50] A further factor might be the level of favourable coverage of the three cities. Correcting for such obvious errors, the theory of self-hating Bostonians quickly collapses.

The relevance of these points is that one of the most familiar condemnations of the Western media – perhaps the most common – is that they are unfair to Israel and apply a 'double standard' to it, perhaps because of anti-Semitism, perhaps because the journalists are self-hating Jews or suffer from other psychic disorders. The 'proof' of the double standard is that Israeli crimes receive more coverage than comparable or worse crimes in Syria, South Yemen and other Arab and Third World states. The fallacy of this 'proof' is that the level of media coverage of Israel is huge compared to that of Syria or any other Middle East country. Furthermore, the reporting of Israel is completely different in character. Chomsky notes, 'One would have to search a long time to find a favourable word about Syria, South Yemen, etc., or any word at all. Such coverage as there is is uniformly negative, generally harshly so, with no mitigating elements.'[51] The coverage of Israel is quite different.

On first sight, the Propaganda Model is a difficult theory to take seriously. The idea that the media systematically distort the news in the interests of the powerful is a very difficult one to accept. Faced with such a proposal, a person can either reject it out of hand or examine the evidence put forward in its support. We have sampled some of the arguments constructed to support the model. It is clear in principle how such a proposal can be tested and that some care has been taken in conducting these tests. Our brief survey cannot do justice to the depth of documentation that Chomsky has developed, but it does give a taste of the rigour with which these uncomfortable and unsettling thoughts can be explored.

2

The Culture of Terrorism

The most familiar image of a state propaganda system is the world of *Nineteen Eighty Four*, where the 'Thought Police' and the 'Ministry of Truth' rewrite history books and newspapers to create a politically correct version of events. At the heart of Orwell's book is the torture chamber in Room 101 of the Ministry of Love, which finally extinguishes Winston Smith's independence of mind.[1] Right thinking is created by the ever-present violence of a police state. In contrast, the Chomsky/Herman Propaganda Model is a non-terrorist propaganda system, which operates without the use of force. They describe the Model as 'brainwashing under freedom', indicating the crucial difference. John Dolan therefore describes the Propaganda Model as a 'non-Orwellian' propaganda system.[2] According to Chomsky, 'The general subservience of the media to the state propaganda system does not result from direct government order, threats or coercion, centralized decisions, and other devices characteristic of totalitarian states, but from a complex interplay of more subtle factors.'[3] 'What you face here is a very effective kind of ideological control, because one can remain under the impression that censorship does not exist, and in a narrow technical sense that is correct': 'You will not be imprisoned if you discover the facts, not even if you proclaim them whenever you can. But the results remain much the same as if there were real censorship.'[4] In Chomsky's view, the forms of propaganda in the West were not perceived by Orwell; the Propaganda Model is 'a stage of indoctrination well beyond anything that Orwell imagined'.[5] The Propaganda Model is a 'guided-free-market' model in which thought control is the product not of violence and terror, but of market forces in a highly unequal society. The 'guidance' given to the market is provided by 'the government, the leaders of the corporate community, the top media owners and executives, and the assorted individuals and groups who are assigned or allowed to take constructive initiatives'.[6] Instead of the horrors of Room 101, there are institutional pressures and the seductions of privilege.

Many of Chomsky's critics are unable or unwilling to concede the non-Orwellian nature of the Propaganda Model. Thus a critic in the British *Spectator* sought to refute the model by pointing out that Chomsky's books were freely available in bookshops in Washington DC. Chomsky agreed that his books could be bought without fear of the FBI, 'a fine response to the charge that the US is a police state, but irrelevant to any that have actually been made'.[7] Chomsky has repeatedly stressed that 'from a comparative perspective, the United States is unusual if not unique in its lack of restraints on freedom of expression',[8] and that the freedom of inquiry and expression in the United States 'is in many respects unusual even in comparison with other industrial democracies such as Great Britain'.[9] The United States does not have an Official Secrets Act or libel laws, and does possess an important Freedom of Information Act.[10] At the same time, writing with Edward Herman, Chomsky notes that 'even the most cursory examination of history' demonstrates that internal freedom is 'quite compatible with exploitative and inhumane external conduct extending over many decades'. For example, the fountainhead of Western democracy, ancient Athens, combined military power and a slave-owners' democracy in an aggressive and ruthless naval imperialism which 'kept the entire Greek world in turmoil from 480 to 404 BC'.[11]

The internal freedom in Western societies is an essential part of the Propaganda Model. It is precisely because of the freedom of thought and expression in Western capitalist democracies that such sophisticated mechanisms for shackling public opinion have arisen. Chomsky suggests that democratic systems of thought control are different from totalitarian ones precisely because it is necessary to control 'not only what people do, but also what they think': 'Since the state lacks the capacity to ensure obedience by force, thought can lead to action and therefore the threat to order must be excised at the source.'[12] Those who rule by violence tend to be 'behaviourist' in their outlook. What people may think is not terribly important; what counts is what they do. They must obey, and this obedience is secured by force. In democratic societies, ruling elites cannot control the population by brute force and must replace external controls on the individual with internal controls – control of thought itself. What matters is not what people are able to do, but what they are able to think. The US propaganda system is in many ways more efficient than the Stalinist model, Chomsky muses. 'Ours is surely a more effective system, one that would be used by dictators if they were smarter. It combines highly effective indoctrination with the impression that the society is really "open," so that pronouncements conforming to the state religion are not to be dismissed out of hand as propaganda.'[13] In a dictatorship the mechanisms of propaganda are opaque and it is entirely clear what the official line is. Chomsky comments, 'In a curious way, this practice frees the mind. Internally, at least, one can identify the propaganda message and reject it.'[14] The US propaganda system is, in contrast, quite transparent. Its victims are unaware of being manipulated.

One of the main techniques for establishing such invisible control is to set up the boundaries of thinkable thought: 'It's thought to be necessary to take over the entire spectrum of opinion, the entire spectrum of discussion, so that nothing can be thinkable apart from the party line, not just that it be obeyed, but that you can't even think anything else. The state propaganda is not expressed; it's rather implicit; it's presupposed.'[15] There is a system of unspoken assumptions which govern people's thinking: these are not asserted, 'it is better that they be presupposed'.[16] These assumptions 'become the framework for thinkable thought, not objects of rational consideration'.[17] We can no longer perceive the ideas that are shaping our thoughts, as the fish cannot perceive the sea. In this way the unspoken underlying principles are removed from inspection.

Once these controls have been established, debate and dissension are not suppressed, they are permitted. Chomsky suggests that it is in fact more effective to encourage debate, so long as all the participants obey the ground rules. Once it is properly framed, debate has a 'system-reinforcing character', as mainstream critics reinforce the basic assumptions of the propaganda system by their loyal opposition.[18] In their 'feigned dissent',[19] even those at the liberal extreme of the media and scholarship, who appear to be opposing elite interests and contesting government policy, actually help to buttress the fundamental doctrines of the propaganda system. 'If even the harshest critics tacitly adopt these premises, then the ordinary person may ask, who am I to disagree?'[20] 'The more vigorous the debate, the better the system of propaganda is served, since the tacit, unspoken assumptions are more forcefully implanted.'[21] Chomsky suggests that 'A useful rule of thumb is this: If you want to learn something about the propaganda system, have a close look at the critics and their tacit assumptions. These typically constitute the doctrines of the state religion.'[22] Much of

Chomsky's work on ideology consists of exactly this: revealing the hidden assumptions of mainstream critics.

One classic example of feigned dissent took place during the Vietnam War, when many of those seen as critics of the war actually reinforced the basic principles of state propaganda. One of these critics was Arthur Schlesinger, a leading Kennedy liberal, near the liberal extreme of the 'responsible approach' to the war. At the other end of the mainstream political spectrum were those like Joseph Alsop, who urged a continuation of the war and predicted victory. Schlesinger believed that Alsop's optimism was unwarranted, but added: 'we all pray that Mr Alsop will be right'.[23] In other words, Schlesinger's opposition to the war was based on its diminishing prospects of success, not on a condemnation of the moral character of the war. Alsop and Schlesinger would be united in approving of the war, if only it could be brought to a successful conclusion. Given their positions at the extremes of 'responsible opinion', Chomsky noted, 'Their views bound a substantial range of American opinion.' He suggested that it was of great importance, therefore, 'to note that each presents what can fairly be described as an apologia for American imperialism'.[24] Schlesinger responded angrily, 'Does Professor Chomsky understand that the foundation of political analysis lies in the capacity to make distinctions? Someone who is unable to see the difference between a supporter and an opponent of the Vietnam War ought to shut up shop as a political seer and return to the linguistics factory.'[25] Chomsky answered,

> Schlesinger objects that I identified his views with Alsop's (thus disqualifying myself as a political commentator). This is a curious charge. What I wrote was that Schlesinger and Alsop are at opposite poles, in the mainstream of American debate over Vietnam. For precisely this reason it is important to take note of the shared premises that lead Schlesinger to 'pray that Mr Alsop will be right' in his forecast that the American war in Vietnam will be successful. Both are apologists for American imperialism. They differ, and are bitterly opposed, over issues that will seem insignificant to those who reject their ideological assumptions. One might question my interpretation, but Schlesinger's inability even to comprehend these simple points is perhaps a further indication of the powerful grip of this shared ideology.[26]

The significance of people like Schlesinger, Chomsky suggests, is that the 'major contribution to the doctrinal system during the Vietnam war period' was made by 'the position of the doves';[27] those who appeared to oppose the war but who in fact supported the right, in principle, of the United States to impose its will on others by force.

In 1984, Chomsky referred to the case of Russian newscaster Vladimir Danchev, who in May 1983 had denounced the Soviet invasion of Afghanistan in five successive radio broadcasts. Danchev was sent to a psychiatric hospital and later returned to his position. Chomsky pointed out that what was particularly remarkable about the broadcasts was that Danchev called the Soviet invasion an 'invasion'. In Soviet ideology there was no such event as the 'invasion' of Afghanistan; rather, there was a Russian 'defence' of Afghanistan against bandits operating from Pakistani sanctuaries, supported by the CIA and other warmongers. Chomsky notes that 'The Russians claim that they were invited in, and in a certain technical sense this is correct. But as the London *Economist* grandly proclaimed, "An invader is an invader unless invited in by a government with a claim to legitimacy." '[28] The significance of the Danchev incident for the United States, Chomsky pointed out, is that in the United States there have been no Danchevs. There are two possible explanations: either Washington has never carried out such an invasion, or, alternatively, 'no American journalist would ever mimic Danchev's courage, or could even perceive that an American invasion of the Afghan type is in fact an invasion or that a sane person might call on the victims to resist'.[29] In the case of South Vietnam, the United States claimed to have been invited in, but, as the Pentagon Papers revealed, South Vietnam was

> essentially the creation of the United States. Without US support Diem almost certainly could not have consolidated his hold on the South during 1955 and 1956. Without the threat of US intervention, South Vietnam could not have refused to even discuss the elections called for in 1956 under the Geneva settlement without being overrun by Viet Minh armies. Without US aid in the years following, the Diem regime certainly, and an independent South Vietnam almost as certainly could not have survived.[30]

In Chomsky's view, Kennedy's decision in 1962 to send the US Air Force to attack rural South Vietnam (where more than 80 per cent of the population lived) was a direct invasion of South Vietnam. He argues that 'as the London *Economist* recognized in the case of Afghanistan (never, in the case of Vietnam), "an invader is an invader unless invited in by a government with a claim to legitimacy," and outside the world of Newspeak, the client regime established by the United States had no more legitimacy than the Afghan regime established by the USSR'.[31]

One of the staples of the propaganda system was that the war was between South Vietnam and North Vietnam, with the United States simply aiding in the defence of South Vietnam. The Pentagon Papers provide irrefutable proof that when the United States undertook its major escalation in February 1965, it knew of no regular North Vietnamese units in South Vietnam, and that five months later, while implementing the plan to deploy eighty-five thousand troops, the Pentagon was still only speculating about the possibility that there might be North Vietnamese Army forces in or near South Vietnam. The first reference to regular North Vietnamese Army units in the south is in a CIA/DIA (Defence Intelligence Agency) memo of April 1965 (months after the full-scale US invasion), while by July 1965 there was concern over 'the increasing probability' of such units in South Vietnam or in Laos.[32] Chomsky comments, 'In the light of these facts, the discussion of whether the U.S. was defending South Vietnam from an "armed attack" from the North – the official U.S. government position – is ludicrous.'[33] If ideological blinkers are removed, it is clear that the United States invaded South Vietnam in exactly the same way that the Soviet Union invaded Afghanistan. Chomsky commented in 1984, 'For the past twenty-two years, I have been searching to find some reference in mainstream journalism or scholarship to an American invasion of South Vietnam in 1962 (or ever), or an American attack against South Vietnam, or American aggression in Indochina – without success.' There is no such event in history. 'Rather, there is an American *defence* of South Vietnam against terrorists supported from outside (namely, from Vietnam), a defence that was unwise, the doves maintain.' In short, there are no Danchevs here.[34]

A later war provides another example of the power of the propaganda system. In the run-up to the Nicaraguan elections of 1990, the US government repeatedly announced that if their favoured party, the UNO coalition, did not win, the economic embargo, which had already caused $3 billion worth of damage, would continue, as would US sponsorship of Contra terrorism. The UNO victory that followed was then hailed on all sides of the mainstream US media as a triumph of 'free and fair' elections. Chomsky constructs the following analogy:

Suppose that the USSR were to follow the US model as the Baltic states declare independence, organizing a proxy army to attack them from foreign bases, training its terrorist forces to hit 'soft targets' (health centers, schools, and so on) so that the governments cannot provide social services, reducing the economies to ruin through embargo and other sanctions, and so on, in the familiar routine. Suppose further that when elections come, the Kremlin informs the population, loud and clear, that they can vote for the CP or

THE CULTURE OF TERRORISM

starve. Perhaps some unreconstructed Stalinist might call this a 'free and fair election'. Surely no one else would.[35]

Anyone who called the 1990 elections 'free and fair', and a welcome step towards democracy, was, in Chomsky's view, 'not only a totalitarian, but one of a rather special variety'.[36] Nevertheless, this was the only reaction throughout the US media. Chomsky claims to have found only a single mainstream reporter willing to recognize and state the elementary truth – Randolph Ryan in the *Boston Globe*. At the liberal extreme of the media, a more typical performance was that of Tom Wicker of the *New York Times*, who recognized that the Sandinistas lost 'because the Nicaraguan people were tired of war and sick of economic deprivation', but who concluded that the elections nevertheless were 'free and fair', and untainted by coercion.[37] What is so striking is the uniformity of articulate opinion. Such intellectual obedience would be impressive in a totalitarian state. Under the conditions of freedom in the United States, it is extraordinary. To have the entire intellectual class (discounting a few shrill voices on the fringe) blanking out years of terror and decay at the hands of Washington was a consummate achievement of the propaganda system and a strong confirmation of the Propaganda Model.

Another triumph of the propaganda system concerned Nicaragua's alleged attempts to acquire Soviet military aircraft. The charge of trying to acquire Soviet MiGs was made on election night in Nicaragua in November 1984, in a transparent attempt to block out coverage of the successful elections. The official story was that the MiGs, later conceded to be non-existent, would be capable of aggressive operations against neighbouring states and pose an unacceptable threat to US security. Something of an insult to the US Air Force, one imagines. Chomsky commented that the missing question in the public furore was quite what the MiGs would be for: 'They need MiGs because they have to protect their air space. The CIA is flying two or three supply flights a day in there in order to maintain a foreign-run army. It's as if Russia had an army up there in the hills around L.A. and since they don't have any popular support you have to keep flying arms in every day, food, uniforms, etc.'[38] Furthermore, at that very moment, the United States was sending in advanced aircraft to El Salvador to help control air strikes in that country.[39] The underlying principle was that the United States had every right to attack Nicaragua and that Nicaragua had no right to defend itself. Again, we see this principle upheld throughout the mass media and by the most liberal figures in Congress. Chomsky comments, 'The assumption across the board was, of course, that no country has a right to defend itself, because the United States has the right to kill and attack anybody it likes.'[40]

It is difficult to find a precedent for such a stance. Chomsky comments, 'If we heard a discussion like this in the Soviet Union, where people were asking whether, let's say, Denmark should be bombed because it has jets which could reach the Soviet Union, we would be appalled. In fact, that's an analogy that's unfair to the Russians. They're *not* attacking Denmark as we're attacking Nicaragua and El Salvador.'[41] He goes further: 'That's beyond Newspeak. I don't think you can find a country in history that has reached this level of indoctrination.... Hitler accused the Poles of aggression, but I don't believe he ever accused the Poles of getting arms to defend themselves against attack. That's a level of fanatic indoctrination that's unique in history.'[42] 'By our standards, Hitler looked rather sane in the 1930s.'[43]

A number of different institutional and individual factors interact to create a system of 'brainwashing under freedom'.[44] The institutional factors are uncontroversial, or should be. The most obvious fact about the mass media is that, almost by definition, in order to reach a mass audience a media organization must be a sizeable corporation, owned either by the state or by rich individuals. In the United States, the field is dominated by huge, private, profit-seeking corporations, 'which are closely interlocked, and have important common interests, with other major corporations, banks, and government'.[45] The entry requirements into newspaper publishing, for example, are considerable. The initial capital costs of acquiring printing and distribution facilities are prohibitive. In the 1970s, Chomsky commented acidly, 'everyone who has twenty million dollars is free to open a newspaper, and one knows what this means'.[46] It would be somewhat surprising if the views expressed through such channels were to undermine the authority and power of those who control and own the means of communication.

The second major factor is what Herman and Chomsky term 'the advertising licence'. In their history of the British press, James Curran and Jean Seaton conclude that the growth of advertising was as significant as the growth in capital costs in choking off the popular radical press which had grown up in the first half of the nineteenth century. Advertising is used by publishers to lower the price of newspapers below the cost of producing them, undercutting competitors. Advertising also pays for improvements in format, features, the publicity budget, and so on. Curran and Seaton comment: 'advertisers thus acquired a de facto licensing authority since, without their support, newspapers ceased to be economically viable'.[47] Chomsky suggests that, 'Like other businesses, the mass media sell a product to buyers. Their market is advertisers, and the "product" is audiences, with a bias towards more wealthy audiences which improve advertising rates.'[48] Given these facts, 'It would hardly come as a surprise if the picture of the world they present were to reflect the perspectives and interests of the sellers, the buyers, and the product.'[49]

It is sometimes suggested that because they have to sell their wares to readers, newspapers are somehow democratic and must reflect the ideas and attitudes of their readers. Chomsky's analysis suggests that there is a constraint on the extent to which a newspaper can mirror its readers' views, or permit the expression of opinions which are outside the elite consensus: 'The media represent the same interests that control the state and private economy, and it is therefore not very surprising to discover that they generally act to confine public discussion and understanding to the needs of the powerful and privileged.'[50] When we take into account the fact that advertisers prefer wealthier audiences for their advertisements, Herman and Chomsky point out, 'The idea that the drive for large audiences makes the mass media "democratic" thus suffers from the initial weakness that its political analogue is a voting system weighted by income.'[51]

There are other factors, like the government's powers of regulation, taxation, licensing, and so on, which give it great influence over media organizations. The Herman/Chomsky model also stresses the need for a steady flow of regular and credible news, from respectable sources – primarily the government and big business. By providing the media with facilities in which to gather, advance copies of speeches, press releases, photo-opportunities, press conferences timed for deadlines, and so on, the government and business organizations in effect subsidize the mass media and 'gain special access by their contribution to reducing the media's costs of acquiring the raw materials of, and producing, news'.[52] Government and elite institutions also provide 'experts', another important source of news and opinion. If for some reason sections of the media fall out of line, there is also the power of what Herman and Chomsky call 'flak': letters, phone calls, petitions, speeches, legal action and parliamentary action against those who produce unwanted news.[53] The prospect of 'flak' can be a deterrent to making a programme or publishing a story, or further down the chain can stop reporters seeking out particular topics because the resulting stories are unlikely to be aired or published. Clearly, the more wealth and power an organization or individual has, the more influential their criticism. In the United States, there are special business-supported groups such as Accuracy in Media, whose sole function is to attack the media for its liberal and left-wing bias. The most significant generator of 'flak' is, however, the government itself, for obvious reasons.

In a scholarly review of 'Vietnam and the breakdown of consensus', two US commentators refer to Chomsky's analysis as 'an almost conspiratorial view of the media'.[54] This is a very common criticism. Chomsky concedes that 'It's a description that is partially correct; it just uses funny words.'[55] There is planning and conscious thought in the Propaganda Model, but it is not a conspiracy in the normal sense of the word. 'With equal logic, one could argue that an analyst of General Motors who concludes that its managers try to maximize profits (instead of selflessly labouring to satisfy the needs of the public) is adopting a conspiracy theory.'[56] In the case of non-media business, is it a 'conspiracy theory' to discover that major corporations are inter-linked with banks and meet internally to increase profit and market share? The Propaganda Model is not a 'conspiracy theory' in the sense of secret controls exercised by officials acting outside normal institutional channels, any more than a 'Profit Model' of General Motors depends on the existence of a Freemasons' Lodge of shareholders and directors. Chomsky traces media behaviour not to state directives or backroom intrigue, but to institutional imperatives. If the explanation is based on the nature of institutions, not the machinations of individuals, it cannot, by definition, be given the name 'conspiracy theory'. Chomsky describes terms like 'conspiracy theory' as 'the intellectual equivalents of four-letter words', which are used to prevent discussion of arguments that cannot be answered.[57]

The Propaganda Model is, then, a guided-free-market model of the media, where institutional pressures combine with self-censorship to produce an extremely controlled intellectual culture. One of the key mechanisms is the recruitment of media personnel, who are selected by media corporations on the condition that they already possess the 'right' attitudes. (Much the same happens in academia, Chomsky suggests.) According to Chomsky, it is the pre-selection of 'right-thinking' journalists and scholars which accounts for much of the censorship in the Propaganda Model. On the other hand, if those who are recruited lack the required attitudes, pressures soon come to bear. 'To put it in the simplest terms, a talented young journalist or a student aiming for a scholarly career can choose to play the game by the rules, with the prospect of advancement to a position of prestige and privilege and sometimes even a degree of power; or to choose an independent path, with the likelihood of a minor post as a police reporter or in a community college, exclusion from major journals, vilification and abuse, or driving a taxi cab. Given such choices, the end result is not very surprising.'[58] Chomsky has given some examples in conversation. One young scholar was driven out of academia for daring to expose a crude piece of anti-Arab propaganda which had been greeted with acclaim by US intellectuals.[59] The personal costs of dissidence can sometimes be quite high, even in 'open' societies. Furthermore, any 'critic must also be prepared to face a defamation apparatus against which there is little recourse, an inhibiting factor that is not insubstantial'.[60]

There are also prior pressures to conform. Chomsky suggests that asking serious questions about your own society is both difficult and unpleasant: 'difficult because the answers are generally concealed, and unpleasant because the answers are often not only ugly – in foreign affairs, roughly in proportion to the power of the state – but also painful'. Understanding the truth about such matters can lead to difficult moral dilemmas. If one is led to action, this may carry significant personal costs. The alternative is considerably easier: simply to 'succumb to the demands of the powerful, to avoid searching questions, and to accept the doctrine that is hammered home incessantly by the propaganda system'. Chomsky suggests that this is the main reason for the easy victory of dominant ideologies, for 'the general tendency to remain silent or to keep fairly close to official doctrine with regard to the behaviour of one's own state and its allies and dependencies, while lining up to condemn the real or alleged crimes of its enemies'.[61] There are also secondary factors in the surrender of intellectual independence. The most powerful of these may be 'elemental patriotism, the overwhelming wish to think well of ourselves, our institutions, and our leaders'.[62] Such a deep-seated bias can have profound effects on one's judgement. There are also advantages in conformism. One advantage is that repeating standard doctrine does not require much work: 'If one chooses to denounce Qaddafi, or the Sandinistas, or the PLO, or the Soviet Union, no credible evidence is required.'[63] The charge has only to be made to be believed. In contrast, a critical analysis of US institutions and the way they function must meet high standards: 'One has to work hard, to produce evidence that is credible, to construct serious arguments, to present extensive documentation – all tasks that are superfluous as long as one remains within the presuppositional framework of the doctrinal consensus.'[64]

In any event, once on the job, news reporters and columnists develop a feeling for what is acceptable, and 'self-censorship thus occurs at their level on the basis of learned and understood limits of subject matter, tone, balance, and the like'.[65] These limits can be conveyed subtly or bluntly. Once a journalist begins to censor herself, it becomes difficult for her to avoid believing the ideas she reproduces. Chomsky suggests, 'Those who choose to conform, hence to remain within the system, will soon find that they internalize the beliefs and attitudes that they express and that shape their work; it is a very rare individual who can believe one thing and say another on a regular basis.'[66] 'It's just too hard a burden to maintain insight and understanding while doing something else. It's a lot easier to accept the values and then just do it. Once you've done that, you're finished. Then you're just a loyal servant.'[67] Journalists may be led into a process of steadily adapting their judgements until they conform to the prevailing norms, supposing some divergence existed in the first place. For many, upbringing and education have already succeeded in fostering a conformist outlook. Chomsky comments, 'you don't get to be a reporter on at least one of the quality journals or the national press unless you've already internalized all those values. There's a long process of indoctrination that begins in kindergarten.'[68] Tom Wicker, a columnist on the *New York Times*, reacted with scorn to Chomsky's analysis of his and other journalists' coverage of Central America. He protested that no one gave him instructions on what attitude to take to the Sandinistas.[69] Chomsky responded,

> That's true. Nobody's telling Tom Wicker what to write.... But he wouldn't have that column unless he already *knew* what to write. That's the point. If he didn't already know it he never would have gotten to that point. Once you've internalized all the values and understand what you're supposed to say and that comes naturally to you, you don't need any pressure. You're now safe.[70]

Chomsky's analysis of the media (and of US foreign policy) has been attacked for being 'simplistic'. Chomsky concedes the truth of this charge: 'The facts are always more complex than any description we may give.'[71] The atomic theory of matter, or indeed quantum electrodynamics, are also 'simplistic' in this sense. There are three options open to those who recognise this constraint, Chomsky suggests:

> (1) We may abandon the effort; (2) we may try to record many facts in enormous detail, a course that reduces in effect to the first, for all the understanding it provides; (3) we may proceed in the manner of rational

inquiry in the sciences and elsewhere to try to extract some principles that have explanatory force over a fair range, thus hoping to account for at least the major effects.[72]

Chomsky argues that the third approach is the one taken in the hard sciences. 'To account for "all the facts" in the physical world has never been the goal of physics in the modern period.... The great success of physics is due in part to the willingness to restrict attention to the facts that seem crucial at a particular level of understanding, and perhaps to look for quite exotic facts that will be crucial for the theory.'[73] It is also important to set facts in the correct perspective, with a proper understanding of their relative importance. The Soviet invasion of Afghanistan was clearly more complex than suggested in the commonly presented picture. This did not stop commentators, quite rightly, from focusing on the central fact: that Moscow invaded Afghanistan without being invited in by any government with a claim to legitimacy. Similar considerations apply to the Propaganda Model's attempt to identify and explain the dominant features of media behaviour.

The Propaganda Model is an attempt to capture the 'major effects' of the underlying social pressures on media performance. Herman and Chomsky note that, 'No simple model will suffice, however, to account for every detail of such a complex matter as the workings of the national mass media.' They concede that the model will unavoidably leave 'many nuances and secondary effects unanalyzed'.[74] Nevertheless, the model has, in Chomsky's view, 'been shown to provide a reasonably close first approximation, which captures essential properties of the media and the dominant intellectual culture more generally'.[75] Herman and Chomsky comment, 'We do not claim this is all the media do, but we believe the propaganda function to be a very important aspect of their overall service.'[76] There are a number of secondary factors that can affect media performance, including the honesty and integrity of journalists and the need to provide a picture fairly close to reality for investors and other decision-makers.

A further qualification to the Propaganda Model is that Chomsky addresses what he describes as the 'elite media', in particular the handful of newspapers which, along with the government and news agencies, 'defines the news agenda and supplies much of the national and international news to the lower tiers of the media, and thus for the general public'.[77] The agenda-setting elite media target the political class, those who are politically active. 'Things have to be done for the rest of the population too, they have to be marginalized.'[78] Chomsky describes this subordinate segment of the media as the 'diversionary media'. One element of this section of the propaganda system is its emphasis on professional sport, which, Chomsky suggests, helps to build up 'jingoist fanaticism'.[79] There are other devices. Chomsky and Herman write,

> On television, the news itself is easily overrated in importance for ideology and attitude formation in comparison with the commercial and 'entertainment' messages that combine dramatic intensity and uniformity of ideological substance. The action-drama-spy series of the immediate pre-Vietnam War era, continuing throughout the war, gave an ideological underpinning to the U.S. intervention. Especially the FBI espionage-type series, featuring the omnipresent Communist threat . . .[80]

In this connection, Chomsky cites the American sociologists Paul Lazarfeld and Robert Merton, who pointed out in 1948 that the mass communications media 'not only continue to affirm the status quo but, in the same measure, they fail to raise essential questions about the structure of society. Hence by leading toward conformism and by providing little basis for a critical appraisal of society, the commercially sponsored mass media indirectly but effectively restrain the cogent development of a genuinely critical outlook.'[81]

There are a number of stages to the argument in support of the Propaganda Model: the detection of media distortion and misrepresentation of contemporary events; the extraction of significant regularities in this distortion; then an explanation of these patterns in terms of the nature of mass media institutions in a capitalist economy. It should be clear from this analysis that the basic features of the Propaganda Model can be applied to other Western economies, with minor adjustments. The general picture is of a media machine acting as a self-regulating system where propaganda is produced voluntarily and in a decentralized way by media personnel who censor themselves on the basis of an internalized sense of political correctness.[82] Chomsky concedes, 'Just how that works in the editorial offices I can't tell you.'[83] This kind of microanalysis is not the task of the Propaganda Model. The model provides an overview of the system at work, making sense out of a confusing picture by extracting the main principles of the system.

In 1985, a US television critic defended the media against the charge of being 'unpatriotic'. Corry suggested that the media were not 'anti-American', despite their adversarial stance, it was simply that they reflected 'a powerful element of the journalistic-literary-political culture', where 'the left wins battles ... by default' because 'its ideas make up the moral and intellectual framework for a large part of the [journalistic-literary-political] culture', and 'television becomes an accomplice of the left when it allows the culture to influence its news judgments [sic]'.[84] Chomsky describes Corry's 'journalistic-literary-political culture' in rather different terms. He describes it as 'an intellectual culture dedicated to terrorist values and policies'.[85] The examples sampled here, which are explored in much greater detail in Chomsky's work, go some way to substantiating this charge. Some critics charge that Chomsky has failed to prove his assertion that the media knowingly print falsehoods and suppress inconvenient truths. Chomsky concedes the truth of this criticism: 'In empirical inquiry, nothing is ever literally *proven*; one presents evidence and tries to show that it can be explained on the basis of the hypotheses advanced. A critic could then rationally argue that the evidence is mistaken, poorly chosen, or otherwise inadequate, or that there is a better theory to explain the facts.'[86] In the absence of compelling arguments along these lines, the Propaganda Model seems well established.

3

Intellectual Self-Defence

The picture outlined so far can seem rather overwhelming. A French interviewer may have been speaking for many readers when he suggested to Chomsky in 1981 that 'Supposing that there are minds that are free enough to read you, the implacable mechanisms that you describe will only make impotent and isolated poor souls of them.'[1] A black woman in California once wrote to Chomsky to make a similar point. She complained that after hearing him on the radio, she felt frustrated and utterly powerless. Chomsky responded that he took her criticism very seriously and apologized for the fact that he had often heard the same criticism before, 'though without responding sufficiently'. His own conclusion was that he should try to overcome his inclination to keep to analysis and 'should emphasize as well the fact that there is a great deal that can be done'.[2] Readers of Chomsky's political writings could be forgiven for feeling that the dominant message of his work is not that 'there is a great deal that can be done'. Chomsky comments, 'I wish I could be more encouraging to readers. *Turning the Tide* was meant to be a more positive book – hence the title. But it just didn't come out that way.'[3] Chomsky's views on the potential for challenging the propaganda system, and on the power of popular movements to achieve social changes, make up a tiny part of *Turning the Tide*, and, indeed, of the thousands of pages of political writing Chomsky has produced over the last few decades. The dominant impression left by his writings is of the power and resilience of what Chomsky himself describes as 'one of the most awesome and effective, if not the most awesome propaganda system that has ever existed in world history'.[4] Chomsky has tended to offer chilling insight and understanding rather than cheerful encouragement. Michael Ferber, a draft resister in the Boston area during the Vietnam War, recalls that organizers generally invited Chomsky and Howard Zinn to speak together at anti-war demonstrations:

> We liked having them both because they were so different. Howard was always funny, always made you feel real good about being in the peace movement, just that wonderfully light, serious touch. Whereas Chomsky was always bristling with facts and figures, and told us ten thousand things we needed to know, and whenever he spoke I always felt that I had to take notes.[5]

When uncovered, Chomsky's thoughts on the possibilities for change are actually quite encouraging. In his view, the propaganda system is 'extremely unstable', because 'Any system that's based on lying and deceit is inherently unstable.'[6] The system of thought control is, he says, based on principles that are 'flimsy and dishonest', and can collapse very quickly, 'as happened during the Vietnam war'.[7] On a smaller scale, Chomsky has referred to the modest but real successes of the East Timor solidarity network in raising the profile of the issue and providing real assistance to suffering people. By his account, there were perhaps half a dozen people in the United States devoting real effort to lifting the curtain of silence on the issue for many years. After some time, 'they actually did succeed in breaking through to the point where a few people in Congress became quite upset about the issue, there were occasional articles and editorials, and some limited news-reporting'. That might seem like a small achievement after the massacre of a hundred thousand people with Washington's support, but it did have an effect: the Red Cross was finally allowed in sporadically and some aid flowed to the victims. 'Tens of thousands of lives were saved. That's not a small achievement for a small group of mainly young people.'[8] 'There are very few people who can claim to have achieved so much of human consequence.'[9] As Chomsky notes, others can share such achievements, if they choose.

There are clearly opportunities for constructive action and means of resisting the power of the propaganda system. Chomsky remarks, 'If the schools were doing their job, which of course they aren't, but they could be, they would be providing people with means of intellectual self-defence . . . so that people growing up in a democratic society would have the means of intellectual self-defence against the system.'[10] As the schools are failing to provide this service, 'individuals have to somehow undertake this task themselves'.[11] The first step in freeing oneself from the grip of the propaganda system 'is to recognize that it exists, to come to understand that the pretended objectivity and neutrality of social and political commentary, or simply news reporting, masks presuppositions and ideological principles that should be challenged', and that often collapse quickly when exposed.[12] What we have to do is adopt towards our own institutions, including the media and the journals and the schools and universities, 'the same rational, critical stance that we take towards the institutions of any other power'. When we are confronted with the productions of Nazi or Stalinist propagandists, 'we have no problem at all in dissociating lies from truth' and recognizing the distortions and perversions that are used to protect the institutions from the truth. 'There's no reason why we shouldn't be able to take the same stance towards ourselves, despite the fact that we have to recognize that we're inundated with this, constantly, day after day.'[13]

During the Iran–Contra scandals, it was revealed that one part of the Reagan programme had been a propaganda offensive entitled 'Operation Truth'. This was described by government officials as a 'vast psychological warfare operation' against the population and Congress of the United States, 'of the kind the military conducts to influence a population in denied or enemy territory'.[14] Chomsky suggests that to gain true intellectual independence from the propaganda system, citizens need to understand their position in society: they are considered 'enemy territory' by the propaganda system.

Because of the sheer volume of media output, it is possible for those with some understanding of the system to gain insight into the reality behind the propaganda even from mainstream sources. Chomsky remarks, 'the enormous mass of material that is produced in the media and books makes it possible for a really assiduous and committed researcher to gain a fair picture of the real world by cutting through the mass of misrepresentation and fraud to the nuggets hidden within'.[15] Hard work can bring real insight: 'you just have to read widely'. If you read the US press carefully, says Chomsky, 'you'll find out a lot'.[16] Walter LaFeber, whom Chomsky describes as 'an outstanding and independent-minded historian', criticized the Propaganda Model on the grounds that it failed to explain 'why so many publications (including my own) can cite [stories that appear in the media] to attack President Reagan's Central American policy'.[17] Chomsky responded that the Propaganda Model was not weakened by the discovery that, 'with a careful and critical reading', material could be unearthed in the media that could be used by those who objected to Reagan's Central America policy on grounds of principle. By analogy, one could not prove that the Soviet press was free by finding material in it that undermined government propaganda. For example, one could not prove the non-propagandistic nature of the Soviet press by finding articles in the 1980s 'undermining the claim that the heroic Soviet military [was] marching from success to success in defending Afghanistan from bandits dispatched by the CIA'.[18] Such information could be found, for example, in the mass circulation weekly *Ogonyok*, or in *Literaturnaya Gazeta*, both cited in the book LaFeber criticized.[19] Every propaganda system is leaky. The more information that flows in the system, the more information will leak out.

Herman and Chomsky explain: 'That the media provide some information about an issue ... proves absolutely nothing about the adequacy or accuracy of media coverage. The media do, in fact, suppress a great deal of information, but even more important is the way they present a particular fact – its placement, tone, and frequency of repetition – and the framework of analysis in which it is placed.'[20] The quantity of coverage and the quality of the treatment are used to indicate to the audience the significance of different issues. By careful shading, and by reporting things only once, facts can be effectively erased. 'That a careful reader, looking for a fact can sometimes find it, with diligence and a skeptical eye, tells us nothing about whether that fact received the attention and context it deserved, whether it was intelligible to most readers, or whether it was effectively distorted or suppressed.'[21] Here, then, is a hint for those interested in intellectual self-defence. As LaFeber notes, 'Chomsky's methods and values are similar to those of I.F. Stone. Neither uses or needs inside information', both rely instead on freely available information, collected and organized into new patterns.[22]

It is often suggested that Chomsky derives advantages from his linguistic training in his efforts to counter official propaganda. Seymour Melman was one of the first to strike this chord in his review of *American Power and the New Mandarins*: 'It took a first class scholar of linguistics to perform the devastating analysis of the "Newspeak" quality of United States official discourse.'[23] Others have added variations on this theme in the years since. Chomsky is not impressed by such claims. For one thing, his work on linguistics is highly abstract and quite separate from the work of sociolinguists on how language is used in society. He remarks that anyone with any familiarity with the field should know that 'I might as well be doing algebraic topology for all that has to do with ideology.'[24] Chomsky suggests that there is also a hidden assumption that ordinary people cannot do such work. The idea is that just as you go to the political scientists to have politics explained to you, you should turn to the professional linguist to learn about ideology. No doubt Melman and others on the Left who have made connections between Chomsky's two areas of work would reject this position, but Chomsky himself feels it underlies such an analysis. Another version of Robinson's 'Chomsky problem', perhaps.

In Chomsky's view, it is not intellectually difficult to combat the propaganda system: 'I frankly don't think that anything more is required than ordinary common sense. . . . A willingness to use one's own native intelligence and common sense to analyze and dissect and compare the facts with the way in which they're presented is really sufficient.'[25] 'With a little industry and application, anyone who is willing to extricate himself [sic] from the system of shared ideology and propaganda will readily see through the modes of distortion developed by substantial segments of the intelligentsia. Everybody is capable of doing this.'[26] 'The alleged complexity, depth, and obscurity of these questions is part of the illusion propagated by the system of ideological control, which aims to make the issues seem remote from the general population and to persuade them of their incapacity to organize their own affairs or to understand the social world in which they live without the tutelage of intermediaries.'[27] A 'willingness to look at the facts with an open mind, to put simple assumptions to the test, and to pursue an argument to its conclusion' are all the equipment required to escape the propaganda system.[28]

The most basic requirement is the ability to think independently of the crushing pressures of the mass media. In many cases, such as the 1990 elections in Nicaragua, the information is there in the media. What is needed is an ability to break through conditioning: 'what you have to be able to do is when you hear the White House announce "We're going to continue with the embargo unless Chamorro wins," when you hear that, you have to be able to *think* enough so you conclude, "Well, these people are voting with a gun to their heads". . . . If you can't think that far, then it doesn't matter where the newspapers are.'[29] 'It's got to get to the point where it's like a reflex to read the first page of the L.A. *Times* and to count the lies and distortions and to put it into some sort of rational framework.'[30] In a sense, Chomsky's writings are themselves a course in intellectual self-defence, helping to build up sceptical reflexes.

It is interesting to note that there are significant variations in the grip of the propaganda system internationally. Chomsky's own career provides some examples. When in England during the 1991 Gulf War, Chomsky was constantly on radio and television. On his return to the United States, his only exposure was on community radio.[31] Similarly,

Chomsky was asked in 1988 to deliver the prestigious Massey lectures for the Canadian Broadcasting Company, the equivalent of the BBC. In Canada, he was asked by a local journalist to explain how, if his Propaganda Model of the media was accurate, he was given such an influential platform for his views, on a government-owned radio network. Chomsky replied, 'I'm afraid this remark may sound a little insulting, but let me try to say it without sounding that way . . . Canada is a much more open society in this respect than the United States, and the reason is that it's less important. . . . What people think about international affairs in Canada just doesn't matter that much to established power. If it did matter that much, Canada would close up too.'[32]

Within the United States itself, we find a similar relaxation of ideological constraints. Chomsky cites the case of Arafat's peace offers in April–May 1984, calling for negotiations with Israel leading to mutual recognition. The offer was immediately rejected by Israel and ignored by Washington. The elite media – the *New York Times* and the *Washington Post* – did not report the facts at all. The local 'quality press' – the *Boston Globe*, *Los Angeles Times*, the *Philadelphia Inquirer*, and so on – reported the basic facts, although they were 'obscured and quickly forgotten, to be replaced by familiar diatribes about Palestinian extremism', according to Chomsky. It was in the *San Francisco Examiner*, reputed to be one of the worst papers in any major city, that a United Press International story giving the basic facts appeared on the front page, under a full-page inch-high headline reading 'Arafat to Israel: Let's Talk'. The proper conclusion, Chomsky suggests, is that 'the less sophisticated press simply does not understand what facts must be suppressed as inconsistent with the party line'.[33] 'In general, the more significant the journal, the more it was determined to suppress the facts, which is an entirely natural stance given the position of the U.S. government on the issue.'[34] Chomsky comments, 'When you get out of the main centers in the United States, out of New York, Boston and Washington, then the controls ease. . . . What happens in areas that are marginal with respect to the exercise of power doesn't matter so much. What happens in the centers of power matters a great deal. Therefore the controls are tighter to the extent that you get closer to the center. As soon as you cross the border to Canada nobody really cares much what happens, so therefore it's much freer.'[35]

As well as there being some openings across the breadth of the press and other mass media, there is room for some movement even within the elite media.[36] One minor countervailing tendency in the media is 'the humanity and professional integrity of journalists', which often leads them in directions which are 'unacceptable in the ideological institutions'.[37] Many journalists would be surprised to hear Chomsky speaking in approving terms of the US 'tradition of professionalism of reporting that is also lacking in much of the world'.[38] There are also dissidents within mainstream journalism, 'journalists who are very savvy about all this and they know that they have a little bit of leeway and they're going to use it. They'll sneak things in, they'll change things, they'll use whatever leeway they have while having no illusions about what's going on.'[39] From his own acquaintances in the field, Chomsky knows that 'There are people who do this very consciously. Literally craft stories for the major journals, judging just how far they can go at a particular moment in saying what they would like to say.'[40] When the Iran–Contra scandals broke, such reporters realized 'that there was going to be a brief period, a couple of months in which the press would be a little more open than before to investigative reporting. They could sneak in things that they knew about perfectly well and now publish them in some form or other.'[41]

This kind of dissidence can sometimes be seen on television. Chomsky explains, '*Newsweek* can censor you, because they've got three days to rewrite your stuff, and the *New York Times* can censor you because they've got a day, but if you send your satellite spot across an hour before air time, your ninety seconds, they run it your way or they don't run it and get scooped. . . . So you've got control of that ninety seconds, and there are people who are in television for that reason.'[42] There are also the rare open dissidents who manage to find some kind of toehold within the major journals, like Alexander Cockburn, whom Chomsky once described as 'a one-man antidote to the entire American press',[43] with a column in the *Wall Street Journal* once a month, and more frequently elsewhere. There are institutional constraints on the extent of such openings, but as Chomsky points out, 'You should always press the institutions to their limits.'[44] For those interested in intellectual self-defence, there are some opportunities even within existing institutions.

Outside the institutions, there are other resources and other opportunities. Individuals and communities interested in intellectual self-defence will want to gain access to other forms of communication and to hear the information that is routinely blocked by the mass media. Chomsky suggests,

> If we had the honesty and moral courage, we would not let a day pass without hearing the cries of the victims of our actions, or inaction. We would turn on

55

the radio in the morning and hear the account of a Guatemalan army operation in Quiché province – one supplied and backed by the US and its Israeli client – in which the army entered a town, collected its population in a central town building, took all the men and beheaded them, raped the women and then killed them, and took the children to the nearby river and killed them by bashing their heads against the rocks. A few people escaped and told the stories, but not to us. We would turn on the radio in the afternoon and listen to a Portuguese priest in Timor telling how the Indonesian army, enjoying constant and crucial US military and diplomatic support, forced villagers to stab, chop and beat to death people supporting the resistance, including members of their own families. And in the evening we would listen to some of the victims who escaped the latest bombing attack on villages or fleeing civilians in El Salvador – an attack coordinated by US military aircraft operating from their Honduran and Panamanian sanctuaries. We would subject ourselves to the chilling record of terror and torture in our dependencies, compiled by Amnesty International, Americas Watch, Survival International, and other respected human rights organizations.[45]

If honesty broke out, 'the daily press would carry front-page pictures of children dying of malnutrition and disease in the countries where order reigns and crops and beef are exported to the American market, with an explanation of why this is so'.[46]

Apart from the documentation produced by human rights groups, there are also the journals of the peace and solidarity movements and similar sources. Chomsky regards the term 'alternative media' as 'demeaning'.[47] He prefers the term 'independent media'. Such channels have their limitations. Chomsky observes that 'to a certain extent the alternative media have become a kind of commercialization of freaki-ness'.[48] Journals such as the *Village Voice* are, according to Chomsky, 95 per cent commercialization of 'odd behaviour', and for that reason 'basically another technique of marginalization of the public'.[49] Never-theless, independent journals, like listener-supported radio, can help communities to protect themselves to some extent from the propaganda system. Chomsky reports that from his experience of travelling around the United States and giving talks, there is a real difference in those towns and cities that have listener-supported radio.[50] In such communi-ties, there is another view of the world, which is presented system-atically and continuously. There is also interaction between broadcasters and listeners, leading to greater community involvement. According to Chomsky, 'It has a very noticeable effect on the communi-ties.... You hear something different and you can think about things other than what you hear in the mainstream indoctrination system.' He concedes, 'Maybe what's coming across the community-supported radio is wrong, but at least it's different, a different kind of wrong. You can think a little better.'[51]

Intellectual self-defence requires hard work. For example, to find out about Central America, Chomsky warns, 'you're going to have to read exotic newspapers, you're going to have to compare today's lies with yesterday's lies and see if you can construct some rational story out of them. It's a major effort.'[52] The same is true of many other issues. To defend yourself successfully from the propaganda system, 'you have to decide to become a fanatic.... You have to work, because nobody's going to make it easy for you.'[53] There are successes. In the case of Central America, a considerable effort was made in the United States in the 1980s to uncover the realities of the region and to expose the responsibility of the US government for much of the horror. This dissidence helped to constrain US policy in Central America. Chomsky recounts a personal experience of the level of sophistication of the solidarity movement in the 1980s. Invited to give a talk in a town in Kansas, Chomsky was asked to meet beforehand with the local Central America solidarity group.

> So I thought, OK, four people will be in somebody's living room. To my surprise it wasn't four people in a living room but a couple of hundred people in a church. It was a town of 30,000 or so. There was a lot of literature, including literature I'd never seen, information I'd never seen, and people who were up and back from Central America, who'd been living there doing solidarity work.... I'm sure they know more about Central America than you'd find at the Central America desk of an American newspaper or many Latin American departments [of universities].[54]

Some people who share Chomsky's values feel his emphasis may be misplaced. Staughton Lynd, a fellow radical, criticized Chomsky in 1969 for concentrating too much on the deceit of intellectuals. Lynd wrote, 'it is perfectly clear that what Chomsky and all of us object to about American policy in Vietnam is only secondarily that the policy has been wrapped in lies. Had it been fully explained to the American people, it would still be just as evil.'[55] It is of course true that the moral level of US policy would not have been altered by a frank explanation of what it amounted to, but this was not the point of Chomsky's critique. The point was that an honest look at the nature of the war would very probably have led the US public to register its opposition. The public was prepared to accept a 'defence of freedom'; it was not prepared, as events were to show, to accept a criminal assault on the people of

Indochina. The deceit was an integral part of waging the war. We should bear in mind that the media did not only doctor the facts of what was going on, they also adopted the assumptions of government propaganda, helping to mould public attitudes and values. It was precisely these attitudes and values that Chomsky sought to challenge.

Some critics have charged that Chomsky is naïve, in that he believes that the provision of suppressed information will by itself lead to dissidence and resistance to state crimes by the general population. Jay Parini, in a sympathetic profile, suggests that while Chomsky's great strength is that he places so much faith in 'the persuasiveness of intricately constructed reason', it is also his 'vulnerability'.[56] In fact, Chomsky has explicitly disavowed any such 'faith': 'I try not to have irrational faith. We should try to act on the basis of our knowledge and understanding, recognizing that they're limited. But you have to make choices, and those choices have to be determined by matters that go well beyond anything that you can demonstrate or prove. In that sense, I have faith – but I would like to think it's at least the kind of faith which is subject to the test of fact and reason.'[57] 'I don't have faith that the truth will prevail if it becomes known, but we have no alternative to proceeding on that assumption, whatever its credibility may be.'[58] This is a version of 'Pascal's wager' which Chomsky often relates at the end of his talks. Pascal raised the question: How do you know whether God exists? If God did exist, a belief in him would bring benefits. If he did not exist, nothing would be lost by believing in him. Therefore, Pascal concluded, one should believe. Chomsky adapts the story: 'On this issue of human freedom, if you assume that there's no hope, you guarantee that there will be no hope.' If you assume that there is an instinct for freedom, that there are opportunities to change things, that hope is possible, then hope may be justified, and a better world may be built. 'That's your choice.'[59]

So far, I have been discussing means of individual self-defence against the propaganda system. This is a somewhat misleading approach. Chomsky has emphasized that intellectual self-defence is not something that can be carried out in isolation. One of the dangers is that 'you can lose your sanity'.[60] 'If you're alone and totally different from everybody in the world, you begin to think you must be crazy or something. It takes a big ego to withstand the fact that you're saying something different from everyone else.'[61] There is also a lot of very hard work involved, and 'The more organizational structure you have, the less fanatic you can be. The more you have to work on things alone, the harder it is.'[62] As long as people are isolated, there is little that they can do.

There is a more fundamental point. Chomsky argues that the way to combat propaganda is not by isolated academic research, but by engaging in social struggle. Research and activism should operate in tandem: 'You don't sit in your room somewhere and dispel illusions.' You need to interact with others in order to develop ideas: 'Otherwise you don't know what you think. You just hear something, and you react to it or you don't pay any attention to it or something.' Learning comes from interest, and if the subject is the social world, 'your interest in it often involves, ought to involve at least, trying to change it'. Learning also comes from formulating programmes, and trying to pursue them, understanding their failures and limitations, gaining experience in various ways. So, according to Chomsky, 'dispelling the illusions is just part of organizing and acting. It's not something you do in a seminar or in your living room.'[63] It might just be possible to dispel illusions about classical Greece by sitting in a library, but if you are trying to dispel illusions about a social process that is

> changing in front of your eyes and that you only get to see little pieces of and so on, that's really not the way to do it. You do it through interactions with other people. So it's really just part of functioning as a person in some kind of a community, and a 'community' means a community of concern, and a community of commitment and activism and so on.[64]

This is not, it has to be said, the main impression given by Chomsky's work. A number of factors, including his splendid isolation, apart from Edward Herman, on the shelves of libraries and bookshops, the lack of acknowledgements in his political writings, and what can seem like an Olympian detachment, may mislead some readers into thinking of Chomsky as an isolated thinker fighting a lonely battle against the might of the Western propaganda system. The picture conveyed by the film *Manufacturing Consent* has no doubt reinforced such an impression. The reality is quite different. A large part of Chomsky's writings come out of the constant round of talks he gives in the United States and around the world, and in the early days at least quite a few essays came out of courses he taught at MIT.[65] Chomsky is also part of an international network of activist intellectuals who are in continuous contact, and which supplies him with much of his material. He once spoke about his participation in this community:

> I spend an awful lot of time, for example, just xeroxing stuff, copying stuff for friends in other countries who are, in their countries, in roughly the situation I'm in here. They do the same for me. That means that although I don't get a

research grant to work on this kind of stuff or time off or whatever, I do have access to resources that mainstream scholars or for that matter the CIA don't have. The CIA or mainstream scholars don't have a very smart and perceptive guy in Israel scanning the Hebrew journals for them picking out the things that are important, doing an interpretation and analysis of them and sending reams of this material to me. . . . The end result is that you do have access to resources in a way I doubt that any national intelligence agency can duplicate.[66]

Such resources and such support are needed not only for the reasons given above, but also because of the resilience of the propaganda system. Not only is there a constant stream of new propaganda campaigns on new issues, there is also the fact that the system renews itself by continually seeking to entrench the approved version of past events, even if these have been entirely discredited. Chomsky remarks, 'It is a great mistake to believe that once the lies of the propaganda system have been exposed about, say, the Vietnam war, then it is pointless to take the topic up again.'[67] The propaganda machine will brush aside unwanted exposés with the same ease that it disposes of unwanted facts, and reconstruct a politically correct version of events. In the case of Vietnam, there has been a ceaseless campaign to instil the correct image of US benevolence in the defence of South Vietnam against Northern aggression. In the absence of a sustained and effective challenge to the propaganda version, the appropriate history will triumph.

The need for a 'community of concern' is even greater when public dissidence entails 'unpleasantness, vilification, a degree of risk, some-times loss of substantial privilege'[68] and other costs. Chomsky notes that these penalties for mental disobedience do not match the torture and horror meted out in the West's client states: 'It is possible even for those who are not saints or heroes to come to understand the world in which we live, and to act to stop the terror and violence for which we share responsibility by turning the other way.'[69] Breaking out of the psychosis of Western ideology does have its costs, but dissidents in the West will not share the fate of Winston Smith. And the potential benefits for the victims of Western power are considerable. To return to the letter which opened this chapter, it may be appropriate to end with other remarks from Chomsky's reply. He wrote:

With enough dedication and commitment, maybe we can finally make it a different world. After all, slavery was finally overcome, to mention just one example; and there are many others. Anyway, thanks for your letter. I will try to keep in mind its message, and I hope very much that you won't personally succumb to despair. It is not warranted. Honest dissidence and committed activism are not easy, but they are possible, and they can make a big difference.[70]

4

Patterns of Intervention

Chomsky was once asked at a public meeting what special qualifications he possessed to speak on world affairs. He replied that he possessed the same qualifications as Henry Kissinger, Walt Rostow and other professional commentators. In other words, 'None whatsoever.' He went on, 'The only difference is that I don't *pretend* to have qualifications. Nor do I pretend that qualifications are needed.'[1] Chomsky believes that 'Those areas of inquiry that have to do with problems of immediate human concern do not happen to be particularly profound or inaccessible to the ordinary person.'[2] National security policy is not intellectually any more challenging than being a well-informed sports fan.[3] Chomsky remarks drily, 'if there is a body of theory, well tested and verified, that applies to the conduct of foreign affairs or the resolution of domestic or international conflict, its existence has been kept a well-guarded secret'.[4] Chomsky notes that although he is without any professional credentials in mathematics, he has often been invited to speak on mathematical linguistics at mathematics seminars: 'No one has ever asked me whether I have the appropriate credentials to speak on these subjects; the mathematicians couldn't care less.... They want to know whether I am right or wrong, whether the subject is interesting or not, whether better approaches are possible – the discussion dealt with the subject, not with my right to discuss it.'[5] On the other hand, when commenting on US foreign policy, 'the issue is constantly raised, often with considerable venom'.[6] He suggests that an emphasis on certification reflects a certain lack of intellectual content in the field in question. Henry Kissinger provided some insight, no doubt unwittingly, into the cult of the expert when he noted that the expert 'has his [sic] constituency – those who have a vested interest in commonly held opinions; elaborating and defining its consensus at a high level has, after all, made him an expert'.[7] Those who have the power to mould public opinion select experts on the basis of their political correctness, not because of their specialized knowledge.

Chomsky has devoted himself to exposing and contesting the assumptions underpinning the consensus of the 'experts'. The most fundamental assumption in mainstream discussion in the United States is the belief that the United States is a benevolent power, motivated by a desire to do good. If those on the very edge of respectability accept this higher truth, they may be admitted to respectable circles. If this principle is adopted, one can even use the otherwise forbidden word 'imperialism'. Thus Ronald Steele criticizes 'American imperialism', but adds that 'the American empire came into being by accident and has been maintained from a sense of benevolence'. He continues, 'We engaged in a kind of welfare imperialism, empire-building for noble ends rather than for such base motives as profit and influence.... We have not exploited our empire ... have we not been generous with our clients and allies, sending them vast amounts of money and even sacrificing the lives of our own soldiers on their behalf? Of course we have.'[8] Hans Morgenthau, a famous 'realist' critic of US foreign policy and an exceptionally independent thinker in mainstream terms, observed in 1967, 'We have intervened in the political, military and economic affairs of other countries to the tune of far in excess of $100 billion, and we are at present involved in a costly and risky war in order to build a nation in South Vietnam.' 'Only the enemies of the United States', Morgenthau suggested, 'will question the generosity of these efforts, which have no parallel in history.'[9]

Similar hymns of self-praise can be found throughout the spectrum of 'responsible opinion'. Chomsky summarizes:

> In the United States, the prevailing version of the 'white man's burden' has been the doctrine, carefully nurtured by the intelligentsia, that the United States, alone among the powers of modern history, is not guided in its international affairs by the perceived material interests of those with domestic power, but rather wanders aimlessly, merely reacting to the initiatives of others, while pursuing abstract moral principles: the Wilsonian principles of freedom and self-determination, democracy, equality, and so on.[10]

The fact that the historical record does not seem to bear out this analysis is set aside. Thus Morgenthau rebukes those who do not accept that the United States is devoted to spreading equality throughout the world. He responds, 'To reason thus is to confound the abuse of reality with reality itself.'[11] In other words, 'reality' is the unachieved and mystical 'transcendent purpose' of the United States. The historical record, on the other hand, is merely an 'abuse of reality', because it does not conform to the requirements of US ideology. The facts do not matter. It must be true that Washington is seeking greater equality, and therefore it *is* true that Washington is seeking greater equality. Chomsky comments, 'The United States is Good, its leaders are Good, the facts are irrelevant, no matter how prominently displayed.'[12]

Norman Graebner, whom Chomsky describes as 'an excellent historian' and a critic of Cold War idiocies, provides another demonstration of the intellectual level needed to maintain the myth of benevolence. Graebner accepts the common assumption that US foreign policy has been guided by the Wilsonian principles of peace and self-determination for all nations. Graebner investigates particular examples where these principles have been contested, and observes: 'It was ironic that this nation generally ignored the principles of self-determination in Asia and Africa where it had some chance of success and promoted it behind the Iron and Bamboo Curtains where it had no chance of success at all.'[13] Again, we have a flat contradiction between theory and evidence. Chomsky comments: 'By similar logic a physicist might formulate a general hypothesis, put it to the test, discover that it is refuted in each specific instance, and conclude that it is ironic that the facts are the opposite of what the principle predicts – but the principle nevertheless stands.'[14] Irony is a very useful category for disposing of uncomfortable facts.

Chomsky once described the Propaganda Model in terms of 'Orwell's Problem'. As Chomsky comments, Orwell was fascinated 'by the ability of totalitarian systems to instill beliefs that are firmly held and widely accepted although they are completely without foundation and often plainly at variance with obvious facts about the world around us'.[15] This seems a classic example.

Morgenthau brings out the issues clearly in another of his proposals. He suggests that the national interest underlying a rational foreign policy 'is not defined by the whim of a man [sic] or the partisanship of party but imposes itself as an objective datum upon all men applying their rational faculties to the conduct of foreign policy'. He cites as illustrations US support for South Korea, containment of China and the upholding of the Monroe Doctrine. At the same time, Morgenthau observes that 'the concentrations of private power which have actually governed America since the Civil War have withstood all attempts to control, let alone dissolve them [and] have preserved their hold upon the levers of political decision'.[16] Under such circumstances, Chomsky asks, can we expect foreign policy to be determined by the application of rational faculties to objective data, or do we rather expect it to be the expression of the interests of those 'concentrations of private power which have actually governed America since the Civil War'? When we investigate, Chomsky suggests, we find that the real interests of the people of the United States were not advanced by 'containing' China, supporting dictatorships in South Korea or ensuring the subordination of Latin American economies to the needs of US-based transnational corporations. On the other hand, he suggests, it can be argued that the interests of Morgenthau's 'concentrations of private power' have been advanced by these policies.[17] If so, it is clear that foreign policy formation is not simply the application of reason and common sense to world affairs, but is controlled by those who hold power.

This simple observation is the basis of much of Chomsky's work on US foreign policy. World affairs are complex and confusing, and can appear chaotic, but, according to Chomsky, there are certain regularities in recent history which when grasped can help to make sense out of the chaos. Chomsky argues that there are systematic patterns in US foreign policy and that these derive from the pursuit of 'a fixed geopolitical conception that has remained invariant over a long period and that is deeply rooted in U.S. institutions'.[18] Chomsky suggests that without a grasp of this underlying concept, 'the chances that you'll understand what is happening in the world are relatively slight; whereas if you do understand it, quite a lot of things fall into place, and you could even get a reputation as a good prophet'.[19] What is this 'fixed geopolitical conception'? Chomsky has sometimes described it as the 'Fifth Freedom'. During the Second World War, President Roosevelt announced that the Allies were fighting for Four Freedoms: freedom of speech, freedom of worship, freedom from want and freedom from fear. Chomsky comments bitingly, 'Roosevelt spoke of Four Freedoms, but not of the Fifth and most important: the freedom to rob and to exploit.'[20] Infringements of the Four Freedoms evoke great concern – when they occur in enemy territory. When they occur in Washington's sphere of influence, they are barely noticed. Chomsky remarks, 'as the historical record demonstrates with great clarity, it is only when the fifth and fundamental freedom is threatened that a sudden and short-lived concern for other forms of freedom manifests itself ...'[21] The fine words have little or no value in practice, except in so far as they are useful in whipping up popular support for an intervention to defend the Fifth Freedom, 'the one that really counts'.[22]

As in the case of the Propaganda Model, this is a startling proposal, which requires a high level of documentation to become persuasive. Chomsky and his associates have by now provided a large number of studies with a considerable amount of corroborating evidence. We can only sample a few of their case studies. Perhaps the best example to take briefly is the relationship between US foreign policy and human rights. The conventional picture, of course, is that the United States is concerned with human rights and seeks to extend these wherever possible. According to Chomsky, the United States has indeed shown concern for human rights — it has opposed them with 'tremendous ferocity, and even violence'.[23] Lars Schoultz, the leading academic specialist on the subject, found that US foreign aid to Latin America 'has tended to flow disproportionately to Latin American governments which torture their citizens ... to the hemisphere's relatively egregious violators of fundamental human rights'.[24] The correlation is strong, includes military aid and persisted through the Carter era, when the US human rights campaign was supposedly at its height. Furthermore, Schoultz demonstrated, this correlation could not be attributed to a linking of aid and need. Michael Klare and Cynthia Arnson in a separate study demonstrated that the United States, then the world's leading supplier of police and prison hardware, provides 'guns, equipment, training, and technical support to the police and paramilitary forces *most directly involved in the torture, assassination, and abuse of civilian dissidents*'.[25]

Chomsky and Herman conducted their own investigation of this topic, comparing changes in the human rights climate in ten US client-states with changes in US economic and military aid in the two or three years before and after major political changes.[26] The 1973 coup in Chile which established the Pinochet regime led to a 558 per cent increase in US economic aid and a 1,079 per cent increase in US and multinational credits. The military coup in Brazil in 1964 led to a deterioration in human rights and an increase in US aid: overall aid and credits by the United States and multinational lending organizations increased 110 per cent in the three years following the coup, compared to the three years before the coup.[27] After the CIA-sponsored coup in Iran in 1953, total US and multinational aid and credits increased nine-fold. After the CIA-sponsored coup in Guatemala in 1954, total US and multinational aid and credits increased 5,300 per cent.[28] There are complicating factors in some cases, but the overall picture is clear enough. Each of the ten countries studied was a major violator of human rights in the 1970s and yet each received substantial amounts of US military and economic aid, and police training assistance. Furthermore, 'the deterioration of the human rights climate in some Free World dependency tends to correlate rather closely with an increase in US aid and support'.[29] When we take into account the systematic pattern of US policies towards these and other Third World countries, these figures make it clear that the alleged commitment to democracy and human rights is mere rhetoric, 'directly contrary to actual policy'.[30]

A correlation is not an explanation. One possible explanation is that US governments have a positive hatred of human rights. This is 'implausible', Chomsky suggests.[31] The correct explanation is that both human rights conditions and US aid are closely correlated with a third, crucial coordinate: 'For most of the sample countries, *US-controlled aid has been positively related to investment climate and inversely related to the maintenance of a democratic order and human rights.*'[32] The investment climate of a country is determined by its tax laws, by its attitude to the repatriation of profit and by the nature and scale of government controls on wages and trade unions. It is easy to see why there should be a close relationship between the climate for foreign investors and human rights violations: 'in the Third World, improvement in the investment climate is regularly achieved by destruction of popular organizations, torture of labour and peasant organizers, killing of priests engaged in social reforms, and general mass murder and repression'.[33] When Chomsky and Herman introduce this element into their matrix, they indeed find a positive correlation between aid, torture and the investment climate. US aid and aid from financial institutions under US control are clearly governed by a concern for the Fifth Freedom, not by any concern for human rights.

As in the case of the Propaganda Model, this is the very opposite of a 'conspiracy theory'. It is an institutional critique based on the nature of social structures, not an accusation against particular individuals or secret groupings. Chomsky has rigorously avoided conspiracy theories of the latter type. For example, he expressed scepticism regarding the 'October Surprise' theory that the roots of the Iran–Contra scandal lie in a deal made in 1980 between Ronald Reagan's campaign team and the Iranian authorities – that the Iranians promised not to release hostages until after the election was over, so that Carter would not be able to claim credit and perhaps reverse his falling popularity ratings, and that in return the Reagan team agreed to supply arms at a later date.[34] Chomsky points out the major weakness of the theory: the arms flow to Iran began under Carter in 1980, *before* Reagan was elected. He suggests that the proper focus for inquiry should be patterns in US policy rather than possible minor variations in them. For example, one topic off the mainstream agenda in the case of the Iran–Contra scandal was the pattern of US arms supplies to enemy states such as Indonesia in the early 1960s, Thailand after the 1973 democracy opening and Brazil under the liberal President Goulart. In all three cases the supply of arms to unfriendly states was accompanied by greater US influence over the military in the target country. In all three cases increased US arms supplies were followed by military coups, with the predictable increases in other forms of US aid as well as the predictable increases in human rights violations.[35] When placed in such a framework, the arms supply to Iran becomes more comprehensible and revealing of the standard operating procedures of US institutions.

Chomsky has also expressed some scepticism about the Christic Institute's 'secret team' analysis of US covert operations: 'My own feeling is that a lot of it is plausible but not demonstrated. How much of it will turn out to be true, I don't know. . . . But I'd watch all of this stuff with a grain of salt. You can get carried away by big complicated conspiracies.' The one aspect of the analysis Chomsky registered complete opposition to was the suggestion that Washington had been manipulated and controlled by a small group of rogue officials. In Chomsky's view, the available evidence demonstrates that the CIA and other agencies are obedient and well controlled by the civilian authorities: 'the record, at least as far as I read it, shows pretty careful planning and control by the civilian authorities, and the idea that maybe the government was hijacked by a secret team, I don't believe it. I think that that's not correct and probably diversionary if it turns attention away from the way the institutions themselves function.'[36]

When we turn to the greatest conspiracy theory of them all, we find Chomsky resolutely sceptical and, again, concerned at the diversion of energy. The belief that John F. Kennedy was assassinated by a high-level conspiracy and that the crime has since been concealed, is, as Chomsky notes, widely held in the grassroots movements and among Left intellectuals and, indeed, 'is often presented as established truth, the starting point for further discussion'.[37] Across this spectrum of opinion, it is also often assumed that President Kennedy was about to break the mould of US politics and that it was his intention to, for example, withdraw from Vietnam that prompted his assassins to act. Chomsky has addressed this second assumption, but not the question of the assassination itself.[38] Examining Kennedy's public statements, the internal record which has been revealed and the historical record, Chomsky finds no basis for the belief that Kennedy deviated from the policy framework set by his predecessors. Chomsky clearly wishes to direct attention away from speculation about the assassination and towards the war itself, and in particular towards an understanding of the roots of policy-making: 'In the present case, there is a rich record to assist us in the quest for the roots of policy planning. People who want to understand and change the world will do well, in my opinion, to pay attention to it, not to engage in groundless speculation as to what one or another personality might have done.'[39]

Throughout his career as a political commentator, Chomsky has concentrated on revealing the systematic patterns in US foreign policy and in media behaviour, generally seeking to relate these patterns to the institutional structures that govern reporting and foreign policy-making. Chomsky has consistently avoided the focus on personalities and individuals which is the defining characteristic of the true conspiracy theory. Chomsky has even gone on record decrying the Left's addiction to conspiracy theories, which drains the movement of a large proportion of its resources, which could be used much more productively.[40] He linked the growth of such theories to the growth of cynicism and fear in society: 'Everybody thinks somebody is doing something to them, and they don't exactly know who.' There is a lack of serious political analysis of the institutional sources of policy and decisions. Consequently, many people are vulnerable to irrationality. 'If I gave a talk somewhere and said that George Bush is from outer space and drinks children's blood or something, people would probably say, why not? Sounds plausible. In this kind of state people are open to anything: religious fundamentalism, conspiracy theory.... So in that circumstance it's extremely easy to say there's some secret team out there who stole our nice country from us.'[41]

In contrast to such tendencies, Chomsky has devoted his own work to a rational analysis of the way that dominant US institutions work, how they determine much of what happens in the world and how they control the perception of these events at home. There is one particular event in modern history which Chomsky has returned to again and again as a classic demonstration of the way that the Fifth Freedom is consciously placed at the centre of state planning and action. During the Second World War, a high-level group of planners was formed, drawn from the State Department and from the Council on Foreign Relations (CFR), a business think tank.[42] In what was called the 'War and Peace Studies Project', these elite planners worked throughout the war to develop war and peace aims for the United States. Their guiding concept was the 'Grand Area', the territory which should be taken under control by the United States 'in a world in which it proposes to hold unquestioned power'.[43] For one of the directors of the CFR, the Grand

Area was the area 'strategically necessary for world control'.[44] In the early years of the war it was thought that part of the postwar world would be controlled by Germany, in which case the task was to develop 'an integrated policy to achieve military and economic supremacy for the United States within the non-German world'.[45] As the tide of the war turned, it became clear that Nazi Germany would be defeated and that, as the Council's president put it, 'the British Empire as it existed in the past will never reappear and ... the United States may have to take its place'.[46]

The critical issue was identified as the acquisition for the US economy of 'the "elbow room" ... needed in order to survive without major readjustments'.[47] This 'elbow room' was to include, at a minimum, the Western Hemisphere, the British Empire and the Far East, and was, in Chomsky's words, 'to be developed as an integrated economic system responsive to the needs of the American economy – or more precisely, those who own and manage it'.[48] The developed nations, such as Germany and Japan, had their place as consumers of US industrial goods. The Third World, on the other hand, was to serve the needs of the industrial societies in various ways. Working within the Grand Area framework after the war, the State Department's Policy Planning Staff made it clear that South East Asia, for example, should be made to 'fulfill its major function as a source of raw materials and a market for Japan and Western Europe'.[49] This attitude was generalized to the whole Third World. In the CFR documents, it is a pervasive theme that international trade and investment are closely related to the economic health of the United States, as is access to the resources of the Grand Area (on terms determined by the United States), so that the Grand Area must be organized, in Chomsky words, so as 'to guarantee the health and structure of the American economy, its internal structure unmodified'.[50] The control of the Grand Area, coupled with the militarization of much of the economy, would protect the United States against recession and domestic reorganization that might threaten business privileges.

George Kennan, credited as the architect of 'containment' and then head of the State Department Policy Planning Staff, noted in 1948 that the United States had 'about 50% of the world's wealth, but only 6.3% of its population'. He argued that 'Our real task in the coming period is to devise a pattern of relationships which will permit us to maintain this position of disparity without positive detriment to our national security.' To achieve this task, Kennan wrote,

we will have to dispense with all sentimentality and day-dreaming; and our attention will have to be concentrated everywhere on our immediate national objectives. We need not deceive ourselves that we can afford today the luxury of altruism and world-benefaction....We should cease to talk about vague and – for the Far East – unreal objectives such as human rights, the raising of the living standards, and democratization. The day is not far off when we are going to have to deal in straight power concepts. The less we are then hampered by idealistic slogans, the better.[51]

Chomsky points out that US elites were as concerned with preserving a 'position of disparity' between groups within the United States as between the United States and other nations. Putting this qualification to one side, we find in these words, and in the record of imperial planning during the war, a clear expression of the real value of the Four Freedoms in US foreign policy, and the overriding importance of the Fifth Freedom. During the war, CFR and State Department planners had made the position clear by urging the president to stress the interests of the peoples of Europe, Asia, Africa and Latin America in his public pronouncements, as 'this would have a better propaganda value' than an honest expression of US war aims.[52]

One region where the pursuit of the Grand Area scheme was to have explosive consequences was Indochina. As we have seen, the purpose of South East Asia was to 'fulfill its major function as a source of raw materials and a market for Japan and Western Europe'. The Viet Minh anti-fascist resistance and other nationalist movements saw things differently. They were therefore targeted as obstacles to the Grand Area project. The United States supported the attempt to reimpose French colonialism on Indochina and the destruction of the anti-fascist resistance, as elsewhere. It is important to stress that the issue for US planners was not Vietnam itself. A US National Security Council working group, meeting in November 1964, feared that if South Vietnam 'fell', mainland South East Asia might also 'fall', and noted that 'if either Thailand or Malaysia were lost, or went badly sour in any way, then the rot would be in real danger of spreading all over mainland South-east Asia'.[53] In particular, there might be unwelcome effects on Japan, 'where the set is clearly in the direction of closer ties with Communist China, with a clear threat of early recognition', and on the rest of South East Asia, which might also 'succumb over time', so that the effects might be 'multiplied many times over'.[54] Chomsky notes that the planners are vague as to how the rot will spread: 'This imprecision cannot be an oversight; these are, after all, the crucial issues, the issues that led the planners to recommend successive stages of aggression in Indochina, at immense risk and cost. But even internal documents, detailed analysis of options and possible consequences, refer to these central issues in loose and almost mystical terms.'[55] Occasionally they indicate that Thailand, for example, might accommodate to Communist China 'even without any marked military move by Communist China...'[56] But the non-military mechanisms of accommodation are never spelt out.

There is only one rational explanation for this imprecision, Chomsky argues. The 'rot' that the planners feared was an 'ideological threat',[57] the threat that successful development directed to national needs in a unified Vietnam could inspire and encourage nationalist movements elsewhere in South East Asia. This is, Chomsky suggests, the rational core of the 'domino theory'. The version released for popular consumption was somewhat different, described by Chomsky in the following terms: 'You know, Ho Chi Minh will get into a canoe and land in Boston and rape your sister and that sort of thing.'[58] Such fantasies appear to have had some hold even within decision-making circles. For example, in 1948, Lyndon Johnson, on the liberal side of mainstream politics, warned that unless the United States maintained its overwhelming military superiority, it would be 'a bound and throttled giant; impotent and easy prey to any yellow dwarf with a pocket knife'.[59] Chomsky points out that 'The fact that policymakers may be caught up in the fantasies they spin to disguise imperial intervention, and may sometimes even find themselves trapped by them, should not prevent us from asking what function these ideological constructions fulfil...'[60] Only those kinds of irrationality which are useful and serve power are permitted to state officials. Chomsky suggests that the rationalizations of foreign policy-makers can be set aside when analysing their motivations and the functions of policy, just as the belief of many corporate executives that they are enhancing social values and serving the community is generally ignored when analysing their performance as profit-maximizers and enhancers of market share for their companies.

The conventional view is that the Vietnam War was an aberration in US policy. Chomsky points out that, when placed in the context of other postwar US interventions, in Guatemala, the Dominican Republic, Lebanon, Iran, and so on, Vietnam was an 'aberration' for the United States only in the sense that 'we lost control'.[61] Charles Glass puts the matter succinctly in an article on Chomsky:

The high moral purpose theory holds that Indonesia (both in its repression of its own citizens and its brutal conquest of neighbouring East Timor), the Philippines, the nineteen military coups in Latin America since 1960, Iran under the Shah, Nicaragua under Somoza, *et al.*, are exceptions to the rule in American foreign policy. To Chomsky and Herman, they are the rule.[62]

Chomsky argues that every postwar US president could have been hanged for violations of the Nuremburg principles. Truman invaded Greece, Eisenhower overthrew the elected government of Guatemala, Kennedy invaded Cuba, Johnson invaded the Dominican Republic, Nixon invaded Cambodia, Ford supported the invasion of East Timor, Carter increased that support, and Reagan, apart from his own activities, supported the Israeli invasion of Lebanon. These are only a few of the crimes that could be charged against these leaders.[63] Apart from ignoring the pattern of US interventionism that Vietnam is part of, it is also conventional to neglect the period before the US invasion of South Vietnam, when the basis of US policy was set. Once this earlier period is forgotten, it is usual to criticize the US intervention in the late 1960s for its 'stupidity' and 'savagery'. These are socially neutral terms that distract attention from institutional factors. All that is required, according to such a critique, is the selection of more intelligent and humane leaders, to carry out more intelligent and humane invasions. This is not to say that stupidity and self-delusion were not factors in the conduct of the war. Hannah Arendt once proposed that irrational factors dominated Vietnam policy. Chomsky comments, 'A case can be made for her view that these were significant factors, but primarily in the 1960s.'[64] In his view, the record exposed in the Pentagon Papers shows that there was, in the 1960s, 'an increasing component of irrationalism and posturing, with much talk of psychological tests of will, humiliation, the American image, and so on'.[65] By 1965, Chomsky notes, 'questions of long-term motive were of diminished importance. We were there. Period.'[66] In the earlier period, however, the documentary record gives quite a different picture. Those who supported French colonialism and moved to undermine the Geneva Accords were implementing a sophisticated plan for securing US power. 'Never was there the slightest deviation from the principle that a non-Communist regime must be imposed, regardless of popular sentiment.'[67] Chomsky comments, 'Given this principle, the strength of the Vietnamese resistance, the military power available to the United States, and the lack of effective constraints, one can deduce with almost mathematical precision the strategy of annihilation that was gradually undertaken.'[68] Such are the sanctions employed to secure the Grand Area and to preserve 'elbow room' for US corporations.

Understood correctly, then, Vietnam was a rather peripheral concern for US planners, which gained significance in relation to other, more important nations. This, too, is a pattern in US foreign policy. According to Chomsky, 'the tinier and weaker the country, the less endowed it is with resources, the more dangerous it is' to US power.[69] He explains, 'if a tiny nothing-country with no natural resources can begin to extricate itself from the system of misery and oppression that we've helped to impose, then others who have more resources may be tempted to do likewise'.[70] This explains the fanatical opposition of the US government to constructive development in countries such as Grenada, Cuba and Nicaragua. When Third World countries begin to have strange ideas about controlling their resources for their own benefit, rather than subordinating themselves to the leaders of the Free World, they can expect disciplinary measures. Typically, these attacks will be couched in terms of 'containing the Communists' or 'defending freedom'.

Anti-communism has been the most obvious regularity in US foreign policy since the Second World War. Why exactly has the United States opposed communism? The conventional answer is that communism is aggressive and expansionist in character, and must be contained. Robert Tucker argued in 1968 that,

> The containment of China has not been pursued simply because China has a communist government, but because of China's outlook generally and her policy in Asia particularly. It is China's insistence upon changing the Asian status quo, and the methods she has used, that explain American hostility.[71]

Chomsky asks, 'What methods did China use in changing the status quo beyond its borders? In what respect were these methods "objectionable" in comparison with American methods in the Far East? In what sense was the forceful reimposition of French colonialism in opposition to a Communist-led Vietnamese nationalist movement an attempt to preserve the status quo after World War II?'[72] Chomsky suggests that Tucker was nearer the mark when he pointed out that US hostility towards – in fact, terrorism against[73] – Cuba was based on the fear that Castro 'would refuse to do our bidding' and 'would stand as a challenge to our otherwise undisputed hegemony in this hemisphere'. Tucker is unable to explain how Castro would refuse to do US bidding and what aspects of Washington's hegemony would be challenged. He remains at the level of generalities: 'America's interventionist and counterrevolutionary policy' can be explained by two factors: 'a reasonably well-grounded fear that the American example might become irrelevant to much of the world'; and the 'will to exercise dominion over others'.[74] Chomsky asks what elements of 'the American example' a foreign society must adopt to allay these fears:

> Was it fear that Guatemala would choose soccer rather than baseball as its national sport that precipitated the 1954 intervention? Was the Bay of Pigs invasion rooted in the fear that Cuban intellectuals would prefer Continental phenomenology to American-style analytical philosophy? Is it our concern that the model of American political democracy might prove 'irrelevant' that explains why the United States executive so prefers Brazil to Chile under Allende?[75]

The real answer, Chomsky suggests, lies in a 1955 study by the Woodrow Wilson Foundation and the National Planning Association, which concluded that the primary threat of communism was the economic transformation of the communist powers 'in ways which reduce their willingness and ability to complement the industrial economies of the West'.[76] This also explains the content of what Tucker vaguely calls the 'will to exercise dominion'.

In other words, it is not the real crimes of the so-called 'communist'[77] states which provoke US anti-communism, it is their refusal to subordinate their economies to the industrial economies of the West. In Chomsky's words, the United States has been hostile to the communist states 'because they separate themselves from the US-dominated world system and attempt to use their resources for their own development'.[78] George Kennan, that influential policy-maker, explained that in Latin America, as elsewhere, 'the protection of our resources' was the critical issue, and that as the main threat to US control of these resources was indigenous, Washington should not shrink from the unpleasant option of 'police repression by the local government'. In general, Kennan suggested, 'it is better to have a strong regime in power than a liberal government if it is indulgent and relaxed and penetrated by Communists'.[79] Chomsky comments that the term 'communist' is used here in its technical sense, 'referring to labour leaders, peasant organizers, priests organizing self-help groups, and others with the wrong priorities'.[80] In this sense, 'communism' is often a synonym for 'nationalism'. Chomsky refers to a top secret document from 1954 which plainly states the perceived threat to the United States in much of the Third World:

> There is a trend in Latin America toward nationalistic regimes maintained in large part by appeals to the masses of the population. Concurrently, there is

an increasingly popular demand for immediate improvement in the low living standards of the masses, with the result that most Latin American governments are under intense domestic political pressure to increase production and to diversify their economics [sic].[81]

The National Security Council memorandum continues by pointing out that 'The growth of nationalism is facilitated by historic anti-US prejudices and is exploited by Communists.' US assistance is therefore required to block 'Communist intervention and subversion'. For the properly indoctrinated, those who exploit irrational prejudices against the United States are, by definition, communists. When used in US propaganda, Chomsky points out, 'communism' is a broad-ranging concept that has 'little relation to social, political or economic doctrines but a great deal to do with a proper understanding of one's duties and function in the global system', as prescribed by the lord of the system.[82] In other words, it is not important what people actually believe and what they think they are, if they interfere with the Fifth Freedom, they are 'communists' and will be treated accordingly. With the demise of the Soviet Union, new terms of abuse may have to replace this useful ideological weapon.

One useful term is 'terrorism'. This term is generally reserved for anti-state violence, but covers a wider spread of activities. The US Army defines terrorism as 'the calculated use of violence or the threat of violence to attain goals that are political, religious or ideological in nature'. Theoretically at least, one could speak of 'US state terrorism'. Within the propaganda system, this concept does not exist – it cannot exist – because of the fundamental principle that the 'United States is Good'. Chomsky has, none the less, documented the existence of US terrorism; we may glance at a few examples. One prime piece of evidence is the judgment of the World Court in the case of the US attack on Nicaragua. In June 1986, the Court found that US actions constituted 'an unlawful use of force' and violations of binding treaties. The Court found that the attacks could not be justified either by the doctrine of collective self-defence (the US claim) or by any right of the United States to take counter-actions in the event of intervention by Nicaragua in El Salvador – as no such right exists in international law.[83] It follows that the US attack on Nicaragua falls into the category of terrorism (or perhaps the more serious category of 'aggression'). It is important to note how distorted the discussion of terrorism has become. During the 1980s, no one personified 'international terrorism' in US ideology more than Muammar Gaddafi. Libya did engage in terrorism, sometimes international terrorism, Chomsky notes, in that it killed fourteen Libyan citizens, four abroad, in the period up to 1985. During this same period, 'the US client regime of El Salvador killed some fifty thousand of its citizens in the course of what Bishop Rivera y Damas, who succeeded the assassinated Archbishop Romero, described in October 1980, after seven months of terror, as a "war of extermination and genocide against a defenceless civilian population"'.[84] Chomsky notes that this was not only state terror, but international terrorism, 'given the organization, supply, training, and direct participation by the Ruler of the Hemisphere'.[85] Another comparison: Chomsky suggests that Iran's most extreme involvement in international terrorism in the 1980s was its involvement in support for the Contras. The terrorism of the Contras, a US proxy army, far exceeded anything attributable to Iran. 'So we could then say, if we were to be honest with ourselves, that the real scandal of the Iran–Contra hearings was that Iran was found dealing with Washington – terrorist commanders in Washington – its major terrorist act.'[86]

In the past, there have been occasions when terrorism has been insufficient, and the United States has had to move to aggression to enforce the Fifth Freedom and maintain the Grand Area. Sometimes, however, lesser means suffice. While there is a consensus in mainstream circles that violence is a legitimate option when the Fifth Freedom is under threat, there are differences between 'doves' and 'hawks': 'It would be wrong to leave the impression that the ideology of the liberal intelligentsia translates itself into policy as a rain of cluster bombs and napalm,' Chomsky noted in connection with Vietnam.[87] Liberals tend to prefer diplomacy, sanctions, international debt and other less obviously bloody mechanisms of control. Chomsky comments, 'The use of force to control the Third World is a last resort. Economic weapons are more efficient, when feasible',[88] GATT and NAFTA being recent acquisitions. In an earlier period, the export promotion policies of the Latin American 'Alliance for Progress', instituted by the Kennedy administration along with other 'aid' programmes, 'had a murderous and destructive impact, probably more so than the death squads that originated in the same aid programs, as they are euphemistically called'.[89] Chomsky notes that some analysts have described these programmes as the 'soft war'.[90] One classic illustration of the difference between the doves and the hawks was the attack on Nicaragua in the 1980s. The doves objected to the use of the Contras, arguing that diplomatic trickery and sanctions would be more effective than terrorism in creating misery, regaining US control and forcing the

Sandinista government out of power, and returning the economy to its proper service role.[91]

Within the mainstream, it is possible to record official 'errors' and 'failures' in the pursuit of noble objectives, but not, Chomsky points out, 'to expose their systematic patterns and to trace these "blunders" to the conscious planning that regularly underlies them or to their roots in the pattern of privilege and domination in the domestic society'.[92] The power of the propaganda system means that much of the energy of anti-intervention movements is taken up with a minute analysis of the situation in various countries around the world. The real problem lies not in Vietnam, or in Nicaragua, or in Haiti, but rather closer to home. Chomsky remarks,

> I've been in 10,000 teach-ins in my life, I don't know how many. Every one of them is about something happening somewhere else. I go to a teach-in on Central America, a teach-in on the Middle East, a teach-in on Vietnam. That's all nonsense. Everything's happening in Washington. It's just the same things in Washington playing themselves out in different parts of the world.[93]

Concentrated private power in the United States requires the state to create and maintain an international order that will foster improvements in the investment climate and other arrangements to entrench privilege. In defence of the Fifth Freedom for US transnational corporations, the state uses a variety of means, generating a pattern of interventions and a constellation of client regimes employing terror and horror. It is his emphasis on these patterns in US foreign policy and their basis in US institutions that marks out Chomsky's work from the mainstream. It is his documentation in depth, his abstention from conspiracy theories and his fair-minded treatment of the facts that mark him out from many other 'radical' commentators. Walter LaFeber, the noted historian, remarks that Chomsky is 'certainly more serious about the past than many professional historians. . . . And he is deadly serious about the use of evidence.'[94] It is difficult to disagree with this assessment.

5

Rational Suicide

One of the devices used to obscure unpleasant patterns in US foreign policy is the doctrine of 'change of course' – the explanation that mistakes were once made, but have now been corrected. This doctrine is particularly useful when invoked in the 'post-Cold War era'. For example, after Indonesian forces carried out a massacre in East Timor in November 1991, in front of Western television crews, and the issue of the occupation was given unprecedented international attention, the *Washington Post* suggested that the United States 'should be able to bring its influence to bear on this issue', noting that the United States had for sixteen years supported an invasion and forced annexation which had killed 'up to a third of the population'. The reason for this support was, according to the *Post*, that 'the American government was in the throes of its Vietnam agony, unprepared to exert itself for a cause' that could harm relations with its 'sturdy anti-Communist ally' in Jakarta. But that was then. 'Today, with the East–West conflict gone, almost everyone is readier to consider legitimate calls for self-determination.'[1] Chomsky points out that this does not deal with quite all of the facts:

> Unexplained is why, in the throes of its Vietnam agony, the US found it necessary to increase the flow of weapons to its Indonesian client at the time of the 1975 invasion, and to render the UN 'utterly ineffective in whatever measures it undertook' to counter the aggression, as UN Ambassador Daniel Patrick Moynihan proudly described his success in following State Department orders. Or why the Carter Administration felt obligated to sharply accelerate the arms flow in 1978 when Indonesian supplies were becoming depleted and the slaughter was reaching truly genocidal proportions.[2]

There was, Chomsky suggests, no real relation between the Indonesian invasion and East–West conflict, but it is often convenient to ascribe US foreign policy 'errors' to the pressures of the Cold War.

Until the 1960s, the conventional wisdom in the West was that the origins of the Cold War lay in Soviet aggressiveness, leading to a defensive reaction by the United States to protect freedom and democracy. This picture was challenged by a number of 'revisionist' critics, and the orthodox view was amended somewhat as a result. Chomsky summarizes some of the revisionist criticisms of the orthodox model: some argue that the perception of a Soviet threat was exaggerated, and US policies, while noble in intent, were based on misunderstanding and analytic error. 'A still sharper critique holds that the superpower confrontation resulted from an interaction in which the United States also played a role (for some analysts, a major role)', and that the contrast between the superpowers is not simply between a nightmare and the defence of freedom, but is more complex – in Central America and the Caribbean, for example.[3] Chomsky notes that in all these variants, it is assumed that the essential doctrines guiding US policy have been containment and deterrence, or even 'rollback', of the Soviet Union.

Chomsky's analysis differs from both the orthodox liberals and the revisionists. According to him, 'the Cold War has been misinterpreted by the left and the right from the beginning'.[4] He suggests that the way to understand the Cold War is to examine the events of the Cold War. 'Needless to say, if we *define* the Cold War as involving nothing beyond the confrontation of two superpowers, with their allies and clients tailing along, it follows trivially that that is precisely what it was.'[5] Putting this definition aside, a different picture emerges. True, there has been some superpower conflict, but this is 'only a fraction of the truth'.[6] Keeping for the moment to external issues, it is clear that the events of the Cold War rarely involved actual superpower confrontation. 'The substance of the Cold War system consists primarily of intervention and subversion by the two superpowers within their own domains: East Berlin, Hungary, Czechoslovakia, Poland, Afghanistan (the sole large-scale example of the use of Soviet forces beyond the borders conquered by the Red Army during World War II) – Greece, Iran, Guatemala, Cuba, Indochina, the Dominican Republic, Chile, El Salvador and Nicaragua, and all too many others.'[7] 'Putting it schematically, for the Soviet Union the Cold War has been primarily a war against its satellites; and for the United States a war against the Third World, with ancillary benefits with regard to domination of the other industrial societies.'[8] The explanation for the adoption of an East–West propaganda framework by both superpowers is that, 'One cannot claim that

Guatemala or Czechoslovakia is a threat to either superpower, but they become so when they are presented as outposts for the real enemy, with missiles and nuclear weapons and an ample record of savagery and subversion.'[9] If the claims are investigated, Chomsky suggests, typically no real evidence of the superpower enemy will be found to support the claims of the aggressor in cases such as Czechoslovakia and Guatemala. At the same time, as Chomsky observed during the Vietnam War, 'Of course, Russian imperialism is not an invention of American ideologists. It is real enough, as the Hungarians and Czechs can testify. What is an invention is the uses to which it was put' by US leaders and propagandists.[10] The central conflicts have then not been East–West, but between the East and its satellites; and the West and its satellites: 'If you look at the actual events of the Cold War, you find, in my view, a kind of tacit compact between the Soviet Union and the United States to allow them to share in world management.'[11] While each superpower would have preferred the other to disappear, in practice each accepted that this would be impossible short of mutual annihilation, and the system settled down to one of 'hostility combined with mutual accommodation'.[12] In place of the standard 'zero-sum game' view of the Cold War, where the gains of one antagonist equal the losses of the other, Chomsky suggests that it would be more realistic to regard the Cold War system as a 'macabre dance of death', in which the rulers of the superpowers use the image of their enemy to mobilize their populations in support of harsh and brutal measures against victims within their respective domains.[13] In 1973, Chomsky characterized the Cold War system as 'a conservative alliance of great powers, each free to control its own domains, with arrangements (e.g. the recent SALT agreements) for a controlled expansion of the system of military production . . .'[14]

When we inquire into the origins of the Cold War, we find that serious diplomatic historians trace the onset of the conflict not to 1950 but to 1917. According to the scholarly consensus, the decision by the Western powers to invade the Soviet Union after the Revolution was a 'defensive' reaction to Soviet aggression. The nature of this 'aggression' is particularly interesting. According to John Lewis Gaddis, the security of the United States was 'in danger' in 1917 because of the 'profound and *potentially far-reaching intervention* by the new Soviet government in the internal affairs, not just of the West, but of virtually every country in the world', namely, 'the Revolution's challenge ... to the very survival of the capitalist order'.[15] The same view of the Soviet threat was voiced in 1947 by George Kennan, when he stated, 'it is not Russian military power which is threatening us, it is Russian political power'.[16] According to this view, the Soviet Union was simply a gigantic 'rotten apple' or 'virus', and the real danger it posed to the West was the demonstration effect of successful independent development, just as in Vietnam or Nicaragua. For Chomsky, 'the Cold War can be understood, in a large measure, as an interlude in the North–South conflict of the Columbian era, unique in scale but similar to other episodes in significant respects'.[17] In the case of Grenada, it took a weekend to reverse unwanted developments; in the case of the Soviet Union, it took seventy years. The underlying rationale is the same.

According to Chomsky, 'The Cold War framework had both positive and negative aspects for US power.'[18] On the positive side, the US propaganda system was strengthened tremendously. 'On the negative side, the Cold War created some space for nonalignment and neutralism,'[19] as minor states gained some room for manoeuvre by playing off the superpowers against each other. The Cold War also impeded US interventionism to some extent. The conventional story is that it was the United States that 'contained' the Soviet Union. The truth, Chomsky suggests, is rather the reverse. Paul Nitze, an influential policy-maker throughout the postwar era, argued in January 1953 that Soviet advances in nuclear weaponry 'would present an extremely grave threat to the United States' because they 'would tend to impose greater caution in our cold war policies to the extent that these policies involve significant threat of general war'.[20] The Pentagon Papers reveal the effect of such caution on US operations in Vietnam.[21] Chomsky points out that,

> The clearest example of the success of deterrence is provided by Cuba, where the US was restricted to large-scale international terrorism instead of outright invasion after the missile crisis brought the world perilously close to nuclear war, in the judgement of the participants; understandably, this is not an example that figures prominently in the Western literature on deterrence.[22]

The Soviet nuclear arsenal tended to inhibit the free exercise of US power in areas where Washington lacked a conventional military advantage. In 1988, Dimitri Simes, a senior associate at the Carnegie Endowment for International Peace, wrote that Gorbachev's new policies and the apparent decline of the Soviet threat made 'military power more useful as a United States foreign policy instrument ... against those who contemplate challenging important American interests', because the United States need no longer fear 'triggering counterintervention' if it resorted to violence to suppress such challenges. Washington's hands would be 'untied' if concerns over 'Soviet counteraction' diminished.[23] Long after the Berlin Wall came down, at the time of the Panama invasion, Elliot Abrams observed that the use of force was more feasible than before, since 'developments in Moscow have lessened the prospect for a small operation to escalate into a superpower conflict'.[24] In the so-called post-Cold War world, US military power can extend to new areas, as it did in the Persian Gulf.

Chomsky argues that it is inaccurate to speak of the Cold War being over. If we understand the Cold War as a system involving parallel processes of subordination within the two blocs, only half the Cold War is over. The Western half continues unabated. All that changes after 1989 is the propaganda rationale for interventions that take place for the same old reasons, in defence of the Fifth Freedom.

According to Chomsky, the Cold War had important internal as well as external features, and here too there will be little change. In a famous report to the National Security Council, NSC 68, in April 1950, months before the Korean War, we find a call for intensive militarization of the economy, with 'a large measure of discipline and sacrifice' from the 'American people'.[25] The purpose of this militarization was to maintain the strength and structure of the US economy through 'military Keynesianism'. The Pentagon system became a system of state intervention in the economy,[26] providing a state-guaranteed market for high-technology rapidly obsolescing waste production, that is to say, armaments. The Keynesian economists Leon Keyserling and Paul Samuelson advised Truman and Kennedy respectively that military spending 'if deemed desirable for its own sake can only help rather than hinder the health of our economy in the period immediately ahead'.[27] Chomsky notes that 'Contrary to much misconception, the beneficiaries [of military spending] are not only, or even primarily, military industry.'[28] For example, in the 1950s, computers were not marketable and the public paid 100 per cent of the cost of research, development and production, through the Pentagon. By the 1960s, they were beginning to be marketable in the commercial system, so the public subsidy declined to around 50 per cent. Chomsky draws the lesson: 'The idea is that the public pays the costs, the corporations make the profits. Public subsidy, private profit; that's what we call free enterprise.' By the 1980s, substantial new expenditures were required for advances in fifth-generation computers and parallel processing systems, and the public share of the costs rose again, to a large extent via the Star Wars programme.[29]

A number of commentators have pointed out that the Pentagon is much less efficient than, for example, the Japanese model of state economic management via its Ministry of International Trade and Industry (MITI). Japanese policy-makers, Chomsky writes, 'make approximately the same judgements as American industrial managers about the likely new technologies. Why do they do better than we do? Very simple. They direct their public subsidy directly to the commercial market.' When Japanese planners decide to work on lasers, business elites and government officials concentrate on ways of producing lasers for the commercial market. In the United States, if the desired product is a laser, 'what we do is pour the money into the Pentagon, which tries to work on a way to use a laser to shoot down a missile 10,000 miles away', hoping there will be a spin-off that will be useful for the commercial market. The efficiency differential is obvious, and 'Out of that comes the trade balance and so on.'[30]

The United States could theoretically opt for the Japanese style of state intervention and choose more conventional forms of subsidy, but 'With the best of will, it is not easy to devise alternative forms of government intervention in the economy that will not conflict with the interests of these private empires.'[31] Chomsky argues, 'What they teach you in economics courses is true but irrelevant.'[32] It is true but irrelevant that social spending is at least as effective as military spending in keeping the economy moving. The problem with spending on civilian needs was spelt out by *Business Week* in 1949:

> there's a tremendous social and economic difference between welfare pump-priming and military pump-priming. It makes the government's role in the economy – its importance to business – greater than ever. Military spending doesn't really alter the structure of the economy. It goes through the regular channels. As far as a businessman is concerned, a munitions order from the government is much like an order from a private customer. But the kind of welfare and public works spending that Truman plans does alter the economy. It makes new channels of its own. It creates new institutions. It redistributes income. It shifts demand from one industry to another. It changes the whole economic pattern.[33]

So, one reason for fear is that civilian spending tends to redistribute income. Chomsky adds, 'A second and worse defect is that it is democratizing. It tends to mobilize and organize people.' If the state becomes involved in building hospitals and schools, the population will become concerned and try to influence decisions. 'That's the worst imaginable tragedy, that you might have aspects of a functioning democracy. On the other hand, if you're building missiles nobody has any thoughts about it, so the public can be properly marginalized.' A third defect is that social spending interferes with managerial prerogatives. If the government is involved in doing something useful, that inevitably interferes with the capacity of private industry to exploit that market. If the government restricts itself to contributing towards the costs of production, such as research and development, and providing a guaranteed state market for waste production, that does not diminish, but enhances managerial prerogatives.[34]

Another reason why Washington has opted for military Keynesianism is that it is much easier to convince the population to pay for the defence of the nation than to tell the truth. An executive with a US aerospace corporation explained:

> It's basic. Its selling appeal is defence of the home. This is one of the greatest appeals the politicians have to adjusting the system. If you're the President and you need a control factor in the economy, and you need to sell this factor, you can't sell Harlem and Watts but you can sell self-preservation, a new environment. We're going to increase defence budgets as long as those bastards in Russia are ahead of us. The American people understand that.[35]

It so happens that 'those bastards' were never ahead of the United States, but such facts are irrelevant to the debate.

Chomsky does not attribute national security policy to a concern for national security. In fact, he suggests that national security is irrelevant to the formation of security policy and suggests some tests. At the end of the Second World War, the United States emerged in a position of global superiority which may never have existed before in history. In terms of security from threat, the United States was also in an unparalleled situation, with no threats in the Western Hemisphere, and total control of the oceans on either coast. There was only one danger to the territory of the United States: the development of intercontinental ballistic missiles, which could reach the United States with thermonuclear warheads. Chomsky notes, 'The record shows no serious efforts to avert the sole potential threat to the security of the United States, indeed, little concern about the matter in the first postwar decade when progress might have been made in this direction.'[36]

When we examine the three major escalations in US conventional and nuclear military capabilities in the postwar era, the evidence is also suggestive. The escalations occurred in the early 1950s, when there was a 40 per cent real increase in the military system; under Kennedy, when a lesser increase included a major escalation of the strategic arms race; and finally under President Reagan, following increases planned by President Carter, when social spending declined while military spending went up as a proportion of government spending, and outlays on the military increased 30 per cent in real terms. The first major increase in military spending is usually justified by the Korean War, and its significance as a sign of Soviet aggressiveness. However, as we have already seen, this round of escalation was initiated by NSC 68, which pre-dated the Korean War. Furthermore, there was no credible evidence of Soviet involvement in the North Korean decision to invade. The Kennedy bout of militarization was justified by an alleged 'missile gap' with the Soviets, which President Eisenhower correctly maintained did not exist. As Kennedy and his officials well knew, this 'gap' was wholly in favour of the United States, at a time when the USSR possessed precisely *four* operational ICBMs at a single missile-testing site. The Reaganites created the concept of 'the window of vulnerability', a period of Soviet missile superiority allegedly created by Carter's failed security policy, to justify their huge spending. General Benny Davis, head of US Strategic Air Command, effectively conceded the fraudulent nature of the 'window' to Congress, after it had served its propaganda function. He admitted that a simultaneous attack on all three legs of the strategic triad – bombers, submarines and land-based missiles – was impossible.[37] Chomsky concludes, 'In none of the three crucial cases was there any significant change in the international environment, any new threat to the US or its allies, to justify the military programs undertaken.'[38] According to Chomsky, national security planners are only marginally concerned with 'national security' – 'a dirty little secret' of state planning.[39]

While security policy is not concerned with US national security, the military system is useful in maintaining an international economic order that has been designed to favour US economic interests, and this is no doubt a secondary factor in the arms race. There are other pressures:

> Unfortunately, a great many factors – the drive for domestic and global power, the need to mobilize popular support for costly government programs, the concern to recycle petrodollars by exploiting the comparative advantage of the industrial powers in advanced technology (the arms trade), the requirement that state-induced production must not harm but rather must enhance the interests and power of the private empires that control the economy and largely staff the state executive in the state capitalist democracies – all converge on military production.[40]

Given the fact that this basic institutional framework continues to exist after the Cold War has officially ended, similar policies can be expected, though accompanied by new rhetoric. Thus the 'post-Cold War' continuation of large arms expenditures in the United States, and in the other nations where military Keynesianism holds sway.[41]

There is a short-term rationality, then, to the arms race which explained its persistence and explains its survival of the Cold War framework. However, the system of shared control between the superpowers was accompanied by severe risks of runaway crises. The system was 'fairly stable in the very short-term, though fraught with immense dangers, possibly terminal catastrophe, in a longer-term framework that planners do not consider'.[42] In a 1986 pamphlet entitled *The Race to Destruction – Its Rational Basis*, Chomsky noted that the nuclear arms race, coupled with recurring local crises and superpower intervention, guaranteed 'a persistent fair probability of nuclear war': 'Even if one takes the probability to be low, the meaning of this fact is that a terminal conflict is highly likely.'[43] To accept a repeated risk of nuclear war was to accept 'a near guarantee of nuclear war in the long run – a "long run" that is unlikely to be very long given the risks that policy makers are willing to accept'.[44] According to a close associate, Theodore Sorenson, President Kennedy was willing to accept a probability of a third to a half of nuclear war during the Cuban missile crisis.[45] What is more significant than the decisions of one particular set of policy-makers is that the behaviour of the Kennedy administration is still regarded as admirable and sensible in dominant circles in the United States and elsewhere.

Chomsky observes that 'The lunacy is institutional, not individual.'[46] Such radically short-term planning is natural in competitive societies, 'where those who contemplate the longer term are unlikely to be in the competition when it arrives'.[47] The idea of political leaders who are apparently devoted to enhancing their own power actively pursuing policies which almost guarantee the destruction not only of their privileges but of much of civilization seems somewhat paradoxical. Chomsky draws an analogy with the business world: if, say, General Motors were to devote its resources to planning for the future, concentrating on what will be profitable in ten years from now, other car manufacturers, who are maximizing profit and power in the short term, would take over the market long before then, with the result that General Motors would no longer be in the market in ten years' time.[48] The primary task for business managers is to remain managers. This depends on their ability to rebuff hostile takeovers and stop attempts by owners to replace them. Their ability to perform these functions depends in turn on their ability to maximize short-term profitability and market share. These kinds of institutional pressures create foreshortened horizons. The picture is not very different for those who manage the state in the interests of those who own the economy. Someone who prioritizes long-term considerations at the expense of immediate gain will be disqualified from the top posts.

The environment is another example of 'the rationality of collective suicide'.[49] Chomsky notes that 'there are tendencies in human society and technological development toward ecological catastrophe, and they're not so far off'.[50] He cites in particular the case of global warming, with its potentially catastrophic effects on sea levels, and notes that we do not seem to be 'equipped socially' to deal with this problem. Our social organizations and our intellectual culture reassure us about the prospects, but there are no good reasons to accept such assurances.[51] Chomsky suggests that if perhaps one-tenth of the funds directed to the Star Wars project had been ploughed into solar energy research, solutions might have begun to emerge, but this is not a course of action that enhances the power and prestige of ruling elites in the short term, and therefore it is not a likely policy outcome. Chomsky concludes, 'That's a kind of social pathology which could very well lead to biological destruction.'[52] 'There's an inherent conflict between capitalism and the environment, just like there's an inherent conflict between capitalism and democracy. They're inconsistent.'[53] Chomsky comments,

No one who gives a moment's thought to the problems of contemporary society can fail to be aware of the social costs of consumption and production, the progressive destruction of the environment, the utter irrationality of the utilization of contemporary technology, the inability of a system based on profit or growth-maximization to deal with needs that can only be expressed collectively, and the enormous bias this system imposes towards maximization of commodities for personal use in place of the general improvement of the quality of life.[54]

In brief,

Predatory capitalism ... is not a fit system for the mid-twentieth century. It is incapable of meeting human needs that can be expressed only in collective terms, and its concept of competitive man [sic] who seeks only to maximize wealth and power, who subjects himself to market relationships, to exploitation and external authority, is anti-human and intolerable in the deepest sense.[55]

Before we turn to the question of possible remedies for these problems, it may be worth reminding ourselves that Chomsky's twin concerns, the US propaganda system and US interventionism, stem from the same root. Patterns of intervention and patterns of indoctrination are both expressions of the concentration of private power in the United States. Distinguishing between Chomsky's work on culture and his analysis of policy should not lead to an unbridgeable demarcation between the two areas. The situation becomes clearer when we explore Chomsky's unconventional definition of the 'state'. He distinguishes between the state and the government, 'where the state is a system of institutions, including private institutions that set conditions for public policy, which are relatively stable, changing slowly if at all. These constitute the actual nexus of decision-making power in the society, including investment and political decisions, setting the framework within which public policy can be discussed and is determined.' The government, on the other hand, 'consists of whatever groups happen to control the political system, one component of the state system, at a particular moment'.[56] It is perfectly possible for the media, for example, to be 'anti-government' while remaining 'pro-state'. For Chomsky, it is roughly true that the state executive – the government – is 'a branch of the ruling class which is governing this particular centralized structure'.[57] There are, of course, many secondary complicating factors, including conflicts of interest between different sectors of business, and the semi-autonomous nature of some government bureaucracies.[58] Nevertheless, to a very large extent, the government is an agency of those who own and manage the private economy.

In general, Chomsky suggests, if we wish to understand anything about the foreign policy of a state, it is a good idea to begin by investigating the domestic social structure: Who sets foreign policy? What interests do these people represent? What is the domestic source of their power? 'It is a reasonable surmise that the policy that evolves will reflect the special interests of those who design it.'[59] Chomsky observed, before 1989, that it is easy to adopt this procedure with official enemies:

Discussing the Soviet Union, no reasonable person hesitates to entertain the possibility that its foreign policy is designed to enhance the power and privilege of the ruling military–bureaucratic elite, that the system of propaganda is committed to denying and concealing this fact, and that the pattern of repression and coercion that results from Soviet intervention reflects the perceived needs of this ruling group. Indeed, this is generally taken to be obvious truth, as it is, to a very good first approximation.[60]

It is more difficult to apply this same rational stance to your own country. When it is applied, this approach is often characterized as a 'radical' analysis. Chomsky challenges this description. Far from being 'radical', he contends that this is a 'very conservative' critique, which would not have surprised the eighteenth-century figures who founded the United States.[61] In general, systems of government will be captured by domestic power structures: it is the function of government to serve the interests of those who hold power. For this reason, Chomsky holds that governments are not and cannot be 'moral agents'.[62] Curling around this power structure, Chomsky suggests, there will always be mechanisms for hiding social realities from the general population, and extracting public acquiescence in rule by the few. There will always be a group entrusted with mystification and indoctrination, to serve the interests of those who hold power: 'Rather generally, throughout history, the power of some state provides a fair measure of its external violence and the hypocrisy of its doctrinal system...'[63] The United States has enjoyed unprecedented power in the postwar era. The levels of hypocrisy have also been rather high.

6

Visions

Chomsky has been criticized repeatedly for concentrating his attention on present evils rather than their relief. A caller put this to him on a radio talk show: 'It seems that, Professor Chomsky, you are merely a critic of society and you don't have a definite program or political alternative or system that you are clearly advocating. In what you write and what you say you give only the barest and vaguest solutions. You talk vaguely of a social revolution or something of this nature, but you don't say concretely what you believe in.'[1] A knowledgeable British critic goes so far as to say that Chomsky presents 'no realizable vision of the future' and that 'Ultimately, the problem with his work is that he offers no advice, and establishes no guidelines.'[2] While understandable, given that guidelines and vision are minor elements in his work, such criticisms are unfounded. Chomsky has in a number of places described his picture of a desirable future society and how we might move towards it. Whether this ideal is 'realizable' or not is, of course, a matter for debate.

Chomsky has argued that without such a vision of the future, the Left will not succeed in its aims. In his view, the Left will not *deserve* to succeed 'unless it develops an understanding of contemporary society and a vision of a future social order that is persuasive to a large majority of the population'. He warned the Left in 1969, 'If its only clearly expressed goals are to smash and destroy, it will succeed only in smashing and destroying itself.'[3] In an advanced industrial society, Chomsky comments, it is far from true that the workers have nothing to lose but their chains. On the contrary, they have a considerable stake in preserving the existing social order. 'Correspondingly, the cultural and intellectual level of any serious radical movement will have to be far higher than in the past, as André Gorz, for one, has correctly emphasized.'[4] In such circumstances, the Left cannot simply satisfy itself with a litany of current injustices, but will have to provide 'compelling answers' to the question of how these evils can be overcome, either 'by revolution or large-scale reform'.[5] As Bertrand Russell once wrote, people must be 'persuaded to the attempt by hope, not driven to it by despair', if socialism is to be achieved.[6] For someone to commit themselves to a movement for radical social change, 'with all of the uncertainty and hazard that this entails', she must have 'a strong reason to believe that there is some likelihood of success in bringing about a new social order',[7] and a clear idea of what that social order might be.

Chomsky observes: 'A movement of the left should distinguish with clarity between its long-range revolutionary aims, and certain more immediate effects it can hope to achieve.'[8] For the moment we shall consider the ultimate goals Chomsky has considered in his work; we turn to more immediate issues in the next chapter.

In the long term, Chomsky agrees with Bertrand Russell that anarchism is 'the ultimate ideal to which society should approximate'.[9] Chomsky disputes the notion that anarchism is a set doctrine, with fixed ideas and a fixed conception of the ideal society. He cites approvingly Rudolf Rocker's characterization of anarchism as 'not a fixed, self-enclosed social system but rather a definite trend' in the historic development of humankind,[10] a tendency towards freedom that expresses itself in different ways at different times. In this view, as outmoded social forms are cast off because of their oppressive nature, new problems of human freedom will be discovered that require new forms of liberation, in a continual struggle. Chomsky invokes the example of sexism, barely recognized as a social evil before the 1960s, now universally acknowledged as a problem requiring attention. On optimistic assumptions, as sexism and other current forms of oppression are overcome, new problems will come into focus and require social reform.[11] In this perpetual struggle for freedom, Chomsky comments, anarchists will always be among the 'revolutionaries trying to overcome these new kinds of oppression and unfairness and constraint that we weren't aware of before'.[12]

George Woodcock, one of the most famous anarchists of the postwar era, has challenged Chomsky's self-identification as an anarchist. He characterizes Chomsky as 'a sympathetic outsider' trying to use anarchism to support his own, quite different, doctrines. Chomsky is not an anarchist 'by any known criterion': he is rather a 'left-wing Marxist', who regards Marxism 'as *primary*' and '*selects* from anarchism those elements that may serve to diminish the contradictions in Marxist doctrine'. He thus impoverishes anarchism by 'abandoning its essential extremities'.[13] This is a good example of what might be termed the doctrinal approach to anarchism, perhaps also the dominant approach. I am not aware of any 'known criteria' for being an anarchist and this seems a weak line of argument, given anarchism's historic diversity. Woodcock's suggestion that Chomsky is primarily a Marxist is also somewhat strange, given the wealth of material now available on this issue. Woodcock's misunderstanding may have been understandable in 1974, but as a judgement of 1992, when his review was republished without qualification, it is very curious.

Chomsky has, it is true, expressed respect for Marx's work; he has described Marx as 'a major intellectual figure', and remarks that 'it would be foolish not to learn from him or to value his contributions properly'.[14] He once described Marx as one of history's 'true revolutionaries', despite the fact that, as an activist, Marx's behaviour 'left much to be desired, in the politics of the First International, for example'.[15] In Marx's thought, there were what Chomsky describes as 'competing strains',[16] including authoritarian elements which were accentuated and refined by Lenin. Though, as Chomsky comments, 'it would obviously be a gross error in interpreting the debates of a century ago to rely on the claims of contemporary social movements as to their historical origins. In particular, it is perverse to regard Bolshevism as "Marxism in practice".'[17] There were also libertarian elements in Marx's thought, now disregarded to a large extent, which were developed further by anti-Leninist Marxists such as Gorter, Pannekoek, Luxemburg and similar figures. Chomsky observes that for the most part, 'Marxism itself has become too often a sort of church, a theology', though 'Work of value has been done by those who consider themselves Marxists.'[18]

In fact, Chomsky dislikes the term 'Marxism'. For him, terms such as 'Marxism' and 'Freudian' belong to the history of organized religion. A human being, 'no matter how gifted, will make some contributions intermingled with error and partial understanding'. The correct attitude is to try to 'understand and improve on their contributions and eliminate the errors'. Identifying yourself as a Marxist or as a Freudian is to treat someone as a god to be revered, not a human being whose contribution is to be assimilated and transcended. This is 'a crazy idea, a kind of idolatry'.[19]

To return to the question of anarchism, Chomsky suggests that the leading idea within the anarchist tradition was defined by Bakunin in 1871. Bakunin described himself as 'a fanatic lover of liberty, considering it as the unique condition under which intelligence, dignity and human happiness can develop and grow'. Bakunin repudiated the 'purely formal liberty conceded, measured out and regulated by the State', and spoke in favour of a richer concept of freedom: 'the only kind of liberty that is worthy of the name, liberty that consists in the full development of all of the material, intellectual and moral powers that are latent in each person; liberty that recognizes no restrictions other than those determined by the laws of our own individual nature'.[20] In this perspective, freedom will vary from person to person to the extent that their endowments and preferences vary.[21] Chomsky comments that these ideas grow out of the Enlightenment; 'their roots are in Rousseau's *Discourse on Inequality*, Humboldt's *The Limits of State Action*, Kant's insistence, in his defence of the French Revolution, that freedom is the precondition for acquiring the maturity for freedom, not a gift to be granted when such maturity is achieved'.[22]

Chomsky traces modern anarchism to eighteenth-century European liberalism – an unusual step. Classical liberalism was concerned with the feudal system, slavery and two powerful institutions: the Church and the State. Enlightenment thinkers opposed all but the most limited state intervention in personal or social life on the grounds that, in Humboldt's words, the state tends to 'make man [sic] an instrument to serve its arbitrary ends, overlooking his individual purposes'.[23] Chomsky argues that the application of these same eighteenth-century principles to the circumstances of the twentieth century lead to an anti-capitalist, libertarian socialist position. With the centralization of effective power in the industrial and financial system of corporate capitalism, classical libertarian ideals demand more than a concern for the coercive role of the Church and the State.[24]

Rocker described modern anarchism as the confluence of Liberalism and Socialism. Such a perspective is perhaps less common today than it once was. Many anarchists today seem to regard 'socialism' as synonymous with 'statism'. Chomsky, in contrast, finds his place within what he regards as a more classical tradition, where socialism is thought of in terms of a society controlled by free associations of workers. He comments, 'To libertarian socialists, at least, socialism and freedom are inseparable. There is no socialism worthy of the name under a party dictatorship.'[25] One of the difficulties for libertarian socialists, according to Chomsky, is that both the major propaganda systems of the modern era colluded in distorting the meaning of socialism. Both Washington and Moscow found it convenient to identify the totalitarianism of the Soviet Union with socialism. 'For the Bolsheviks, the goal of the farce was to extract what advantage they could from the moral prestige of Socialism; for the West, the purpose was to defame Socialism and entrench the system of ownership and management control over all aspects of economic, political, and social life.'[26] Chomsky argues that the meaning of socialism has been no less distorted by self-proclaimed 'democratic socialists', who hold, for example, that 'All social democratic ideals fundamentally relate to how we distribute our wealth and allocate our resources: that is what socialism is about.'[27] In response, Chomsky cites Rudolf Rocker, who argued that 'In the prison, in the cloister, or in the barracks one finds a fairly high degree of economic equality, as all the inmates are provided with the same dwelling, the same food, the same uniform, and the same tasks.'[28] Freedom is an essential element of socialism. In fact, Chomsky suggests, 'anarchism may be regarded as the libertarian wing of socialism', and he cites Rocker once again: *'socialism will be free or it will not be at all.* In its recognition of this lies the genuine and profound justification for the existence of anarchism.'[29] To a properly brain-washed intellectual, the idea of a 'libertarian socialist' is inconceivable, and Chomsky's description of himself as such 'makes him at any rate the most important oxymoron alive'.[30]

While Chomsky's roots may be in the Enlightenment, he is very much of the modern age. 'What attracts me about anarchism personally are the tendencies in it that try to come to grips with the problems of dealing with complex organized industrial societies within a framework of free institutions and structures.'[31] Chomsky has often expressed his prefer-ence for that tendency in anarchism which 'merges, or at least interrelates very closely with a variety of left-wing Marxism, the kind that one finds in, say, the Council Communists that grew up in the Luxemburgian tradition, and that is later represented by Marxist theorists like Anton Pannakoek [sic], who developed a whole theory of workers' councils in industry and who is himself a scientist and astronomer, very much part of the industrial world'.[32] In this inter-relation of ideas, 'radical Marxism merges with anarchist currents'.[33] Going back to Woodcock, there is a considerable gap between favouring this kind of 'merging' – with left-wing, unorthodox, Marxism – to regarding Marxism as 'primary'. My reading would be that Chomsky regards anarchism as 'primary', or at least his preferred stretch of the anarchist spectrum, and selects those elements in the Marxist tradition that help to enrich this tradition.

Unlike many inside and outside anarchist circles, Chomsky rejects the idea that anarchism is suitable only for pre-industrial, agrarian societies. For him, the ideas of libertarian socialism are 'exactly the appropriate ideas for an advanced industrial society'. He argues that 'anarchism in that sense suggests certain principles of organization which are extremely realistic'.[34] Where there is a sufficiently high level of technology and communications, where onerous but necessary labour can be eliminated by mechanization, it seems 'entirely possible, in fact essential, to move toward these social forms so very much appropriate to advanced industrial society'.[35] For Chomsky, 'industrialization and the advance of technology raise possibilities for self-management over a broad scale that simply didn't exist in an earlier period.... At present, institutions do not permit [workers] to have control over the requisite information, and the relevant training to understand these matters.'[36] These are social defects, which could be remedied. If they were remedied, 'With modern technology, tools can be tools' and human beings can be human beings.[37]

Chomsky notes that 'One striking difference between Marx and the anarchists was expressed in Bakunin's remark about how a revolutionary would try to build the structures of a future society within the present society.'[38] Marx was for the most part a theorist of capitalism rather than of a future socialist society. Anarchists, on the other hand, have spent some time on the possible arrangements of a future society. Summarizing the classical anarchist consensus, Chomsky suggests, 'one can imagine a network of workers' councils, and at a higher level, representation across the factories, or across branches of industry, or across crafts, and on to general assemblies of workers' councils that can be regional and national and international in character'.[39] From another point of view, there might be a system of governance involving local assemblies, which might also be federated regionally, nationally, perhaps even internationally, across trades and industries, and so on. Both systems would control themselves directly, without a coercive authority above them. There would be 'two modes of immediate organization and control, namely organization and control in the workplace and in the community':[40]

In any institution – factory, university, health centre or whatever – there are a variety of interests that ought to be represented in decision-making: the workforce itself, the community in which it is located, users of its products or services, institutions that compete for the same resources. These interests should be directly represented in democratic structures that displace and eliminate private ownership of the means of production or resources, an anachronism with no legitimacy.[41]

Exactly how the two networks would interact, and whether both are required, Chomsky does not say: 'these are matters over which anarchist theoreticians have debated and many proposals exist, and I don't feel confident to take a stand. These are questions which will have to be worked out.'[42] Such a conception of socialism runs directly counter to the Stalinist model of a centralized bureaucratic state. For Chomsky these ideas are derived from early anarchist thinkers, and he describes himself as a 'derivative fellow traveller' of anarchism, rather than as an 'anarchist thinker' as such.[43] The basic principle is that 'In a decent society, socially necessary and unpleasant work would be divided on some egalitarian basis, and beyond that people would have, as an inalienable right, the widest possible opportunity to do work that interests them.'[44]

There is an inherent tension in capitalist democracy between democracy and authoritarianism. Capitalist work relations are totalitarian and there are hierarchical structures of authority in the workplace 'of a kind that we would call fascist in the political domain', Chomsky suggests.[45] There is tight control at the top, and strict obedience is established at every level – 'there's a little bargaining, a little give and take, but the line of authority is perfectly straightforward.'[46] This tension between political democracy and economic fascism could in principle be resolved in one of two ways: by political dictatorship or by the extension of democracy to the workplace. For Chomsky, this extension of democratic control is both desirable and possible: workers should control the work they do, the purposes it is carried out for, the conditions under which it is performed, the relationships between their own and other sectors of the economy and the interrelationships between the workplace, the community and the environment. If it is found that workers do require specialized 'managers' to coordinate their work – and Chomsky is reluctant to concede such a possibility – then 'there is no reason why managers should be answerable to private capital rather than the work force and the community'.[47] Managers could be elected by workers or neighbourhood councils rather than appointed by distant shareholders.

Joshua Cohen and Joel Rogers note that anarchist views are typically criticized for resting 'on implausible accounts of human motivation, for being inattentive to the ways that decentralization can exacerbate political and material inequalities, and for ignoring the attractions and requirements of economic efficiency'. Chomsky's approach to anarchism, they conclude, 'avoids at least the most obvious versions of these objections'.[48] However, they suggest that there are weaknesses in his presentation. For Chomsky, the optimal solution to the question of government is that participation in the various levels of administration should rotate through the population. It should be temporary and partial: 'that is, the members of a workers' council who are for some period actually functioning to make decisions that other people don't have the time to make, should also continue to do their work as part of the workplace or neighbourhood community in which they belong.'[49] This rotation would help to prevent the rise of an administrative elite. Cohen and Rogers suggest that modern societies have created complex problems, such as pollution and other third-party costs, which cannot be overcome by such part-time administrators.[50] Chomsky's attitude to the question of administrative complexity is pragmatic. If professionalization proves to be necessary, as in the case of steel production or other industrial processes, then 'the natural suggestion is that governance should be organized industrially, as simply one of the branches of industry, with their own workers' councils and their own self-governance and their own participation in broader assemblies', as happened in Hungary in 1956, for example.[51]

Perhaps an example will help to clarify this rather abstract debate. Chomsky accepts that the production of plans for social or industrial units requires the work of a group of technicians – professional planners. He suggests that these workers should be organized like other workers into their own 'industry' of plan-making. The fact that they were making the plans and explaining the consequences of different decisions through the use of planning models would not give these technicians the right to set the parameters of the plans, to determine social priorities or to control the implementation of plans. They would have no special power. Just as others produced steel girders for use by different community and economic concerns, so the planners would produce plans to order, for other workers to adopt or reject as they saw fit. What is required in this scenario is an educated and informed working class, capable of understanding complex planning. Chomsky argues that it is precisely the achievement of industrial society that such a level of consciousness and education is now possible.

Chomsky notes, 'The problem of how to combine planning with democracy, and so to preserve and significantly extend and enrich liberal values, will not be solved on paper, but only through a combination of practical experience and intellectual analysis.'[52] He suggests that 'What is far more important [than the writings of proponents] is that these ideas have been realized in spontaneous revolutionary action, for example in Germany and Italy after World

War I and in Spain (not only in the agricultural countryside, but also in industrial Barcelona) in 1936.'[53] In addition to the experience of these revolutionary outbreaks, there is also the history of small democratic communities such as the Israeli kibbutzim, 'which for a long period really were constructed on anarchist principles' and were 'extraordinarily successful by almost any measure that one can impose'.[54]

Rosa Luxemburg, in her critique of Leninism, argued that a true social revolution requires a 'spiritual transformation in the masses degraded by centuries of bourgeois class rule': 'it is only by extirpating the habits of obedience and servility to the last root that the working class can acquire the understanding of a new form of discipline, self-discipline arising from free consent'.[55] Luxemburg's emphasis on the spiritual dimensions of class struggle is intriguing. Chomsky was asked by the British broadcaster Peter Jay, 'How far does the success of libertarian socialism or anarchism really depend on a fundamental change in the nature of man [sic], both in his motivation, his altruism, and also in his knowledge and sophistication?' Chomsky replied,

> I think it not only depends on it but in fact the whole purpose of libertarian socialism is that it will contribute to it. It will contribute to a spiritual transformation – precisely that kind of great transformation in the way that humans conceive of themselves and their ability to act, to decide, to create, to produce, to enquire – precisely that spiritual transformation that social thinkers from the left-Marxist traditions, from Luxembourg [sic] say, through anarcho-syndicalists, have always emphasized.[56]

Here we enter the debate over 'human nature' and the potential for social change. Harry Bracken notes that 'No issue discussed by Noam Chomsky has generated as much debate as his comments on human nature.'[57] Chomsky stands firmly by the position that humans possess genetically inherited mental capacities. He suggests that among these capacities are 'some that relate to intellectual development, some that relate to moral development, some that relate to development as a member of human society, some that relate to aesthetic development'.[58] Chomsky argues that socialist principles, or indeed any political beliefs, must be based, fundamentally, on a picture of human nature. It is a curious fact that Marxists have tended to adopt the empiricist position that the mind is empty of structure at birth and that 'human nature' is a product of historical circumstances alone. Chomsky sees contradictions in such a position. 'For example, I don't think it's possible to give a rational account of the concept of alienated labour on that assumption, nor is it possible to produce something like a moral justification for the commitment to some kind of social change, *except* on the basis of assumptions about human nature and how modifications in the structure of society will be better able to conform to some of the fundamental needs that are a part of our essential nature.'[59] Chomsky argues that, 'any social or political theory, whether conservative, reformist or revolutionary, is based on some implicit concept of human nature, a biological given. Thus if we are opposed to slavery, it is because we think that in some sense these institutions are an infringement on essential human nature.'[60] 'Maybe the assumption is not explicit, in fact, it almost never is explicit. But the fact is that if there is any moral character to what we advocate, it is because we believe or are hoping that this change we are proposing is better for humans because of the way humans are.'[61] For Chomsky, 'it's crucially important to try to bring those assumptions forth, and to see whether in fact we can find any evidence bearing on them'.[62] There is very little evidence. Chomsky suggests that it may even be impossible for humans to understand the question of human freedom.[63] In the absence of such evidence, one must rely on intuition and the slight indications given by the world around us.

Humans have many capacities and options. Which of these capacities reveal themselves depends to a large extent on the institutional structures which form our social environment. If dominant institutions were to allow free rein to pathological killers, then psychopaths would take charge of society, and in order to survive one would have to allow those elements of one's nature to manifest themselves. If the institutions were to encourage pure greed at the expense of other human emotions and commitments, society would reflect this basis. However, 'A different society might be organized in such a way that human feelings and emotions of other sorts, say solidarity, support, sympathy become dominant.' In that case, different aspects of human nature and personality would reveal themselves.[64] Chomsky observes:

> It is no wonder that 'fraternity' has traditionally been inscribed on the revolutionary banner alongside of 'liberty' and 'equality'. Without bonds of solidarity, sympathy, and concern for others, a socialist society is unthinkable. We may only hope that human nature is so constituted that these elements of our essential nature may flourish and enrich our lives, once the social conditions that suppress them are overcome. Socialists are committed to the belief that we are not condemned to live in a society based on greed, envy, and hate. I know of no way to prove that they are right, but there are also no grounds for the common belief that they must be wrong.[65]

For Chomsky, 'my own feeling is that the fundamental human capacity is the capacity and the need for creative self-expression, for free control of all aspects of one's life and thought';[66] 'I do not doubt that it is a fundamental human need to take an active part in the democratic control of social institutions.'[67]

Perhaps the most common argument against anarchism is that human nature cannot be changed and requires a coercive apparatus to constrain the ugly tendencies in human nature.[68] In slightly different form, this argument is sometimes posed in terms of the need for a state apparatus after a social revolution. Chomsky cites the anarcho-syndicalist Fernand Pelloutier: 'Must even the transitory state to which we have to submit necessarily and fatally be the collectivist jail? Can't it consist in a free organization limited exclusively by the needs of production and consumption, all political institutions having disappeared?' Chomsky comments, 'I do not pretend to know the answer to this question. But it seems clear that unless there is, in some form, a positive answer, the chances for a truly democratic revolution that will achieve the humanistic ideals of the left are not great.'[69]

Short of anarchism, there are other, still quite remote possibilities. Chomsky cites approvingly Bertrand Russell's suggestion that 'guild socialism' was a reasonable prospect for the industrial societies. According to Russell, this would entail workers' control of industry, a democratic parliament representing the community, some restricted forms of state management, a guaranteed right to all of the material necessities of a decent existence, and 'the organization of citizens with special interests into groups, determined to preserve autonomy as regards their internal affairs, willing to resist interference by a strike if necessary, and sufficiently powerful (either through themselves or through their power of appealing to public sympathy) to be able to resist the organized forces of government successfully' when their cause was generally thought of as just.[70] Even this halfway house to anarchism seems somewhat distant.

Asked in 1976 about the prospects for anarchism in the West, Chomsky replied, 'I don't think I'm wise enough, or informed enough, to make predictions and I think predictions about such poorly-understood matters probably generally reflect personality more than judgment.' He did venture the opinion that the tendencies in Western society towards the concentration of power would continue, and that these developments would 'continually lead to revulsion, to efforts of personal liberation and to organizational efforts at social liberation'.[71] It was impossible to judge whether these efforts might succeed. It is perhaps suggestive, though, that socialist attitudes have grown up and appear to persist even among the most depoliticized populations. According to Chomsky, 'Gary Hart's pollsters found in 1975 that the overwhelming majority believe that workers and the community should control business enterprises.'[72] He also claims that the communist credo, 'from each according to her ability, to each according to her need', is so uncontroversial that in one study over 50 per cent of those polled believed the phrase formed part of the US Constitution.[73] There is perhaps some basis in popular attitudes for a revival of the anarchist ideas Chomsky endorses. Whether the opportunities for such a revival will be taken up is another matter.

7

Strategies

Mike Ferber, one of the leading figures in the draft resistance movement of the 1960s, recalls the heady days of 1968, when he was receiving letters from Paris still smelling of tear gas, revolts were breaking out from China to Czechoslovakia, and the student movement was filled with anticipations of crisis and overthrow. 'Chomsky, through it all, seemed incredibly calm.' On occasion, Chomsky would welcome the increasing numbers engaging in protest. 'Then he'd shake his head and say, "It'll be a long struggle".' Ferber observes that there were few older, 'really steady', supporters of the draft resisters. He names Chomsky and Dave Dellinger as two who made such a commitment, 'seeing the opportunities to do things, but not getting carried away'.[1] Chomsky in no way conforms to the usual stereotype of a 'revolutionary'. His approach to social change is permeated by the calm, serious attitude Ferber describes.

Just as some have criticized Chomsky for his alleged lack of social vision, others have complained of his lack of advice on how to move forward. David Finkel, in an unpublished review of *The Chomsky Reader*, notes that Chomsky's political writings are 'widely admired, particularly among "non-party" activists, for qualities lacking in so much of what passes for theory in mainstream social theory and in many leftist orthodoxies'. He points out, however, that mounting a critique is only the first step in social change; the second step is turning 'the destructive criticism of the existing system into a *constructive* and *responsible* theory and practice'. Chomsky's writings on this second stage are, Finkel suggests, 'vague'.[2] Chomsky concedes something to this type of criticism. He notes that 'Friends who share my interests and concerns have often criticized the work I do, maybe rightly, because they say it's much too critical of superficial phenomena, in a sense.'[3] Atrocities in Vietnam, in Latin America, in the Middle East, in East Timor, are matters that have enormous human significance, but they're superficial in a sort of technical sense; that is, they are the end result of much deeper, central factors in our society and culture. The criticism is that I ought to pay more attention to the central factors and to ways of changing them, to revolutionary strategy, for example. Well, I've been resistant to that, rightly or wrongly, but I see the point, certainly.[4]

While he has been 'resistant' to paying more attention to questions of strategy and social change, Chomsky has made some remarks on the subject, such that one can construct a skeleton argument of his views.

As we have seen, Chomsky distinguishes between the long-range aims of the Left and the 'more immediate effects' that may be achieved; between the large-scale structural reform of US institutions and more limited changes needed to terminate and prevent particular atrocities and interventions. In some circles it is customary to counterpose these two kinds of social change as the objects of two very different social strategies, and of two very different kinds of politics. The question is often put in terms of choosing either 'revolution' or 'reform'. During the 1960s, when he was heavily involved in civil disobedience and support for draft resisters, Chomsky noted:

> In general, problems of resistance are particularly complex for those who do not find it possible to adopt a position of revolutionary disdain for American social institutions, but who see basic and perhaps fatal flaws in our uncertain democracy. The problems thus arise for those who see no realistic alternative, for the moment, to the present social order, but who feel that submission to the instruments of war and repression would be grotesque, and obedience to government dictates detestable.[5]

In the current situation, where the institutions of society are not crumbling but remain strong, and where there is an almost complete absence of alternative institutions, Chomsky suggests, 'It is far from clear that the alternatives are sensibly to be posed as "reform or revolution." There is the possibility of working towards what André Gorz calls "structural reform".'[6] Such 'non-reformist reform' would be intended gradually to restrict the powers of the state and of capital, and increase democratic control, without accepting the newly reformed institutions as necessarily permanent or legitimate.

By accepting that the present social order would continue to exist for the foreseeable future, Chomsky was merely acknowledging reality. By granting that there were valuable elements in US institutions and in US democracy, and that these should be preserved and defended, Chomsky was breaking with much of the New Left. The contrary tendencies within present-day US society are, for Chomsky, an expression of the tension between democracy and capitalism. Chomsky's view, as we have seen, is that the tension should be resolved in favour of democracy, by, among other things, replacing authoritarian control of work by owners and managers by direct control by workers or, if necessary, by managerial authority accountable to workers rather than shareholders. This kind of shift in power relations could theoretically take place in a number of different ways, but 'could only follow a very serious internal conflict in the United States' – Chomsky suggested this might 'just be a conflict of ideas – I hope so'.[7] He notes, 'any revolutionary I've ever heard of must prefer peaceful non-violent means if these are possible. But it's rarely been possible because of the resistance of those who want to preserve their privileges.'[8] Chomsky accepts that it is likely that, 'at some point, the ruling class will simply strike back by force', popular movements will be forced to defend themselves 'and that probably means violent revolution'.[9] There are other dangers. For example, if a libertarian social revolution were to take place in Western Europe, 'then I think the problem of defence would be very critical'.[10] A Western European socialism worthy of the name would face military threats from the United States and perhaps Russia.[11] An anarchist revolution in the United States, on the other hand, might not face an immediate military threat.

Despite the undoubted influence on him of pacifists such as A.J. Muste, Chomsky himself is not an absolute pacifist. He has argued that violence in the course of social change can be justified: 'one can and *must* give an argument' for the use of violence:[12] 'any recourse to violence must be justified, perhaps by an argument that it is necessary to remedy injustice'.[13] This is simply part of the larger question of justifying struggle in any sense:

> A social struggle, in my view, can only be justified if it is supported by an argument – even if it is an indirect argument based on questions of fact and value that are not well understood – which purports to show that the consequences of this struggle will be beneficial for human beings and will bring about a more decent society.... if you can't give an argument you should extract yourself from the struggle.[14]

Foucault, in contrast, argues that one must engage in class struggle simply in order to gain power, not on the grounds that it might lead to a more just society. In his view, current notions of justice are irretrievably contaminated by present class society and are therefore not legitimate. During his debate with Foucault, Chomsky argued that the concept of justice did exist in some fashion outside of historical circumstances: 'I think there is some sort of an absolute basis – if you press me too hard I'll be in trouble, because I can't sketch it out – ultimately residing in fundamental human qualities, in terms of which a "real" notion of justice is grounded.'[15] This is an extension of Chomsky's position on human nature: he believes that part of the inherited framework of human nature is a moral sense which is capable of generating the concept of justice, given the appropriate conditions for development.[16]

Following on from the issue of revolutionary violence, it may be worth discussing another very old question, that of the factors that precipitate revolutionary crisis. Chomsky appears to agree with the proposition that an economic crisis may be necessary for social revolution to come onto the agenda. In his view, 'As long as a complex social system is more or less working, satisfying at least basic needs, and sometimes considerably better than basic needs, to substantial parts of the population [sic], and is not creating totally intolerable conditions for large numbers, I would imagine that it would persist. That has been true generally in industrial capitalism.'[17] A necessary condition is not, however, a sufficient condition. A crisis by itself does not lay the basis for a better society. Other elements are required, though this is sometimes disputed. Some political groupings have been able to avoid developing strategies of change or visions of the future by relying on the advent of 'inevitable' crises to create opportunities. Chomsky rejects such an unprincipled approach, in part because of the dangers of a reactionary popular response: 'The trouble is that when you bring people down to the level of utter destitution, they sink below despair, they don't get politicized. They try to survive. If this happens to substantial parts of the population it becomes a potential mass base for a fascist society.'[18] This is a particular danger in the United States, which has an extraordinarily depoliticized and atomized population. Chomsky argues that in the United States fascist values are 'deeply rooted in everybody's mind already'.[19] From a cultural point of view, fascism meant an attack on the ideals of the Enlightenment, an attack on the idea that humans had natural rights, that they were fundamentally equal, that it was an infringement of human rights if some groups were subordinated to others, that there were real bonds of unity and solidarity among people across cultures, and so on. Because of the pervasive nature of fascist values, and the depoliticization and privatization of social life, there is, Chomsky suggests, great potential for fascism to gain sway in the United States, particularly

> among the general population, the less educated, less articulate part of the population which also is typically the most depressed part of the population, there you can find at times appeal by charismatic figures who promise to lead them out of their problems and to attack either the powerful or some other bogeyman, the Jews or the homosexuals, or the communists, or whoever is identified as responsible for their troubles.[20]

Charismatic religious leaders are particularly dangerous, given the phenomenal growth of religious fanaticism in the United States. Chomsky comments, 'Fortunately the leading figures in this movement have been extremely corrupt, which is a very good thing. Every time I find that one of them wants nothing but gold Cadillacs or free sex, etc. I applaud.'[21]

Simply relying on the 'inevitable crisis of capitalism' does nothing to combat the danger of a lurch to the right in the face of depression and unemployment. What is needed is the awakening and self-organization of the population. There is another kind of threat to such a development: the Leninist model of the vanguard party. Chomsky warns that the goals and organizational forms of the Left must take shape through the active participation of the population in political struggle and social reconstruction.[22] The Left 'must not succumb to the illusion that a "vanguard party," self-designated as the repository of all truth and virtue, can take state power and miraculously bring about a revolution that will establish decent values and truly democratic structures as the framework of social life'.[23] It is necessary to 'build the organization of the future in the present society somehow'.[24] Marx considered the workers' association as 'the real constructive effort to create the social texture of future human relations'.[25] Bakunin urged that the workers' organizations should create 'not only the ideas but also the facts of the future itself' in the pre-revolutionary situation.[26] This is the core of the libertarian case against Bolshevism and its Trotskyite and Stalinist variants. The 'facts of the future' are to a large extent inherent in the forms of today. During the Russian Revolution, peasants and workers set up self-governing 'soviets' or workers' councils which assumed real power. In Chomsky's view, these were the beginnings of socialism: 'Lenin and Trotsky, upon assuming power, immediately devoted themselves to destroying the liberatory potential of these instruments, establishing the rule of the Party, in practice its Central Committee and its Maximal leaders – exactly as Trotsky had predicted years earlier, as Rosa Luxembourg [sic] and other left Marxists warned at the time, and as the anarchists had always understood.'[27] Chomsky comments, 'Failure to understand the intense hostility to socialism on the part of the Leninist intelligentsia (with roots in Marx, no doubt), and corresponding misunderstanding of the Leninist model, has had a devastating impact on the struggle for a more decent society and a liveable world in the West, and not only there.'[28]

We are some way from seeing large sectors of the population, in the United States or elsewhere in the West, dedicated to changing basic social structures, and organized in democratic, anti-authoritarian associations. Chomsky suggests that a necessary precursor to such a mass revolutionary movement might be a mass reform movement: 'a movement for social change with a positive programme that has a broad-based appeal, that encourages free and open discussion and offers a wide range of possibilities for work and action'.[29] This movement could be devoted to 'badly needed reforms, anti-imperialist and anti-militarist, concerned with guaranteeing minimal standards of health, income, education, industrial safety and conditions of work, and overcoming urban decay and rural misery'.[30] Within or related to such a movement, there might develop 'a variety of more radical movements that explore the possibility of dismantling the system of private and state power and democratizing basic social institutions through cooperatives and community and worker's control, and that organize and experiment to these ends'.[31] A revolutionary movement could develop from this radical fringe. If this two-stage picture is a reasonable one, then it is clear that the first priority is to create a coalition of interests and groups, some greater coalescence of single-issue campaigns: 'What we don't have and should have is mass popular organization. Then critical discussion and analysis, and serious thought about social issues, can become significant.'[32]

Naturally, a reformist movement has by its nature only limited aims, and can hope only for limited successes. This can cause problems. In the late 1960s, the US New Left began to lose much of its libertarianism. According to Chomsky, 'Around '67 or '68, everybody had to be more of an orthodox Marxist-Leninist than the guy sitting next to him [sic] and all sorts of strange things happened then.'[33] The problem, he suggested, was the gradual realization that for all the efforts of the New Left, revolutionary changes were not on the agenda. All that could be accomplished with existing techniques and organizations was the creation of better trade unions, the inclusion of previously excluded groups in the existing electoral system, and so on.[34] There were certain 'almost built-in limits to what could be achieved by the earlier movement. And those were given by very powerful institutional facts about this society that just couldn't be transcended by that kind of movement.'[35] This led to disillusionment and a search for messianic solutions in Marxism-Leninism and elsewhere. If this analysis is correct, there is a strong argument for the development of a revolutionary theory and a revolutionary strategy that will help activists and organizers to resist the temptation of authoritarian solutions to problems of social change. It is very curious then that Chomsky has written so little about this subject, a matter we return to below.

Rather unusually for an anarchist – perhaps we are becoming accustomed to his lack of orthodoxy by now – Chomsky is favourably disposed to the idea of forming a reformist mass party in the United States, as part of this wider effort. Such an organization could, in his view, be important 'in impeding the drift towards what Bertram Gross recently called "friendly fascism" and in defending both democratic rights and the most elementary needs of the poor and the exploited. It might also provide a framework for badly needed discussion of the mythology of American state capitalism, rarely challenged in recent decades.'[36] Chomsky is under no illusions: reformist parties like the British Labour Party 'do not pose a really serious problem to the dominant structure of the society'. None the less, the existence of such parties provides a certain continuity for protest and resistance: 'There's some degree of continuity and there are even possibilities of learning and building and being a little better next time.'[37] Chomsky discounts the fear of some radicals that a reformist party of working people and the underclass would divert energies from more radical social change. On the contrary, such an organization 'might very well offer new scope to educational and organizational efforts of a more radical nature'.[38] Once again, radical tendencies may find space within larger movements to persuade and to organize. The danger of co-option and absorption by capitalism is unavoidable: this is so even in the case of workers' control of industry. Chomsky notes that much of the postwar literature on industrial democracy is devoted to exploring how workers' participation can help discipline and supervise the workforce while eliciting improved performance. 'What can be said of workers' councils is true, *a fortiori*, of any other attempt at radical reconstruction of existing institutions.'[39] 'Those who oppose a programme of social action merely on grounds that it might be "co-opted" doom themselves to paralysis: they are opposed to everything imaginable.'[40]

Chomsky notes that 'Marx was, in a sense, you might say, an opportunist. I don't mean this critically. Rather, he rightly felt that different approaches were necessary in different circumstances as a means for social change. Parliamentarian measures in some cases, revolutionary efforts in others.'[41] Chomsky advocates participation in the electoral system.[42] He is apparently a member of the Democratic Socialists of America, a Socialist International affiliate in the United States, which has a handful of supporters among Democratic Party congressional representatives.[43] Chomsky suggests that 'even the engagement of the population in the political arena would be useful progress towards democracy in the United States, meaning not just watching the candidates on television and clapping for them, but actual participation, real participation in formation of programs, in meaningful selection and recall of representatives, etc.'[44] Chomsky has no illusions about the two major US parties:

> It is completely true, and I think we should be realistic about it, that as things now stand, the differences among candidates are slight.... Nevertheless, there's a difference. You've got to remember that this is a very powerful country, there's nothing like it in the world and in history. You've got to multiply those little differences in policy by the power of the United States. When you do that you get big effects for the victims.

Setting aside the propaganda, the difference between the Carter and the Reagan administrations was not enormous – they both carried out and supported violence – but there was a difference, and that kind of difference 'is paid for in the lives of many, many people'.[45]

There are two forces which interact to limit the amount of political space in the mainstream in the United States. One is particular to the United States: the greater cohesion and strength of the business classes. The other pressure is found in all the capitalist democracies. Throughout the West, the private business sector 'sets limits on what the state can do'. Actions that 'erode business confidence' lead to capital flight, investment cutbacks, and in general an intolerable deterioration of the social and economic climate, 'facts that state managers committed to significant reform could hardly disregard, in the unlikely event that they should attain political power'.[46] This problem rarely arises in the United States because of the narrow confines of the political mainstream, but in countries 'that function in a more democratic fashion, where there really are policy options, say in Latin America, you see it all the time'.[47] 'In a capitalist democracy, the primary concern of everyone must be to ensure that the wealthy are satisfied; all else is secondary. Unless the wants of investors are satisfied, there is no production, no work, no resources available for welfare, in short, no possibility of survival.'[48] The power over investment decisions grants power over political decisions.

For Chomsky, 'Meaningful democracy presupposes the ability of ordinary people to pool their limited resources, to form and develop ideas and programs, put them on the political agenda, and act to support them.'[49] The kinds of popular organizational structures needed include: 'effective unions with real worker participation that devote themselves to serious problems of the social order, groups dedicated to worker self-management and community control, information systems independent of private and state power, political clubs and parties based on active participation of broad constituencies'.[50] Chomsky notes that trade unions are 'unique within capitalist democracy in providing some way for people of limited resources to enter meaningfully into the political system'.[51] In the absence of such organizational structures and resources, democracy amounts to choosing among candidates selected by and representing the interests of one or another power base in society, generally from the private economy. A general election thus becomes merely 'an opportunity to ratify elite decisions'.[52] It is for this reason, Chomsky suggests, that almost half the US population ignores the presidential election. In such circumstances, 'people are intelligent enough to understand that they are not voting the issues. They are voting for Coca-Cola or Pepsi-Cola.'[53]

Chomsky notes that there is a hierarchy of responsiveness: 'Your congressional representatives can be influenced much more easily than your Senator, and the Senator can be influenced somewhat more easily than the President, who is usually immune.'[54] Contra aid was an example where a congressional decision, in this case to send aid to the Contras, had very important effects, and could have been altered by popular pressure. 'That came close. A little more political activism could have swung that vote, which would have made a tremendous difference in the amount of torture and murder and destruction in Central America. We didn't do it, we failed, and it could have been done at the congressional level.'[55] Other achievements are theoretically possible through the parliamentary structures.

For example, it might be possible to put enough pressure on Congress to essentially compel the government to join the comprehensive test ban, to extend it to a comprehensive test ban on both nuclear weapons tests and missiles. Every arms analyst will tell you what that means: that the threat of a first strike erodes ... it's a literally costless and certainly verifiable way of achieving what SDI, 'Star Wars,' [was] theoretically supposed to achieve.[56]

This would start to modify the system of military Keynesianism, and 'if it was combined with another parallel citizens' effort to block intervention and hence undermine the necessity for a nuclear umbrella to permit it to continue, you can imagine very significant changes in the country. But that takes a scale of protest that's well beyond a group of people sitting in here and there at their Congressman's [sic] office or inviting their representatives to their house.' Chomsky argues, 'Sure elections can matter, if they are just the forward edge of a citizenry that's really insisting on participating and determining policy at every stage of the game from planning through implementation. If elections are just something you just show up for every once in a while, you're just playing a game that's being run by elites.'[57]

There are, broadly speaking, two kinds of strategy for influencing state policy: 'One way is to try to influence the choice that will be offered by the two major political parties and to exercise this choice on Election Day. Another, very different approach is to try to modify the objective conditions that any elected official must consider when he [sic] selects a course of action.'[58] As the US political system is currently constituted, Chomsky argues, policies are determined by representatives of private economic power. In their institutional roles, these individuals 'will not be swayed by moral appeals', but can only be affected by the 'costs consequent upon the decisions they make'.[59] If decision-makers are swayed by considerations outside of the cost/benefit calculus as this is determined by corporate elites, they will be quickly replaced in favour of those who are more reliable. Chomsky points out that 'The closer to the centers of power one stands, the more these factors operate.'[60] Chomsky argues that 'Those who are serious about inducing changes in public policy will therefore consider ways to modify this calculus of costs', and to increase such costs dramatically generally means actions outside the usual channels.[61]

At the time of the Vietnam War, Chomsky and others within the anti-war movement argued that the government was impervious to reasoned argument and could only be contained by the non-violent imposition of social and economic costs. The internal record revealed in the Pentagon Papers demonstrates the accuracy of this insight.[62] Civil resistance imposed two kinds of cost on policy-makers. The first was relatively obvious. Planners feared domestic disruption. For example,

Chomsky notes, 'the timing of Nixon's November 3, 1969, announce-
ment of troop withdrawals, as well as its content and manner, strongly
suggest[ed] that this was an effort to respond to (and defuse) the
massive fall demonstrations; or in other words that the fall actions were
the immediate cause of this tactical adjustment'.[63] After the Tet
offensive of 1968, the Joint Chiefs of Staff pointed out that the
deployment of additional troops to Vietnam was hampered by the need
to ensure that 'sufficient forces would still be available for civil disorder
control' at home.[64] The anti-war movement also managed to impose
other costs on the government – 'more abstract ones'. Chomsky
suggested that 'These cannot be calculated in dollars and cents, but they
are no less real for that.'[65] McGeorge Bundy, a leading member of the
foreign policy establishment, publicly turned against the bombing of
North Vietnam in October 1968, and called for the withdrawal of
troops, because of what he described as 'the increasing bitterness and
polarization of our own people'. There was, he said, 'a special pain in
the growing alienation of a generation which is the best we have'.[66]
Chomsky comments,

> the only serious 'cost' that can be imposed by these young men and women is
> the threat that the managers of the society of tomorrow, the Yale graduating
> class, for example, will separate themselves from 'the system,' choosing jail
> rather than military service and questioning the legitimacy of our institutions
> in other ways. The important decisions are in fact made by the McGeorge
> Bundys of the world and they are telling us, loud and clear, that they will
> retreat from aggression only when the cost to them is 'plainly unaccept-
> able'.[67]

The future cohesion of the intellectual and managerial classes was
threatened by the war, and this, in a technological society, was quite
threatening.

Note that we are discussing the contribution of different kinds of
tactics by US citizens in securing an end to the war. We are not
discussing the relative contributions to securing US withdrawal made
by the US protest movement as against the effect of the Vietnamese
resistance.

According to Chomsky, it was by escaping the bounds of the political
system that the anti-war movement managed to force 'tactical modifications' on government planners unable to defeat the Vietnamese
resistance.[68] It was 'the effective direct action of spontaneous movements – both in the United States and among the conscripted army in
the field – that were out of the control of their "natural leaders" [that] in

fact played the primary role in constraining the warmakers.'[69] Direct action and mass protest made more conventional forms of protest against the Vietnam War meaningful: 'Without these actions, lobbying of Congress, letter writing, political campaigning and the like would have proceeded endlessly with as much effect as they had in 1964, when the American people voted overwhelmingly against escalation of the war in Vietnam, voting for the candidate who at that time was secretly preparing the escalation that he publicly opposed', Lyndon Johnson.[70] Chomsky himself engaged in a wide range of activities. He wrote in 1967, 'I've tried various things – harassing congressmen, "lobbying" in Washington, lecturing at town forums, working with student groups in preparation of public protests, demonstrations, teach-ins, etc. in all of the ways that many others have adopted as well. The only respect in which I have personally gone any further is in refusal to pay half of my income tax, last year, and again this year.'[71] Later, as draft resistance and large-scale civil disobedience became major factors, Chomsky became involved in these forms of resistance also, either as a supporter or a participant. There is little written record of Chomsky's activism, and he himself has never written for publication about his experiences, apart from the one essay, 'On Resistance'. However Chomsky does appear occasionally in contemporary reports or histories of the anti-war movement.

In October 1965, the first demonstration against the Vietnam War in the Boston area was organized by the Cambridge Committee to End the War in Vietnam, with Chomsky, Russell Johnson of the American Friends Service Committee, and a State Representative as speakers. The counter-demonstrators outnumbered the demonstrators and a local newspaper reported that 'The peace rally, planned as a climax to the well-organized march, came to grief as speakers tried vainly to make themselves heard.' State Representative Irving Fishman was allowed only nine words – 'Last week, I took the floor of the House ...' – before being drowned out by the crowd. The other speakers were even less fortunate.[72] Chomsky recalled the demonstration over twenty years later:

The first public meeting on the Boston Common, sort of Hyde Park, was in October 1965. I was one of the so-called speakers, but there was no speaking. There were hundreds of cops around and we were very glad, because they prevented us from being murdered. Students were marching over from the universities ready to kill you, and the Boston Globe, the liberal newspaper, was applauding the counter-demonstrators, as was radio ...[73]

A meeting a few months later was held in a church on the assumption that this would be a safe venue. This assumption proved to be incorrect: the church was attacked and defaced.[74]

Chomsky was at the pivotal demonstration at the Pentagon in October 1967, when tens of thousands of demonstrators gathered in peaceful protest, only to be attacked by soldiers and federal marshals. Chomsky and many others were arrested while demonstrating against the war.[75] Four years later, during the 'Mayday' demonstrations in Washington DC, when fifteen thousand people gathered to disrupt business as usual in the capital in protest against the war, Chomsky was, in his own words, 'a minor – and, to be honest, reluctant – participant'.[76] Dr Spock, also arrested, described himself as 'chagrined' to discover that Chomsky's affinity group had evaded arrest for much of the day while he, Spock, had been arrested and jailed by 7 a.m. Chomsky's group apparently adopted the tactic of lying in the road at various crossroads until the police appeared, then rising and moving on to another intersection.[77] Chomsky, whose group included Howard Zinn and Daniel Ellsberg (one of the government analysts who released the Pentagon Papers), recalled the occasion a few months later in slightly rueful tones: 'Howard and I, who've been in the Movement for years, kept asking ourselves, "What the hell are we doing here disrupting traffic?" But Dan maneuvered our little affinity group like a platoon in Vietnam.'[78]

Chomsky took part in a number of other protests in 1971. He was, for example, one of 253 people arrested in a sit-down blockade of Hanscom Field airbase near his home in Massachusetts. The defendants argued in court in August that the Pentagon Papers demonstrated that the government ignored less dramatic protests.[79] The judge was unconvinced. In 1972, Chomsky joined a blockade of a building owned by the United Aircraft Sikorsky Division, who were manufacturing training and assault helicopters for Vietnam. He was arrested and charged with disorderly conduct. The headline in the *New York Times* read: 'Chomsky among 60 seized at protest'.[80] Apart from sit-down blockades and suchlike, Chomsky's involvement in resistance had two main strands: tax resistance and support for draft resisters. Chomsky's tax resistance began in 1966 when he and 360 others declared publicly that they were refusing to pay part or all of their taxes to protest against the Vietnam War, thereby risking jail sentences of up to a year and fines of up to $10,000.[81] At a press conference in Boston in 1967, Chomsky, Louis Kampf and a number of others urged people not to file their Federal income tax returns.

Chomsky pointed out, 'By April 15 every American citizen must decide whether he [sic] will make a voluntary contribution to the continuation of the war.' He added, 'I am willing to go to jail. A patriotic person should be willing to do so.'[82] His involvement in tax resistance does not seem to have led to any unfortunate outcome. His involvement in support for draft resistance, though, very nearly did have serious consequences.

As draft resistance became more widespread, Chomsky became heavily involved in efforts to organize practical and political support for resisters, efforts which resulted in the formation of RESIST, a group based initially on the example of those French intellectuals who had supported and sheltered deserters during the war in Algeria.[83] It is no exaggeration to say that Chomsky was a central figure in RESIST, and indeed in support for draft resistance more widely.[84] In Massachusetts in 1968, subscribers to the national newspaper of the grouping known as 'The Resistance' were asked to make their cheques out to either 'N.E.R.' (New England Resistance) or to 'Noam Chomsky'.[85] One of the many support actions Chomsky participated in was the transportation of draft cards in 1967 from a ceremony in the Arlington Universalist Church in Boston to the Justice Department in Washington DC, where he and other supporters handed them in on behalf of the resisters. The evidence of resistance was preserved rather than burned, and it was delivered to the government in a way that could not be ignored.[86] In October 1968, MIT student groups offered sanctuary to Mike O'Connor, a soldier then AWOL, in the Stratton Student Center. The sanctuary lasted for six days, during which time thousands of students came to protect O'Connor from arrest. Many slept in the hall with the young resister, many others moved their classes to the Student Center in solidarity.[87] According to Louis Kampf, the sanctuary was a student initiative that grew out of the political courses he and Chomsky were teaching together at MIT.[88] Chomsky comments that the sanctuary 'dramatically changed the political climate on the campus', and laid the basis for a one-day research strike in March 1969 which finally involved over 50 colleges.[89]

In 1973, Chomsky backed an effort to nominate all US draft resisters, deserters and war resisters within the armed forces for the Nobel Peace Prize.[90] As is well known, Chomsky's first book was dedicated to 'the brave young men who refuse to serve in a criminal war'.[91] It was his direct involvement with draft resisters which came close to landing him in jail. When in January 1968 the FBI finally put a case together against draft resisters and their supporters, the indictment was a haphazard affair, including people who were not centrally involved as well as people like Mike Ferber, a leading young resister. Chomsky was an unindicted but named co-conspirator of the 'Boston Five'. It was clear that he would soon be targeted. In February, Chomsky told a reporter, 'I'll be surprised if I don't get indicted this Spring.'[92] Many years later, Chomsky confessed,

> In the late 1960s I certainly expected I was going to spend five years in jail. I was involved in organizing resistance. There are two reasons that didn't happen. One, the FBI was too incompetent to figure out what was going on. That's not a joke, and it's something important to bear in mind. The other was, the Tet offensive came along and shifted government policy, so they began to cancel the prosecutions that were underway. But my wife went back to college to be able to support the children. Those were pretty difficult days.[93]

The results of all the various kinds of anti-war activities, across the United States, were impressive and lasting. Chomsky summarizes: 'In 1965, teach-ins, demonstrations, town forums, extensive lobbying, and other forms of protest reached substantial proportions, and by 1967 there were enormous mass demonstrations, large-scale draft resistance, and other forms of nonviolent civil disobedience.... By 1971, to judge by the polls, two-thirds of the population regarded the war as immoral and called for the withdrawal of American troops.'[94] Chomsky notes that as late as 1982, 'after years of dedicated brainwashing with no audible response, over 70% of the general public regarded the war as not merely a "mistake" but "fundamentally wrong and immoral"'.[95] These kinds of achievement began with the work of a handful of people in the early 1960s. At that time, Chomsky admits, 'I thought it was utterly hopeless. I never thought there was the slightest possibility that anything could be done to overcome the jingoist fanaticism that had virtually no break in it at that point.' Chomsky spent his evenings 'talking in somebody's living room to three neighbors, two of whom wanted to lynch me, and taking part in demonstrations so small that we had to be protected by the police to keep everybody from killing us. This went on for a while. I never thought a serious movement would develop.'[96]

Chomsky's involvement in civil disobedience and resistance stemmed from a considered, unexcitable commitment, as Mike Ferber's remarks indicate. Chomsky noted, 'As I indicated in my essays, I arrive at these conclusions reluctantly; they are hardly comfortable ones.'[97] Unlike certain elements in the student movement, Chomsky found the public

activities involved in protest and resistance uncomfortable and somewhat distressing: 'I don't like public life. I don't like demonstrations. I
don't like being maced. I don't like giving a talk to a big crowd. There
are all sorts of things I much prefer not to do.'[98]

Before leaving the subject of civil disobedience it is important to make
two points. Chomsky accepted that civil disobedience had to be
justified; an argument had to be made that appropriate circumstances
existed to justify such action. It had to be plausibly shown both that the
policy opposed was illegitimate and that civil disobedience could be
effective in restricting and terminating the contested policy.[99] The latter
test was as important as the former. Chomsky has never taken the
position, common in peace movement circles, that civil disobedience is
somehow inherently moral and legitimate. Civil disobedience and other
forms of resistance are, for him, only legitimate when there is an
intolerable evil to be overcome, and when the activities proposed can be
expected to lead to a reduction in human suffering, with the minimum
of harmful consequences. In the absence of popular understanding, on
the other hand, civil disobedience 'may be only a form of self-indulgent
and possibly quite harmful adventurism'.[100]

A more significant point, perhaps, is that civil disobedience can, in
Chomsky's view, only be significant in certain circumstances, and is
therefore of 'very narrow social significance'.[101] Civil disobedience is
effective under two conditions: when the issue at stake is 'a marginal
class interest of the ruling class which will be conducted *if* the costs
aren't too high at home', and where a large part of the population
understands that the policy in question is wrong.[102] Under such
circumstances, civil disobedience can help to mobilize the population
and act as 'a catalyst to mass popular action',[103] creating greater
pressure on decision-makers. In the case of Indochina, control of
Vietnam was not a necessity for US state capitalism, and the population
was gradually brought to see that the assault on that country was quite
criminal. So civil disobedience could have an important role. However,
when more central issues are involved, civil disobedience will start to
become ineffective, and different strategies are required. Chomsky
comments,

> Intervention in Timor, or even in Indochina or Central America, is a rather
> peripheral concern of the managers of the US global system, despite the
> enormous resources sometimes devoted to such enterprises and the genuine
> fears of 'contagion' and 'rotten apples'. Liquidation of these projects of terror
> and coercion will not seriously affect the domestic order or the Fifth

Freedom, and therefore committed popular efforts can make a real difference. Other tasks are much harder, those that begin to touch the structure of
power and privilege; serious efforts to confront the military system are a case
in point.[104]

Where more important interests are at stake, the scale of activity and
commitment rises correspondingly. This is the case, for example, with
the nuclear arms race, or with US economic policies towards the Third
World. Chomsky notes that if the Left is to combat imperialism and the
problems caused by international economic organizations, 'it too will
have to be international in its organizational forms as well as in the
cultural level it seeks to attain'.[105] No easy feat.

What is a good strategy? Chomsky replies, 'Everything is a good
strategy.'[106] 'It's surprising what a few letters to a Congress person
might do sometimes.' Scale, however, is everything. Dissidence has to
be 'sustained and organized'. Single demonstrations are tolerable for
state managers: 'What they can't live with is sustained organizations
that just keep doing things and keep building and where people learn
more and learn lessons from the last time and do it better next time and
reach others.' 'It's not just letters to Congress. It's also pressure on
newspapers and everything else.'[107] If this kind of pressure can build a
mass reform movement, and if out of that a more radical movement can
be constructed, then there is the possibility that deeper social changes
can take place that will terminate US militarism and interventionism at
the root.

What is enough? 'Nothing is enough.'[108] Successful organizing and
mobilization bring with them the risk of repression and state violence.
However, Chomsky warns that the search for confrontation is a sign of
'intellectual bankruptcy', and is ultimately self-defeating. He suggests
that those who take their own rhetoric seriously will seek to delay any
confrontation until they can hope to emerge successful.[109]

Chomsky puts forward one central principle that he feels should
guide political activism. He suggests that the

primary principle, especially for people like us, who are, for the most part,
among the privileged in society, should be the principle that we keep clearly in
mind who we are responsible to. I suggest we are responsible to the people of
Vietnam, to the people of Guatemala, to the people of Harlem. In
undertaking some form of action, we must ask ourselves what the consequences will be for the people who are at the wrong end of the guns, for the
people who can't escape. That's a consideration of overwhelming importance. Even a very well intentioned act, if it strengthens the forces of

121

repression, is no gift whatsoever to those whose fate we, in some sense, bear in our hands. This is a simple and elementary fact, and I think it should be ever present in one's mind.[110]

For this reason, if for no other, violent tactics cannot be justified. Chomsky notes that 'It is quite easy to design tactics that will help to consolidate the latent forces of a potential American fascism.'[111] 'We must not abandon the victims of American power, or play games with their fate. We must not consent to have the same repression imposed on still further helpless victims or the same blind fury unleashed against them. Acts that seem perfectly justified in themselves when regarded in a narrow sense may be very wrong when considered in the light of their probable consequences. And a failure to approach those who can be reached, a failure to act with strength and determination when one can do so in a constructive way, is no less thoughtless and indefensible.'[112]

Chomsky argues that as long as the present institutional structures remain unchanged the only thing 'we can do is to try to slow down the worst catastrophes' by trying to block 'the next crazy weapons system and ... the next intervention in the Third World, knowing that all we are doing is putting a band-aid on a cancer. You just do that because you want the world to exist a little longer and because you have the responsibility to try to protect people who are being tortured and murdered.'[113] He once said, 'Talk about erosion of the state system is so far off that I don't think it's useful to even think about what would be needed' to overthrow it.[114] Chomsky explains,

> To the extent that one can reach the general public on these issues – it's very limited because the media and journals don't really permit it – but to the extent that one can, well, East Timor or Vietnam are topics that you can talk to people about in a way that is meaningful to them, whereas talking to them about institutional change and the possibility that they might play a role in changing the institutions is like talking to them about Mars.

Talking about abolishing wage slavery, for example, is 'just too remote from the options that people actually have for them to even pay any attention to that'. It is difficult to know how to reach the point where such questions can be raised but it is 'Certainly not just by talk. Those are things that people have to live; aspirations and understanding have to grow out of experience and struggle and conflict.'[115]

The immediate tasks, in any event, are quite clear. Single-issue campaigns can be built up that may one day interact to form larger mosaics. The labour movement can be revitalized and strengthened. There are also connections between organizing activism and organizing intellectual self-defence. Chomsky observes,

> Whether one sees oneself as dedicated to reform or revolution, the first steps are education of oneself and others. There will be little hope for further progress unless the means to carry out these first steps are preserved and enhanced: networks of local organizations, media and publishers who do not bend to state and private power, and so on. These first steps interact: the organizations will not function without access to information and analysis, independent media and publishing will not survive without the participation and intellectual and financial contributions of popular organizations that grow and develop on the basis of shared concerns, optimally based in the community, workplace, or other points of social interaction.[116]

The propaganda system is a major obstacle. Chomsky comments, 'Separatism, subcultures or actions that remain meaningless or offensive to much of the population, lack of an articulated vision of the future, acceptance without awareness of the doctrines of the state religion – these are among the many reflections of the enormous power of the Western system of fragmentation and ideological control, and of our inability, so far, to combat it, except sporadically.'[117]

Chomsky's reluctance to devote effort to 'revolutionary strategy' stems, we now see, from his judgement that such work is premature. Talking about such matters is almost meaningless to the bulk of the population. The structure of power means that people's options are radically limited. Furthermore, the propaganda system has to a large extent crushed the capacity for independent thought. There is also, perhaps, another reason for Chomsky's avoidance of questions of strategy and tactics. He claims, 'I'm not very good at advice. I mean, if I could give you advice, I'd be doing it myself.'[118]

> I don't think I'm in any position to tell people what to do. I felt the same way back in the 1960s when I was talking to young people whose lives were on the line. . . . If you tell people to get seriously involved in dissidence, they're going to change their lives. This is not the kind of thing you can dip your toe into and then walk away from. If you're serious about it, it's going to affect you. . . . I don't feel in any position to tell people how to make those choices. I wouldn't tell my own children how to make them.[119]

8

The Function of the University

Despite the fact that he is an academic and has lived much of his life within a university setting, Chomsky has devoted surprisingly little of his writings to the university itself. During the debate about the universities in the 1960s, however, Chomsky did contribute some thoughts. In general terms, he follows Wilhelm von Humboldt, the linguist and Enlightenment thinker, who defined the university as 'nothing other than the spiritual life of those human beings who are moved by external leisure or internal pressures toward learning and research'.[1] Chomsky comments, 'The extent to which existing institutional forms permit these human needs to be satisfied provides one measure of the level of civilization that a society has achieved.'[2] This general observation aside, Chomsky believes that it is pointless to discuss the university outside the terms of a particular historical situation, just as it would be futile to study any other social institution in such a way. Chomsky remarks, 'To one who believes, as I do, that our society must undergo drastic changes if civilization is to advance – perhaps even to survive – university reform will appear an insignificant matter except in so far as it contributes to social change.'[3] We find, then, some connection between this topic and those we have just been discussing.

According to Chomsky, the New Left had a salutary effect in breaking through the postwar complacency of academia. He commented in 1971, 'The universities have been opened, as never before in my lifetime, to new ideas and independent thinking outside of the natural sciences.'[4] Student radicalism mounted what he described as a 'belated and very healthy challenge' to academic subservience to state and private power. This is something of a minority view of events. For most academics, the challenge posed by the students was seen as an unacceptable intrusion, and they responded by publicly decrying the 'politicization' of the university. For Chomsky, this concern was somewhat overdue. He asked,

> how many study projects at political science departments are concerned with the questions of, say, how poorly armed guerillas can withstand a fantastic military force by an outside aggressive power [sic], or how many political science programmes are concerned simply with the problems of mass politics or revolutionary development in third-world countries, or, for that matter, in our own society? The answer is obvious in advance.

Such bias was, and remains, evidence of another kind of politicization, a politicization which had been warned against by President Eisenhower, and by Senators Rickover and Fulbright, well-known mainstream figures.[5]

The rise of the student movement provoked a feverish debate on the question of 'why students rebel'. Chomsky suggested that the question was wrongly put: 'The serious question that we must face is not why students rebel, but rather why students are virtually *alone*, in the white middle classes, in their rebellion, and why they rebel only now, and not before.'[6] Surveying the unprecedented war of destruction in Vietnam, the accumulation and employment of chemical weapons by the United States, the readiness of US officials and politicians to contemplate global nuclear war during the Cuban missile crisis, the dangers of a domestic race war, impending repressive legislation and US aggression overseas, Chomsky suggested that there was no need to explain why a movement of protest, radical political action, and resistance had arisen: 'The real question is why so few join it.'[7] Students, unlike other sectors of the white middle classes, have no particular stake in the existing structure of power and privilege. They are at a stage in their lives when they are relatively free to think and explore and act. When people are given this kind of freedom, and the reality is extremely grim, 'then they are likely to be appalled and try to do something about it. And the reaction to that is student unrest, of course.'[8] 'No elaborate explanations are necessary,' Chomsky suggests.[9] Again, something of a minority view. Chomsky remarked in 1973, 'We read that student activism results from a need for instant gratification, or is an exercise in irrationality or an outburst of left fascism. One can no doubt find cases to which such charges apply, but those who castigate the student movement as dominated by such tendencies are either unaware of the facts or are playing a more cynical game.'[10] He observed that it would be 'superficial, and in fact rather childish' to be mesmerized by the occasional absurdities of phraseology or offensive acts committed by the student movement, while at the same time missing the 'great significance of the issues that have been raised and that lie beneath the tumult'.[11] George Kennan, for example, expressed concern at the 'extremely disturbed and excited state of mind of a good portion of our student youth, floundering around as it is in its own terrifying wilderness of drugs, pornography, and political hysteria'. Chomsky noted that Kennan did not express any similar concern at the disturbed and excited state of mind of those responsible for the fact that the tonnage of bombs dropped on South Vietnam exceeded the total expended by the US Air Force in all theatres of the Second World War.[12]

For a time, under the weight of student pressure, US universities were forced to open up and support what Chomsky describes as 'islands of activism or independent critical thought'.[13] By 1973, though, Chomsky observed that ideological controls had been 'reasonably effectively reestablished',[14] in part through the firing of radical faculty. Student activism declined. Chomsky commented that it was not obvious that the students had merely lost their interest in such matters, as many alleged: 'it is possible that they were simply no longer willing to endure beatings, imprisonment, vituperation, and idiotic denunciations for what was in fact courageous devotion to principle'.[15] The reduction in student activism after the 1960s was not as great as it seemed, however. As activism gradually spread to other sectors of the population, the broader movement made 'the student movement look relatively less significant'.[16]

Chomsky was not uncritical of the student movement, and one of his main criticisms concerned the issue of university reform. 'George Orwell once remarked that political thought, especially on the left, is a sort of a masturbation fantasy in which the world of fact hardly matters. That's true, unfortunately, and it's part of the reason that our society lacks a genuine, responsible, serious left-wing movement.'[17] Chomsky suggested that the students had presented 'a very inadequate analysis of the university and its defects': 'They tend to think that the university is controlled by the trustees and the administration, who send out edicts which are binding on faculty members and require that they work on counter-insurgency and the development of weapons. The fact of the matter is that the situation is really much more serious.'[18] In reality, Chomsky argues, the administration has almost no impact on the content of research. The reason academics devote themselves to counter-insurgency research, or preserving imperialist ideology, or working on new weapons, 'is that they do so out of their free choice'.[19]

Chomsky sees the universities as 'relatively free, fairly decentralized institutions in which the major decisions are made by the faculty at departmental levels'.[20] In a frank discussion with other faculty members at MIT, Chomsky admitted to some ambivalence. Given the dominant role of the university as an instrument of state policy, Chomsky conceded that someone who was aware of, and actively opposed to, the growing militarization of US society at home, and the uses of US power overseas or even at home, could very easily be led to believe that she 'ought to try to smash the universities'.[21] Chomsky even confessed that a part of his own personality had 'a certain great accord with that':

> if smashing the universities, let's say, could prevent endless escalation of the arms race, could prevent militarization of American society, could prevent the increasing concentration of political and economic power in the society, could prevent concentration overseas, could prevent imperialist wars and so on and so forth, well, I think that would be very justifiable.[22]

However, at this point, 'the other side of my schizophrenic view reacts and says that's pretty senseless because the universities are probably the most free and open institutions in the society, the attack against them is launched largely because they are also the weakest, and the most easily attacked precisely because they are relatively free and open'.[23] The consequence of 'smashing the universities' would not be the correction of social evils, but the replacement of universities by more authoritarian and repressive institutions. This would be a net loss for those committed to radical social change.

If Chomsky is correct in his analysis of the university, it follows that the central focus of reform should be not the trustees and the administration, 'but rather the cast of mind and the general intellectual and moral commitments of very substantial segments of the faculty themselves'.[24] The focus of much of the student movement on institutional restructuring, electing people onto committees or even on ending military research was misguided. 'Many of these things could be undertaken without leading to any objective change in the character of the society and what it does.'[25] At places like MIT, people like the head of the political science department 'learned long ago that you don't do your really unspeakable work in your capacity as a university professor. You do your work in your capacity as a member of a corporation which has been set up for that purpose. From the point of view of the Vietnamese, or the people in Harlem, it makes no difference.'[26] It would be quite possible to move all oppressive research work off campus, and create a righteous university, without the victims of US power deriving any benefit whatsoever. We should distinguish therefore between two values: the purity of the university, and the needs of the victims. Chomsky argued that there was 'no particular point in trying to develop pure universities in a criminal society'.[27] The crux of the matter is what the primary value is to be:

> If one's commitment is to the purity of the campus, if that's the highest principle, then, of course, one will say: Take weapons research off campus, because then the campus is more pure. If, on the other hand, one is concerned with the human consequences of what one does, then the question to raise is: What are the human consequences of having weapons research done on campus or off campus?[28]

Instead of severing links in a cosmetic fashion, Chomsky proposed, in all seriousness, the creation of 'Departments of Death', where all repressive research and development could be carried out on each campus. He said later,

> my proposal, and I meant this quite seriously, was that universities ought to establish Departments of Death that should be right in the center of the campus, in which all the work in the university which is committed to destruction and murder and oppression should be centralized. They should have an honest name for it. It shouldn't be called Political Science or Electronics or something like that. It should be called Death Technology or Theory of Oppression or something of that sort, in the interests of truth-in-packaging.[29]

As long as the present structure of power continues, such work will be done. The question is whether it is done on campus or off. The advantage of keeping it on campus is that it would then be visible, and a possible focus for protest and activism, 'rather than moving it somewhere where it can be done silently, freely', with, perhaps, exactly the same people doing exactly the same work.[30] Chomsky commented,

> I would rather have the laboratories right in the middle of the campus, where their presence could be used to politicize future engineers, for instance, rather than having them hidden away somewhere while the campus is perfectly clean and cloistered. I feel this way about chemical and bacteriological warfare too. I would prefer to have a building in the middle of campus, called Department of Bacteriological Warfare, rather than have it right off the map at Fort Detrick or some place nobody knows of. It could be actually

retrograde, in this sense, to try to cut all connections between the university and the Department of Defense.[31]

Chomsky admits, 'Well, I don't think I convinced many people of this, so maybe there's something wrong with my reasoning, but as I see it, at least, these positions are entirely consistent.'[32]

Universities are economically parasitical, and given present social realities must depend upon government subsidies and often on corporate funding. On the issue of ending military funding for research, Chomsky pointed out that 'radical students will certainly ask themselves why support from the Defense Department is more objectionable than support from capitalist institutions – ultimately from profits derived by exploitation – or support by tax-free gifts that in effect constitute a levy on the poor to support the education of the privileged'.[33] On the related issue of university connections with the CIA, Chomsky remarked that he had never become particularly interested in the topic: 'The institution pretty much serves the interests of the state where it can. Whether it's being directly funded by the CIA or in some other fashion seems to me a marginal question.'[34] In fact, Chomsky advocated direct, open funding by the CIA: 'At least everything would be open and above-board.'[35]

The basic problem here is that the university cannot by itself change the nature of society, and must inevitably mirror the inequitable nature of the larger society. Chomsky remarks, 'Those who believe that radical social change is imperative in our society are faced with a dilemma when they consider university reform. They want the university to be a free institution, and they want the individuals in it to use this freedom in a civilized way.'[36] The only way to resolve this tension, according to Chomsky, is to uphold and defend absolutely the principle of academic freedom, while opening up new options in academic work and in connections between the university and the community. For Chomsky, 'One legacy of classical liberalism that we must fight to uphold with unending vigilance, in the universities and without, is the commitment to a "free marketplace of ideas".'[37] He agrees with 'critics who warn of the dangers of politicizing the universities, which should be, so far as possible, independent of the influence of external powers, state or private, and of militant factions within'.[38] Chomsky expressed an unreserved opposition to the use of coercion to prevent military research and other such activities, for a number of reasons:

> Once the principle is established that coercion is legitimate, in this domain, it is rather clear against whom it will be used. And the principle of legitimacy of

coercion would destroy the university as a serious institution; it would destroy its value to a free society. This must be recognized even in the light of the undeniable fact that the freedom falls far short of ideal.[39]

This might seem an instrumental or opportunistic attitude to freedom of research. It is not the basis of Chomsky's defence. He regards academic freedom, and the freedom of expression, as absolute values, important in themselves. For such reasons, he 'supported the rights of American war criminals not only to speak and teach but also to conduct their research, on grounds of academic freedom, at a time when their work was being used to murder and destroy'. He later conceded that this was a position 'that I am not sure I could defend'.[40]

Chomsky's most famous defence of academic freedom was in relation to the 'Faurisson affair', when Robert Faurisson, a professor of French literature at the University of Lyons, was deprived of research facilities and driven from his position for denying that gas chambers were used to kill Jews under the Nazis. A court later convicted Faurisson of the crime of failing his 'responsibility' as a historian, and 'de laisser presendre encharge, par autrui, son discours dans une intention d'apologie des crimes de guerre ou d'incitation à la haine raciale', among other charges. Chomsky, in the company of hundreds of others, signed a petition in 1979 deploring this infringement of academic freedom. Subsequently he wrote a short essay on the need to defend freedom of expression, which was used without his knowledge as the preface to a book about the gas chambers by Faurisson. Chomsky's critics used these actions in defence of Faurisson's civil rights to smear Chomsky as a supporter of Holocaust denial.[41] Le Matin claimed that Chomsky regarded the idea of genocide itself as 'un mythe imperialiste'.[42] The New Republic, a liberal US journal, suggested that Chomsky was 'an agnostic' as to whether or not six million Jews were murdered.[43] The acme of hysteria came from Canadian academic Werner Cohn, who reported that Chomsky was 'in a certain sense, the most important patron' of the modern neo-Nazi movement, and was engaged in a private 'war against the Jews'. According to Cohn, Chomsky had concealed his true allegiances by ensuring that these shameful activities were 'well-known only in France'.[44] Anyone with the slightest knowledge of Chomsky's work will know, as Brian Morton points out, that from his earliest writings to his latest, 'Nazism has served him as a benchmark of pure and unquestionable evil.'[45] Chomsky wrote in his first book of political essays that in accepting the presumption of legitimacy of debate over certain issues – for example, in debating with Nazi propagandists – one had already lost one's humanity.[46] Cohn and others were perfectly aware of Chomsky's commitment on these issues, and his comment, for example, that the Zionist case 'relies on the aspirations of a people who suffered two millennia of exile and savage persecution culminating in the most fantastic outburst of collective insanity in human history'.[47] In another book, again long before the world had heard of Faurisson, Chomsky described the Nazi regime as '*sui generis*' in implementing 'the final solution' and other 'forms of criminal insanity perfected by the Nazi technicians'.[48] When one turns to the petition itself, and to the preface Chomsky unwittingly contributed to Faurisson's book, there is no mention of Faurisson's opinions, only a defence of his right to freedom of research and freedom of speech. Chomsky commented on the significance of the Faurisson affair in an interview in 1988: 'The Faurisson affair really is important, as a demonstration of the victory of fascism, the commitment of the intelligentsia to Stalinist doctrine, their cowardice in concealing all of this beneath a flood of lies, and the ways this is used to undermine criticism of Israel – the real heart of it all, obviously enough.'[49] Unable to answer Chomsky's long-standing critique of the Israeli occupation and other policies of the Israeli state, Chomsky's critics prefer to smear and defame.

As Chomsky pointed out during the Faurisson affair, there are other questions of historical 'revisionism'. The work of those who rewrote the history of US aggression in Indochina, ascribing it to 'error', not only insulted the memory of the dead, as Faurisson was convicted of doing, but also contributed to the continuing sanctions against and torture of Vietnam, and helped to lay the basis for future aggression by the US state, something which Faurisson could not be accused of. Chomsky also noted that,

> if the Journal of the American Jewish Congress publishes, as it recently did, an article claiming that the Nazi genocide of the gypsies is an exploded fiction, I don't say that the American Jewish Congress's editors should be brought to court for Nazi apologetics and for denying an act of genocide which was in fact quite comparable to the Holocaust. If they want to publish their disgraceful lies, they should have the right to do so. If they were brought to court, I would defend their right to say what they want.[50]

Returning to the question of university reform, we see that Chomsky is 'very much out of sympathy with the idea that things ought to be stopped, no matter how bad they are, even, or certainly stopped by force, but even stopped.' He comments, 'I'd like to see them stopped by the weapon of persuasion and often contempt.'[51] Chomsky makes a comparison with the natural sciences, a typical manoeuvre for him, both in linguistics and in politics: 'If the physics student believes his [sic] professor doesn't understand which way is up, then he should demonstrate this to the professor. It won't do any good to storm the physics building. If the student knows which side is up I think he has a fair chance of showing it.'[52] Real reforms will come not by imposing restrictive rules on research, or by closing buildings, but 'by constructing alternative programmes inside the university which can succeed in gathering towards them the better, the more creative students, and the better faculty members'.[53]

The new options which might be opened up in academia were demonstrated by Chomsky's own work at MIT, teaching courses in political and social thought. Together with Louis Kampf, now Professor of Literature and Women's Studies, Chomsky began teaching a course entitled 'Intellectuals and Social Change' in 1965, and another course, entitled 'Contemporary Issues in Politics and Ideology', which began in 1971. The two courses ran in alternate years thereafter until they were discontinued in 1987.[54] Activists and observers came from as far away as Maine and Connecticut to join MIT students on the courses, which became a focus for activism. Teaching assistants, including two future presidents of Students for a Democratic Society (SDS), were encouraged to make the course student-led and -organized as much as possible. One former student, now Professor of Linguistics at Maryland University, describes Chomsky and Kampf as 'geniuses' at 'being able to get you to see things that are apparently different as very similar to one another; you know, all they do is just change the honorifics...'[55] 'To be young and to be exposed to it on a page by page analysis is really ... a very powerful thing to have done.'[56] Chomsky and Kampf issued reading lists of conventional texts such as Roger Hilsman's *To Move a Nation*, J.K. Galbraith's *The New Industrial State*, and W.W. Rostow's *The United States in the World Arena*. They would then proceed to test these standard works to destruction, by exposing and exploding their basic assumptions. The courses also extended to community organization and other activism outside as well as inside the university.[57]

In general, 'To the extent that reform does not reach the heart of the university – the content of the curriculum, the interaction between student and teacher, the nature of research, and in some fields, the practice that relates to theory – it will remain superficial.'[58] Chomsky commended the work of those seeking to construct alternative programmes of study and action, of teaching and research, that would be 'more compelling on intellectual and moral grounds', and that could change the character of the universities by changing not their formal structures – relatively insignificant matters – but the actual work of students and faculty. If such programmes could be fostered, the university could 'reorient the lives of those who pass through it'.[59]

This might be interpreted as a call to 'radical scholarship'. Chomsky denies the existence of any such category. He comments, 'Personally, I believe that *objective* scholarship free from the ideological restraints which are imposed by the general political consensus and distribution of force would lead to radical conclusions.'[60] Naturally, the burden of proof for this contention rests with him and with those who believe as he does. He notes, 'The failure to develop radical scholarship in this sense is not, if you check, a result of the decrees of trustees and administration. Rather, it follows from the unwillingness of students and faculty to undertake the very hard and serious work that's required, and to face, calmly, but firmly, the abuse that is quite inevitable.'[61] There are bound to be personal costs for those who attempt to develop such scholarship – harassment, slow promotion, unemployment, and so on. Chomsky comments, 'if these considerations are enough to deter people, then I think the people are not to be taken seriously'.[62] The lifestyle of the conformist intelligentsia can be tempting, but

> if a person can't resist that sort of temptation, it's rather sad. I think that honesty requires of scholarship that it go in the directions that are determined by internal processes. Obviously there are inducements that lead one away from that. But I don't see any reason why people should not be able to resist these inducements ... I don't believe that Marx would have failed to do his work, let's say, had he been given a government subsidy to work in the British Museum. If one believes that, well, it certainly is rather demeaning to Marx.[63]

Despite the extremely hostile attitude of much of the academic world to his political work, Chomsky continued to teach without apparent problems at MIT, even teaching courses in contemporary affairs 'with no harassment or difficulty'.[64] Chomsky was asked during the Vietnam War how he had managed to carry on teaching at MIT, one of the centres of US military research. He responded, 'there are two aspects to that: one is the question how MIT tolerates me, and the other is how I tolerate MIT'.[65] MIT tolerated him, he suggested, because despite everything, there was a libertarian strain in US society which meant that even an institution that produced weapons of war could be 'willing to tolerate, in fact, in many ways even encourage' someone involved in civil disobedience against the war.[66] Despite being a largely Pentagon-funded university, MIT has a very good record on academic freedom and freedom of dissidence, 'one of the best around, better than most universities', according to Chomsky.[67] On the second question, of how Chomsky tolerated MIT, Chomsky noted that there were many who believed that radicals should dissociate themselves from oppressive institutions. He disagreed emphatically. 'The logic of that argument is that Karl Marx shouldn't have studied in the British Museum which, if anything, was the symbol of the most vicious imperialism in the world, the place where all the treasures an empire had gathered from the rape of the colonies, were brought together.' Marx was correct in 'using the resources and in fact the liberal values of the civilization that he was trying to overcome, against it.' Furthermore, Chomsky's presence at MIT served to some extent – in his view 'marginally' – to help to increase student activism against the war and against much of the work done at MIT.[68] He commented during the war,

> It seems to me particularly crucial to raise these questions with the MIT student body, because of their potential influence and role in decision making. I have no particular illusions about any success that may be achieved along these lines, but as far as I can see, the actions that are most meaningful are educational activities of this sort and personal refusal to participate in any way in implementing the warlike activities of the government.

Chomsky did consider leaving not only MIT but the country, as a protest against the war. His judgement, which he admitted could have been a rationalization, was that, 'what little impact someone like myself can possibly have would be lost by leaving the country'.[69]

Chomsky's continued presence at MIT was constrained by his self-imposed condition that he would not spend the bulk of his time on activism. He commented in 1968, 'If I wanted to spend the dominant part of my time on resistance, I would leave the university. Similarly, if someone says that he [sic] wants to work principally on bombs or counter-insurgency, I think he should leave.'[70] Chomsky has made it abundantly clear that he is much more interested, intellectually, in linguistics than in politics: 'I'd be delighted if all these external problems would go away and I could return to my linguistics – problems like Vietnam, repression in other parts of Asia and Latin America, the preservation of permanent poverty, racism.'[71] In April 1968, Chomsky observed: 'For an American intellectual now it seems that there are some rather difficult choices, given the present state of affairs. One choice is to become a full-time political activist', which could be amply justified by the current state of the world and the role of the United States in world affairs.[72] The second alternative would be to renounce political involvement 'and make use of the very rich resources that this country provides and the very high status and pleasant life it affords to anyone who becomes fully professional'.

> Now those choices may be difficult and may have their own problems, but when you have made either of these two decisions your way is pretty clear from then on. On the other hand there is a middle ground which I would like to occupy, and I think that people are going to have to find ways to occupy: namely, to try to keep up a serious commitment to the intellectual values and intellectual and scientific problems that really concern you and yet at the same time make a serious and one hopes useful contribution to the enormous extra-scientific questions.... Now exactly how one can maintain that sort of schizophrenic existence I am not sure; it is very difficult. It's not only a matter of too much demand on one's time, but also a high degree of ongoing personal conflict about where your next outburst of energy should go.[73]

Chomsky notes wryly, 'A lot of my activist friends can't understand why I waste my time on linguistics.'[74] Elsewhere he comments, 'For reasons of personal sanity, and perhaps a measure of self-indulgence, I also expect to spend as much time and energy as I can on intellectual problems that have always intrigued me.'[75]

Returning to the question of university reform, Chomsky suggests that, ideally, US universities ought to force students to face the fact that their work as professionals is related to the exercise of power, and that in the course of their work they will make political judgements which affect the world at large. That is to say, engineers and sociologists and physicists and other professionals make decisions which affect the lives of other human beings. This cannot be avoided – even if you decide to do nothing, this will have some effect on others. This power confers some responsibility. Having faced this problem, students may choose to transfer the burden of decision to others and abrogate their responsibilities. There is little anyone can do about such a decision, but 'what the university can do is at least make it very hard to avoid facing that problem'.[76] Anyone considering a career as an engineer, for example, should, in Chomsky's view, intensively study the history of the Cold War as presented by people from a very wide range of persuasions. He noted that a large number of engineers had testified, before an internal MIT inquiry into the future of the 'special' military laboratories, to the effect that they were building weapons because otherwise the United States would be overwhelmed by its enemies. He commented, 'Now personally I think that's an absolute myth, but that's not what's important. What's important is that they arrived at that position on the basis of zero knowledge, you know, never having had the issue presented to them. They just arrived at that position because it's in the air.'[77] The fact that they had arrived at this position in such a nebulous way was, for Chomsky, a grave defect in MIT. Furthermore, 'it's a terribly important decision that they arrived at – in fact the fate of civilization may depend on that decision'.[78] Chomsky sought the opportunity, alongside others with different attitudes, to present his view of the background to the Cold War to scientists and engineers; 'And I'm confident enough of my own interpretation of the cold war to believe that if it were presented among others, it would really win over a lot of people to believe they shouldn't be involved in things like weapons production because their involvement in weapons production is based on a complete misconception about what the cold war is about.'[79] These questions should properly be faced by students 'at a time in life when they are relatively free from external pressures, free to explore the many dimensions of the problems and supported by a community with like concerns, rather than isolated in a competitive job market'.[80]

As modern capitalism stands, it requires large numbers of young people to acquire knowledge and skills at university under conditions of relative freedom and openness. 'Dogmatism and achievement are incompatible, in the long run,' Chomsky suggests. While it is to be expected that some of these young people may restrict themselves to conformism and narrow self-interest, 'it is predictable that there will also be free and compassionate and independent minds to challenge prevailing orthodoxies and search for ways to translate a perception of social injustice to some form of action'.[81] Chomsky notes that 'We take it for granted that creative work in any field will challenge prevailing orthodoxy. A physicist who refines yesterday's experiment, an engineer who merely seeks to improve existing devices, an artist who limits himself [sic] to styles and techniques that have been thoroughly explored, is rightly regarded as deficient in creative imagination.'[82] Creative and exciting work will always seek to challenge the conventional assumptions of the field. Whether in physics, in music or in social affairs, 'Honest inquiry is inherently "subversive", in any field.'[83] The difference between the sciences and the humanities is that, in science, Nature is always there to keep you honest. In the humanities such constraints are much more relaxed. 'At least the sciences do instil habits of honesty, creativity and co-operation. All these properties are dangerous from the point of view of society.'[84] In physics, a student will not be able to survive unless she becomes 'radical' and questioning. In the ideological disciplines, the reverse is generally the case. Chomsky suggests that in the 'domain of social criticism the normal attitudes of the scientist are feared and deplored as a form of subversion or as dangerous radicalism',[85] that is to say, the 'questioning and iconoclastic approach that is highly valued and carefully nurtured in the physical sciences, where an imaginative worker will very often hold up his [sic] basic assumptions to searching analysis'.[86] Chomsky's political analysis, like his linguistics, can be understood as an attempt to follow the approach of the natural sciences in the social sciences: testing theories against the facts and attempting to derive models with explanatory power.[87] For Chomsky, the culture of science is the real 'counter-culture' to the reigning ideology. It is for such reasons that Chomsky has suggested that those studying the social sciences should do so 'in the context of the physical sciences, so that the student can be brought to appreciate clearly the limits of their intellectual content. This can be an important way to protect a student from the propaganda of the future...'[88]

One of the mechanisms for containing thought and promoting conformism is the guild structure of universities. In Chomsky's words, this structure 'has often served as a marvelous [sic] device for protecting them from insight and understanding, for filtering out people who raise unacceptable questions, for limiting research – not by force, but by all sorts of more subtle means – to questions that are not threatening'.[89] One example is the failure of the United States to compete effectively with Japan. The crucial issue is the relative efficiency and effectiveness of the Pentagon and MITI systems of state subsidy and coordination of high-technology business.[90] This vital question for US society is, Chomsky submits, 'unstudyable' because of the way that the social sciences have been organized: the economics department is interested only in abstract models of a pure free enterprise economy; the political science department is concentrating on voting patterns and electoral statistics; the anthropologists are studying hill tribesmen in New Guinea; and the sociologists are studying crime in the ghetto. 'There isn't any field that deals with this topic. There's no journal that deals with these topics. There's no academic profession that's concerned with the central problems of modern society.... This is a subtle form of design to prevent inquiry into power.'[91] The disciplines are constructed so that certain questions cannot be posed.

The fact that there has been little in the way of new, objective research and scholarship has little to do with academic repression, Chomsky suggests. He traces it rather to a lack of commitment on the part of 'radical' students and faculty to do the hard work necessary to deepen and humanize their disciplines. The stakes are high. Chomsky suggests that 'a movement of the left condemns itself to failure and irrelevance if it does not create an intellectual culture that becomes dominant by virtue of its excellence and that is meaningful to the masses of people who, in an advanced industrial society, can participate in creating and deepening it'.[92] The university can play a critical role in this effort, if those within it can be persuaded to take seriously the professed values of neutrality, objectivity and honesty. Chomsky notes that such values were embedded in the founding document of SDS in 1962. The 'Port Huron Statement' commented:

> The university is located in a permanent position of social influence. Its educational function makes it indispensable and automatically makes it a crucial institution in the formation of social attitudes. In an unbelievably complicated world, it is the central institution for organizing, evaluating, and transmitting knowledge.... Social relevance, the accessibility to knowledge, and internal openness – these together make the university a potential base and agency in the movement of social change.
>
> Any new left in America must be, in large measure, a left with real intellectual skills, committed to deliberativeness, honesty, and reflection as working tools. The university permits the political life to be an adjunct to the academic one, and action to be informed by reason.[93]

Chomsky's efforts to promote 'real intellectual skills' in the student movement have gone largely unrecorded, though not forgotten by those who were active in those days. Jim Peck, a longstanding activist, notes that 'In the early days of the antiwar movement, Chomsky willingly came and spoke with just a handful of people, with students in all disciplines – from physics to Asian studies – urging them to use their minds and not just their bodies to oppose the war.'[94]

SDS later explicitly rejected its early intellectual and political orientation as it moved towards a Leninist position and eventually disintegrated. Writing in 1970, Chomsky noted that 'Many in the New Left now think of such ideas as part of their "liberal past," to be abandoned in the light of the new consciousness that has since been achieved.'[95] He disagreed. Chomsky argues that the Left 'badly needs

understanding of present society, its long-range tendencies, the possibilities for alternative forms of social organization, and a reasoned
analysis of how social change can come about'. This is exactly the stuff
of new, objective scholarship.[96] Chomsky observes, 'I think the Left
historically has suffered from the passion with which it's taken
positions. I think one has to build up its intellectual substance
significantly.'[97]

In many ways, Chomsky is a defender of traditional intellectual
values. For him, 'The major contribution that a university can make to a
free society is by preserving its independence as an institution committed to the free exchange of ideas, to critical analysis, to experiment,
to exploration of a wide range of ideas and values, to the study of the
consequences of social action or scientific progress.'[98] It remains to be
seen whether this freedom will bear fruit in any of the ways Chomsky
hopes for.

The Responsibility of Intellectuals

As many commentators have noticed, there is, in a sense, something curiously uncomplicated about Chomsky's political writings. Some speak of the 'untheoretical' nature of his writings, others of his 'simplistic' attitudes. One early reviewer wondered whether 'the ultimate question that Chomsky poses' was, 'Is it now necessary to revert to a "pre-ideological" stance?'[1] In a sense this is correct. Chomsky's moral and political principles rest ultimately on a very simple basis. Much of his work is based on the observation that human beings are responsible for the foreseeable consequences of their actions. No great theory can be wrought out of such material, it can hardly be called an ideology. This is a truism of ethical thought. In order to be moral individuals, we must seek to minimize or, if possible, eliminate the harm caused by our actions – and our inaction. At the collective level, we must take responsibility for what our society does and take action to ensure that the suffering inflicted by our social institutions is minimized or, if possible, prevented completely. This is the responsibility of peoples. These are Sunday school lessons which are almost embarrassing to repeat. None the less, this is a necessary foundation for understanding Chomsky's politics.

Chomsky's first adult political essay was entitled 'The Responsibility of Intellectuals', and this responsibility is at the heart of his political writings, the question around which almost all of his writings entwine. The central issue, Chomsky argues, is the question of honesty: 'It is the responsibility of intellectuals to speak the truth and to expose lies.'[2] The duty to tell the truth is particularly important for intellectuals because of the special privileges they possess: they 'are in a position to expose the lies of governments, to analyze actions according to their causes and motives and often hidden intentions'. In the West, intellectuals also have the power that comes from 'political liberty, from access to information and freedom of expression': 'For a privileged minority, Western democracy provides the leisure, the facilities and the training to seek the truth lying hidden behind the veil of distortion and misrepresentation, ideology, and class interest through which the events of current history are presented to us.' The responsibilities of intellectuals are therefore 'much deeper' than the responsibility of peoples which we have already noted.[3]

Chomsky points out that simple honesty is not enough: 'Obviously we demand a commitment to discover the truth, and beyond that, concentration on what is important.'[4] Importance can be gauged by how information leads to action. Chomsky illustrates with a thought experiment. Imagine, before the collapse of the Warsaw Pact, being presented with two pamphlets on human rights violations in the United States, one put out by commissars in East Germany, the other produced by Church and civil rights groups in the United States. We know immediately which document is important, leaving aside questions of accuracy. What East German intellectuals said about US crimes might have been true, but it was not important for their domestic and international audience; what was important for this audience was a discussion of the treatment of dissidents in the Soviet zone, or Soviet terror bombing in Afghanistan. From this we deduce that one index of the 'importance' of an action is: 'What are its likely consequences for victims of oppression?'[5] This is a principle of overriding importance.

There are two aspects of this simple principle. One is that 'The proper focus of concern for us lies in areas where we have a responsibility for what is happening *and the opportunity to mitigate or terminate suffering and violence*. This is particularly true in a democratic society, where policies can be influenced, often significantly so, by public opinion and action.'[6] Chomsky adds, 'There is no way to give a precise measure of the scale of our responsibility in each particular case, but whether we conclude that our share is 90%, or 40%, or 2%, it is that factor that should primarily concern us, since it is that factor that we can directly influence.'[7] This is the basis for Chomsky's concern with US foreign policy: 'The main reasons for my concern with U.S. foreign policy are that I find it in general horrifying, and that I think that it is possible for me to do something to modify it, at least to mitigate some of its most dangerous and destructive aspects.'[8] Chomsky notes briskly, 'In some intellectual circles, it is considered naïve or foolish to try to be guided by moral principles. About this form of idiocy, I will have nothing to say.'[9] Chomsky's decision to focus on foreign policy also stems from his sense that 'while many people here do excellent and important work concerning crucial domestic issues, very few concerned themselves in the same way and with the same depth of commitment to foreign policy issues'. In the arena of foreign policy, Chomsky has set out to focus his energies on areas that are not only important, but also ignored.

> In the current period, the regions where U.S. foreign policy is having the most devastating impact – both in terms of immediate effects and long-term consequences – are Central America and the Middle East, in my judgment. I have personally chosen to concentrate most of my efforts on the Middle East, in part because of special knowledge and interest, in part because there are many people doing outstanding and important work on Central America, while the Middle East is generally avoided for reasons too complex to enter into here.

Chomsky summarizes: 'Putting it a bit crudely, it is best to tell people that which they least want to hear, to take up the least popular causes, other things being equal.'[10]

The other aspect of our basic principle is that our actions on behalf of the victims of oppression should not cause them or others greater suffering. This may sound simple, but it is one of the most hotly contested aspects of Chomsky's stance. If one follows this principle, it may not always be appropriate to criticize oppression. The principle that one should try to help the victims of oppression may sometimes lead to dilemmas where attempting to help a group of suffering people may lead to greater oppression for them, or for others. Chomsky illustrates this with another example from the Soviet era. Should a Russian intellectual in 1988 have written criticism (even if it were accurate) of the terror and atrocities of the Afghan resistance in the Soviet press, knowing that such criticism would enable the Soviet Union to mobilize its own population for further atrocities and aggression? Would that be a morally responsible thing to do? Chomsky comments, 'if you want my answer I would say no, it's not a morally responsible thing to do'. An intellectual, like any human being, has the moral responsibility to consider the human consequences of what they do: 'If you write, you have a moral responsibility to consider the consequences of what you write.'

> To take another example, suppose that I was a German citizen in 1938. Would it have been morally responsible for me to write an article in the Nazi press about the atrocities carried out by Jewish terrorists in Palestine, or

about the crimes of Jewish businessmen, even if it was all accurate? Would it have been morally responsible for me to write those truths in the Nazi press?

Again, for Chomsky, this would not be morally responsible. 'These are just truisms. If we are capable of recognizing truisms about others, then we're just cowardly and dishonest if we refuse to apply the truisms to ourselves. This leads to moral dilemmas.'[11]

By analogy, US intellectuals should consider whether their criticism of the victims of US power or of enemy states may entrench US ideology, and thereby help to consolidate the popular basis for US interventionism and terrorism. Similar questions arise for other Western societies. I should stress immediately that Chomsky does not suggest that criticizing the enemy states or groups is illegitimate. However, there is one set of circumstances in which such criticism is definitely inappropriate, according to Chomsky. Responding to the work of the British left-wing group 'Solidarity' during the Vietnam War, Chomsky agreed with their analysis of North Vietnam, and agreed also with their right to criticize the regime: 'I think they are also perfectly correct in saying we ought to criticize that society. However, not while the bombs are falling, in my opinion.... There were plenty of things wrong, let's say, with England in 1943. But I don't think that was the time or the place to point them out, particularly if you happened to be living in Nazi Germany.'[12] In fact, Chomsky has been a strong critic of Third World national liberation movements and of other enemies of the United States. He comments, 'I have devoted a great deal of time and energy, and have been willing to face some personal risk, in attempting to defend radical nationalist movements in the Third World from the subversion and violence of the industrial democracies, but without illusions as to their character.'[13] However, his criticisms have been channelled so as to minimize their usefulness for the US propaganda system. The *Boston Globe* described one private encounter in 1988:

While in Israel for an academic conference last spring, Noam Chomsky, the brilliant linguist and iconoclastic political critic, addressed a group of Palestinian intellectuals. After 20 years of harsh and unrelenting criticism of Israel's treatment of Arabs – criticism that has, in part, tempered Chomsky's access to establishment media and fashionable academic circles – the Palestinians might well have expected Chomsky to preach to the converted. Instead, a flap erupted when Chomsky, a professor of linguistics and philosophy at the Massachusetts Institute of Technology, called the PLO a 'terrorist' organization. 'Noam is not a person who tells people what they want to hear,' James Higginbotham, an MIT professor and colleague of Chomsky, said in a pointed understatement.[14]

The report neglects to mention that Chomsky has also described the policies of the Israeli government as terrorism.

From the simple principle that our actions should be designed not to harm the victims of oppression, we have arrived at a point where rather delicate dilemmas can arise. Such dilemmas also arose in relation to the superpower enemy. Chomsky argued during the Soviet era that criticizing Moscow, while having little effect on the actions of the USSR, could serve to contribute to the violence of the American state, by reinforcing the (often accurate) images of Soviet brutality. Such images were important propaganda tools, used to frighten Westerners into conformity and obedience, thereby lessening public constraints on state violence. This problem did not stop Chomsky from criticizing the Soviet Union: his explanation of the dynamics of US interventionism was almost always advanced in parallel with his analysis of Soviet imperialism. When lecturing in Managua in 1986, Chomsky was challenged by a questioner: 'We feel that through what you say and write you are our friend but at the same time you talk about North American imperialism and Russian imperialism in the same breath. I ask you how you can use the same arguments as reactionaries such as Octavio Paz, Vargas Llosa, etc.'[15] Chomsky answered, 'I think that what we ought to do is to try to understand the truth about the world. And the truth about the world is usually quite unpleasant. One of the truths about the world is that there are two superpowers, one a huge power which happens to have its boot on your neck, another, a smaller power which happens to have its boot on other people's necks.'[16] In November 1984, Chomsky commented,

> we should of course protest as strongly as we can the brutal internal repression and aggressive violence of the 'Communist' system, recognizing however that this honest protest will be converted into an instrument of Western aggression just as protest over Western atrocities within the Soviet bloc lends itself to the needs of ruling groups, enhancing their capacity to enforce their own domination and oppression.[17]

Chomsky's protests against Soviet totalitarianism extended beyond his commentary. In 1973, Chomsky was one of several US radicals who signed a statement denouncing Soviet repression of intellectuals and citizens, which was read out by the Reverend Paul Mayer at the World Congress of Peace Forces in Moscow.[18] He lobbied on behalf of persecuted individuals in Warsaw Pact countries, and was once stung by a journalist's questioning to reveal that 'There are a fair number of people in the United States and Canada from the Soviet Union and Eastern Europe who are there because of my personal activities on their behalf.'[19]

Chomsky made it clear that he saw no reason to avoid critical analysis of the USSR, and added, 'Nor would I criticize someone who devotes much, even all his [sic] work to this task. But we should understand that the moral value of this work is at best very slight, where the moral value of an action is judged in terms of its human consequences.'[20] In other words, the consequences of such criticism for the victims of Soviet power would not necessarily be very great, and might even be negative. Criticism from an enemy state can sometimes have a positive effect, but may often lead to a hardening of attitudes among the general public and the government. If this outcome seems likely, then public support for the oppressed group in question, while apparently admirable, could in fact be immoral. It is not the voicing of criticism in itself which is of moral value – it is the foreseeable consequences of one's actions, or inaction. Having said all this, and having noted the complex judgements that can arise, it is important to note Chomsky's insistence that criticism of any state is legitimate – 'provided that it is honest'.[21] It is just that, as A.J. Muste observed, so long as we are not dealing with 90 per cent of the problem of violence – 'the violence on which the present system is based, and all the material and spiritual evil it entails' – there is 'something ludicrous and perhaps hypocritical' about our concern over the 10 per cent of violence employed by the rebels against oppression, or the larger share of violence employed by rival powers.

There are other responsibilities for intellectuals, apart from honesty, according to Chomsky:

> It seems to me that the responsibility conferred by our freedom should lead us to protest, to resistance, even to sabotage – as in the case of the Catonsville 9 and the Milwaukee 14 – if this will bring a disgraceful war to a quick end, or if it will help to reverse a lunatic race to mutual annihilation, or bring about the withdrawal of American armed force wherever it serves as an agency of repression – including even American ghettos, where the police sometimes function as a kind of army of occupation.[22]

Apart from this, intellectuals should 'try to articulate goals, to try to assess, to try to understand, to try to persuade, to try to organize ...

further tasks for intellectuals are to develop an objective scholarship, and also to act collectively and individually to confront repressive institutions when that is the effective politics of the moment rather than merely an exciting thing to do'.[23]

The main issue in relation to intellectuals remains their role in the creation and analysis of ideology. Despite self-serving illusions to the contrary, Chomsky argues, Western intellectuals have typically been, in Gramsci's phrase, 'experts in legitimation'. The role of intellectuals has been to 'ensure that beliefs are properly inculcated, beliefs that serve the interests of those with objective power, based ultimately on control of capital in the industrial societies'.[24] Many devices figure in this process of legitimation. We have discussed some of the techniques used in the mass media. Much the same functions are carried out by academic scholarship. Chomsky remarks that 'Ideas that circulate in the faculty club and executive suite can be transmuted into ideological instruments to confuse and demoralize.'[25] As other means of social control become less significant, such ideological weapons are 'matters of no small importance to poor and oppressed people here and elsewhere',[26] particularly as economic growth can no longer be used to mask the issue of redistributing wealth. 'In the post-affluence period, the ideological institutions have dedicated themselves with renewed vigour to convincing the intended victims of the great benefits of the Higher Truths designed for subject peoples.' To take one important, current, example, 'The wonderful news about the marvels of free market economies is broadcast to the people of the South who have been devastated by these doctrines for years, and East Europeans are invited to share in the good fortune as well.' As the Third World model of social stratification is extended to the Western countries as well, 'Market doctrine thus becomes an essential ideological weapon at home as well, its highly selective application safely obscured by the doctrinal system.'[27] Chomsky points out that no developed country has ever industrialized without major state intervention; that the supposed 'free market' miracles of the Far East are actually tightly controlled state capitalist enterprises; and that the nations of the North who impose free market policies on the South refuse to implement similar policies at home, and in fact create serious barriers to free trade to protect their own economies and home-based transnational corporations.[28] All of these facts must be suppressed, and the free market/free trade doctrines must be hammered home to weaken popular forces both in the Third World and in the West. Intellectuals play a large part in such ideological attacks. There are other examples.[29]

It is not difficult to understand why the intelligentsia should choose to serve power rather than truth. As Chomsky told an audience in Managua, 'people who are sophisticated enough to apply class analysis and trace actions to their economic and other roots should apply the same kind of analysis to intellectuals and their interests'.[30] 'If it is plausible that ideology will in general serve as a mask for self-interest, then it is a natural presumption that intellectuals, in interpreting history or formulating policy, will tend to adopt an elitist position, condemning popular movements and mass participation in decision making, and emphasizing rather the necessity for supervision by those who possess the knowledge and understanding that is required (so they claim) to manage society and control social change.'[31] Chomsky argues that it is a dream of the intellectuals – 'almost a disease of the intelligentsia' – to use state power attained on the basis of popular struggles to create a properly managed society controlled by intellectuals. This is the basis for Leninism. It is 'the exact *opposite* of socialism'.[32] Chomsky suggests that 'The Leninist model has had great appeal to the intelligentsia in certain places and periods because, beneath a façade of concern for the welfare of the masses of the population, it offers a justification for the acquisition of state power by the revolutionary intelligentsia...'[33] Fascism is 'in many respects not a dissimilar position'.[34]

One of Chomsky's recurrent themes is that modern Western liberalism is also 'not a dissimilar position' to Bolshevism.[35] Bakunin commented a hundred years ago:

According to the theory of Mr Marx, the people not only must not destroy [the state] but must strengthen it and place it at the complete disposal of their benefactors, guardians, and teachers – the leaders of the Communist party, namely Mr Marx and his friends, who will proceed to liberate [humanity] in their own way. They will concentrate the reins of government in a strong hand, because the ignorant people require an exceedingly firm guardianship; they will establish a single state bank concentrating in its hands all commercial, industrial, agricultural and even scientific production, and then divide the masses into two armies – industrial and agricultural – under the direct command of the state engineers, who will constitute a new privileged scientific-political estate.[36]

Chomsky remarks that there is a striking resemblance between these predictions and the predictions of Daniel Bell, an influential postwar liberal, who suggested that, in the new post-industrial society, 'not only the best talents, but eventually the entire complex of social prestige and social status, will be rooted in the intellectual and scientific communities'.[37] The difference was that Bell, the liberal intellectual, was welcoming the future that Bakunin had warned against, an interesting contrast. Chomsky argued that 'a substantial part of the liberal intelligentsia does aspire to government service'; 'they really are the Bolsheviks, basically'.[38]

In a modern industrial society, Chomsky suggests, the educated classes have two routes to power – through the private economy or through the state – two centres of power that are closely linked in a capitalist society. Those who take on a leadership or a propaganda role in the private economy are generally not given the honorific term of 'intellectual'; they are 'managers' or 'PR specialists'. Those outside the private economy will typically seek prestige and power by association with the state. This can be done either through the vanguard party, or else by association with capitalist state organs 'as commissars in the Western system of indoctrination'.[39] The latter category includes mainstream liberals. Chomsky cites the views of representatives of the two traditions. Lenin in 1918 proclaimed that '*unquestioning submission* to a single will is absolutely necessary for the success of labour processes that are based on large-scale machine-industry', and that 'today the Revolution demands, in the interests of socialism, that the masses *unquestioningly obey the single will* of the leaders of the labour process'.[40] Someone else, somewhat later, expressed the same doctrine in slightly different terms:

> God – the Communist commentators to the contrary – is clearly democratic. He distributes brain power universally, but He quite justifiably expects us to do something efficient and constructive with that priceless gift ... the real threat to democracy comes not from overmanagement, but from undermanagement. To undermanage reality is not to keep it free. It is simply to let some force other than reason shape reality.[41]

Thus reason demands submission to centralized management. Chomsky comments, 'Apart from the reference to God, it would be hard to tell whether the quote is from Lenin, or – as indeed is the case – Robert MacNamara, a typical example of the scientific and educational estate in state capitalist democracy.'[42]

Another indication of the common ground across the two traditions is the ease with which individuals have crossed over between them. When Bolshevik intellectuals have seen their chances of power via control of popular struggles fading away, 'it has been an easy transition

149

to celebration of liberal state capitalism and association with or service to its dominant elites': it 'comes as no surprise, then, that quite commonly the roles shift; the student radical becomes the counter-insurgency expert'.[43]

Chomsky ascribes much of the vilification directed at him to the fact that he concentrates much of his fire on mainstream liberals for their feigned dissent, their contributions to the propaganda system, and their commitment to serve power rather than truth.

We may note in passing that one reason for the lack of a substantial anarchist intelligentsia is that anarchism does not answer to the class interests of intellectuals. 'Anarchism offers no position of privilege or power to the intelligentsia. In fact, it undermines that position.' In an anarchist society, 'people whose major professional concern is knowledge and the application of knowledge would have no special opportunity to manage the society, to gain any position of power and prestige by virtue of this special training and talent. And that's not a point of view that the intelligentsia are naturally drawn to.'[44]

Chomsky has been accused, by Arthur Schlesinger among others, of betraying the intellectual tradition. Chomsky responds, 'That's true, I agree with him. The intellectual tradition is one of servility to power, and if I didn't betray it I'd be ashamed of myself.'[45] For Chomsky, the organized and articulate intelligentsia in the United States is itself 'anti-intellectual', in the sense that its activities and commitments 'are deeply opposed to intellectual and often moral values'. There are individuals who are different, of course, but in general, 'this has been an extremely corrupt and dangerous group'. Chomsky made it clear that he was not referring to intellectuals in the sense of scholars of fourteenth-century manuscripts, but to intellectuals in the sense of those who hold that they have something important to say about society and human life and human action.[46] If we define 'intellectuals' as those who use their minds, the bulk of the population can be considered intellectuals.[47] The term 'intellectual' is, however, generally reserved for those entrusted with the inculcation of ideas, or their articulation. In other words, those whose role is 'telling people what they should believe, or, you know, framing ideas for people in power so they can do things better'. Chomsky comments, 'I think people *should* be anti-intellectual in this respect, it's a healthy reaction.'[48] For him, one of the valuable aspects of the United States is precisely this, that there is very little respect for intellectuals as such. Things are different elsewhere. 'In France, if you're part of the intellectual elite and you *cough*, there's a front page story in *Le Monde*.' This is, Chomsky suggests, one of the reasons for the 'farcical' nature of French intellectual life: 'It's like Hollywood, you're in front of the television camera all the time, and you got to keep doing something new, so they'll keep focusing on *you*, and not the guy at the next table.' The need for media attention puts a premium on startling novelty and what Chomsky describes as 'crazy' ideas.[49]

Chomsky argues that 'By and large the privileged intellectuals are very reactionary, including the ones who are called liberals or left-liberal. They want to serve power.'[50] The intellectual classes have taken over the function of preventing heresy.[51] However, in the process, the intelligentsia has become the victim of its own propaganda. The intelligentsia is 'the most subject to effective indoctrination', and 'tends to have the least understanding of what is happening in the world, in fact, tends to have a sort of institutionalized stupidity'.[52] The suggestion that the educated classes are the most brainwashed is 'pretty close to tautological', according to Chomsky; education is itself a form of indoctrination. Furthermore, the educated are 'subjected to the constant flow of propaganda which is largely directed to them because they're more important, so they have to be more controlled'.[53]

As the recipients of privilege, the intelligentsia are naturally drawn to identify with elite interests and perceptions. On the other hand, in the United States especially, the population at large does not have such a class interest and hardly participates in the democratic system, 'and people learn from their own lives to be skeptical, and in fact most of them are'.[54] The general population learns a great deal about the nature of society simply from its own experience of oppression. After speaking to a group of rich liberals in Los Angeles, Chomsky commented that many of those at the gathering were 'naïve, with no concept of what goes on in the world and their role in it'. He added, 'Talk to a group of welfare mothers and they know much more about the world than someone living in a stockade in Beverley Hills.'[55] This phenomenon was documented during the Vietnam War when a study of public attitudes towards the war demonstrated that 'lower-status groups' tended to be less supportive of government policy. In the words of the study's author, one explanation for this was that 'with less formal education, political attentiveness, and media involvement, they were saved from the full brunt of Cold War appeals during the 1950s and were, as a result, inadequately socialized into the anticommunist world view'.[56] Chomsky notes,

As late as 1982, after years of dedicated brainwashing with no audible response, over 70% of the general public regarded the war as not merely a 'mistake' but 'fundamentally wrong and immoral,' a position held by only

45% of 'opinion makers' (including clergy, etc.) and by a far smaller proportion of elite intellectuals, to judge by earlier studies that showed that even at the height of anti-war activism after the Cambodia invasion of 1970, only a tiny fraction of them opposed the war on principled grounds.[57]

Chomsky observes that the widening gap between the population and the intelligentsia over the Vietnam War did not just happen by itself: 'It was the product of dedicated and committed efforts over many years by innumerable people, the most important of them unknown outside of the small circles in which they worked.'[58] This effort to introduce an element of real democracy and popular input into the political system created problems for state planners. In the eyes of ruling elites, including liberal elites, the mobilization of oppressed sections of the population during the ferment of the 1960s was deeply unwelcome. In the words of the Trilateral Commission, a liberal think tank, there was a 'crisis of democracy'. In a document of this name, three Trilateral Commission scholars complained that, during the 1960s, 'previously passive or unorganized groups in the population', such as 'blacks, Indians, Chicanos, white ethnic groups, students and women ... became mobilized and organized in new ways to achieve what they considered to be their appropriate share of the action and of the rewards'.[59] The demands of these groups could not be met without a redistribution of resources. This being out of the question, the Trilateralists entered a plea for 'a greater degree of moderation in democracy' to overcome the 'excess of democracy' in the 1960s.[60] In other words, 'democracy' means not popular participation and control of political and social life, but disenfranchisement of the population and elite hegemony. Chomsky suggests that this view of democracy is quite traditional, tracing it back to the seventeenth century, when the contemporary historian Clement Walker warned, 'There can be no form of government without its proper mysteries', mysteries that must be 'concealed' from the commoners. John Locke, at the libertarian end of the spectrum, argued that 'day-labourers and tradesmen, the spinsters and dairymaids' must be told what to believe: 'The greatest part cannot know and therefore they must believe.'[61] There are modern variants of this doctrine, as we have seen.

The crisis of democracy was to a large extent overcome, as popular forces were tamed and in some cases destroyed. However, Chomsky does not accept the common perception that the anti-war movement simply disintegrated and faded away: 'True, it stopped being a visible mass movement. But the number of people involved in movement activity wasn't noticeably different in the 1970s than the '60s.'[62] One major development was the women's movement, which had a dramatic effect on society and culture. Chomsky notes, 'The fact that people ignore this, and think the movement "died" in the 1970s, proves some of the justice of the feminist critique.'[63] Mobilization against nuclear power, against the arms race and other social problems took the place of the single anti-war cause. The fragmentation of protest was one factor in the loss of visibility.

Despite this lower profile for popular movements, US society had been deeply affected by the experience of the anti-war movements, and social attitudes had been altered, perhaps permanently. In Chomsky's words, there was a 'notable improvement in the moral and intellectual climate' after the ferment of the Vietnam War period.[64] The general population was considerably less willing to tolerate massacre and invasion as options for US foreign policy. The establishment had a name for this, too: the 'Vietnam Syndrome', obviously some kind of terrible disease. For Chomsky, the Vietnam Syndrome had such symptoms as 'insight into the real world and accompanying feelings of sympathy and concern for the victims of aggression and massacre'.[65] The Vietnam Syndrome was supposed to have been cured by the time Reagan was elected, but the patient suffered an unexpected relapse. When Reagan began preparations to invade Central America in 1981, a large-scale protest movement spontaneously arose in response. This was successful in preventing the direct use of force, and compelled the administration to resort to indirect terrorism via the local governments. Chomsky commented in 1988 that several hundred thousand people had been killed in Central America in the previous decade, but without the high level of domestic dissidence in the United States, the situation would have been a lot worse: 'What took place is bad enough. B-52 bombing would have been worse, much worse.'[66] Such successes may not seem very significant when we survey the horrors that were inflicted by US terrorism, but for those Central Americans who would not otherwise have survived the onslaught, the results may seem different. Chomsky contrasts this citizen intervention with the situation thirty years earlier, when Kennedy's attack on South Vietnam was greeted with approval and silence: 'As late as 1965, anti-war activists felt lucky to be able to speak to groups of neighbors in private homes or to address meetings in colleges where the organizers outnumbered the audience, and public meetings were broken up by militant counter-demonstrators.' Reagan's White Paper on El Salvador in 1981, which was only laying the propaganda basis for attack, not authorizing military activity, 'succeeded only in organizing a large-scale and spontaneous popular movement of protest', and the government was forced to back down from 'more ambitious plans'.[67] Such are the lasting results of the organizing drives of the 1960s.

Chomsky remarked in April 1992, 'I don't think the US is going to intervene more than it did in the past. It's not deterred any longer by Soviet power, but it's deterred internally.'[68] He cites a Bush administration National Security Policy Review which concluded that in the future 'much weaker enemies' must be defeated 'decisively and rapidly', because domestic 'political support' is so thin.[69] The options have narrowed considerably. And it is here that we find once again the vital connection between Chomsky's two areas of concern. Throughout his career, Chomsky has insisted that 'the level of culture that can be achieved in the United States is a life-and-death matter for large masses of suffering humanity'.[70] By 'culture' Chomsky means the intellectual and moral climate of society: the level of honesty and decency among the general population. This is why 'one who is seriously opposed to the use of force to control the empire – the "integrated world economy" dominated by American capital, to use the technical euphemism – must pay careful attention to the actual state of American opinion'[71] and work to alter its condition. Chomsky concludes that, 'For those who stubbornly seek freedom, there can be no more urgent task than to come to understand the mechanisms and practices of indoctrination.'[72]

We can see some effects of the 'crisis of democracy' in Chomsky's own work. One result of the rise in popular understanding and sophistication is that Chomsky is more widely read than he was even in the 1960s. As the years have gone by, mainstream critics have claimed with ever greater vigour that Chomsky is an isolated figure even on the Left, because of his various errors of judgement and extreme political views. At the very same time, Chomsky's readership has broadened and grown,[73] and his access to the mainstream media has also grown, admittedly from a very low baseline in the 1960s.[74]

Another effect of the change in the intellectual climate on Chomsky's work has been his ability to speak more freely. 'During the 1960s and early '70s, at the peak activity of the peace movement, if I was talking to selected peace movement audiences, radicals, I could not say the things that I say to general audiences today.'[75] For example, talking to even the most radical peace movement groups in the 1960s, Chomsky would not have discussed the US invasion of South Vietnam; 'They wouldn't have understood what I was talking about.'[76] Chomsky commented in 1989:

The kinds of things that I am now saying about institutional structures I did not say in the late sixties, not because I didn't believe in them, but because I felt that audiences wouldn't understand what I was talking about. I would not talk about the nature of capitalism. I would not talk about the fact that if you're forced to rent yourself to an owner of capital, that's better than slavery, but it's very far from being a system that a free human being could accept. I didn't talk very much about these things because they were too remote from consciousness and understanding. Now I talk about anything to any audience. No matter who it is, I say approximately the same thing, and I don't feel any constraints any more. The audiences that you reach today are just a lot more sophisticated.[77]

In the same year Chomsky told an interviewer, 'I say about the same things to everybody, whether it's redneck farmers in Eastern Kentucky or journalists in London.'[78]

Chomsky notes that even the most brilliant works remain, in a sense, irrelevant if they are 'too far off the received doctrinal position that's associated with real power'. 'They can't reach people, people can't use them, people can't understand them.'[79] Telling the unvarnished truth can be 'equivalent to speaking in some foreign tongue'.[80] Chomsky's political writings attempt to bridge the gap between what can be comprehended by many people today, what can be meaningful for them and what really exists. He does this by discussing questions that, apart from their intrinsic worth, do seem immediate and comprehensible to people, and which can be tackled without deep institutional change. In other words, Chomsky provides material which, while it loosens the grip of the propaganda system, can at the same time be immediately useful to ordinary people and popular movements.[81]

There are only two ways to escape from the power of the propaganda system: 'One way is to escape "formal education" and "media involvement," with their commitment to the state propaganda system. The second is to struggle to extract the facts that are scattered in the flood of propaganda, while searching for 'exotic' sources not considered fit for the general public – needless to say, a method available to very few.'[82] Most people, though knowledgeable and interested in sports and similar activities, do not apply their intellects to problems of immediate human concern. In part, this is a rational response: 'The way the system is set up, there is virtually nothing people can do anyway, without a degree of organization that's far beyond anything that exists now, to influence the real world.'[83] 'The gas attendant who wants to use his [sic] mind isn't going to waste his time on international affairs, because that's useless; he can't do anything about it anyhow, and he might learn unpleasant things and even get into trouble. So he might as well do it where it's fun, and not threatening – professional football or basketball or something like that.'[84] 'That's why there were gas chambers, because people just want to think about something else', something less unpleasant.[85] Note, though, that 'the plea that we did not know is valid for passive consumers who believe that the media present the world as it actually is. It is not valid for those who have any familiarity with the ideological institutions or participate in them, and who therefore must surely be aware that it takes effort and enterprise to find important and unwelcome facts.'[86] We have come back to the special responsibilities of intellectuals.

Chomsky suggests that the intellectual can make an important contribution to the struggle for peace and justice by agreeing to serve as a 'resource', providing information and analysis to popular movements. Intellectuals have the training, facilities, access to information and opportunity to organize and control their own work, to enable them to make 'a very significant contribution to people who are trying to escape the confines of indoctrination and to understand something about the real world in which they live; in particular, to people who may be willing to act to change this world'. For the same reasons, intellectuals can be active and effective as organizers. Furthermore, by virtue of their privilege, intellectuals are also often 'visible' and can exploit their privilege in valuable and important ways.[87]

There is another aspect of 'visibility' which is relevant here. Chomsky argues that those who concentrate on his own high profile are 'putting the cart before the horse': 'I have visibility because people ask me to come and speak, or because people ask me to write.'[88] It is the organizers of these talks, the local people, who are 'doing the real work', organizing and maintaining projects and campaigns. Chomsky remarks, 'if it's anybody's movement, it's their movement. I'm a small participant.'[89] If the popular movements collapsed, Chomsky's profile would also collapse, as he would have no organized audience outside the mainstream; and the mainstream would continue to embargo his work. 'I would no longer be visible as a political commentator because there would be nowhere for me to open my mouth, except to my friends.'[90] David Barsamian once suggested to Chomsky that he was in 'a singular position in the intellectual life of the country today', a 'life-preserver' for many people, organizations, bookstores and community radio stations. People depended on him for information and analysis. Chomsky responded that to the extent that this was true, it was not a particular comment on him, but a comment on the intellectual class in general, 'which has simply abandoned this responsibility of honest inquiry and some degree of public service'. At its simplest level, 'there just aren't enough speakers available' on important issues:[91] 'There are about five people in the country who do this kind of thing.' According to Chomsky, all of them receive quite enthusiastic responses, all over the United States. Chomsky notes that he often speaks in places where they have never heard of him. He suggests that there is a 'hunger' for information and analysis on these questions among the general public.[92] The few people who are available to speak are 'deluged' with invitations. Chomsky comments,

> I can't accept a fraction of them, and am generally scheduled several years in advance. The 'left intellectuals' (or whatever the right word is) are either involved in unintelligible varieties of postmodernism (mostly nonsense, in my opinion), or otherwise talking to one another. Most of the 'intellectual community' is, as usual, serving power in one or another way. It leaves a huge gap, a matter of great importance these days, I think.[93]

Chomsky freely admits that he is not an exciting orator: 'I'm not a particularly charismatic speaker, and if I had the capacity to do so I wouldn't use it. I'm really not interested in persuading people, I don't want to and I try to make this point obvious. What I'd like to do is help people persuade themselves. I tell them what I think, and obviously I hope they'll persuade themselves that that's true, but I'd rather have them persuade themselves of what *they* think is true.'[94] Chomsky eschews rhetoric in favour of information and analysis. 'I think that there are a lot of analytic perspectives, just straight information, that people are not presented with.... I think by and large audiences recognize that. I think the reason people come is because that's what they want to hear.'[95] Chomsky comments, 'People typically ask me, "Who should I believe?" and my typical answer is, "If you ask that question, you're in trouble, because there's nobody you should believe, including me." '[96] 'I'm not trying to convert, but to inform.... I feel that I've achieved something if people are encouraged to take up this challenge and learn for themselves.'[97]

Who can be persuaded to do this? Chomsky comments that on the rare occasions when he has an opportunity to discuss these issues, 'whether in print or in person with people in the media or the academic professions, I often find not so much disagreement as an inability to hear'. With such heavily indoctrinated people, 'if you don't happen to take part in [the dominant] system of illusions and self-deception, what you say is incomprehensible'.[98] However, outside of elite circles,

> There are a vast number of people who are uninformed and heavily propagandized, but fundamentally decent. The propaganda that inundates them is effective when unchallenged, but much of it goes only skin deep. If they can be brought to raise questions and apply their decent instincts and basic intelligence, many people quickly escape the confines of the doctrinal system and are willing to do something to help others who are really suffering and oppressed.[99]

This is the audience Chomsky seeks to address.

One of the ways in which Chomsky serves as a 'resource', little known perhaps, is his direct communication with hundreds of individuals around the world. Otero suggests that 'the volume of Chomsky's correspondence exceeds that of the letters written by any other single individual'.[100] Ed Robinson, of Non-Corporate News, comments, 'When I write letters to old friends, it usually takes them at least 6 weeks to write back. When I first wrote to Noam Chomsky, after reading his book *Turning the Tide* in 1986, he replied within a week. I'm not sure, exactly, what this says about my friends, Noam Chomsky, or both.'[101] Norbert Hornstein reports another experience:

> I got to know Chomsky because he wrote an article [about Israel] in *Ramparts* and it upset me tremendously. . . . I wrote him a very hot ten-page handwritten letter going through every sentence and trying to show him that he was wrong. [At the time] I was an undergraduate, a nameless undergraduate. . . . I got back within a week a ten-page single-spaced typed letter going through all of my claims and suggesting that I take a look at the following sources, which I duly did. I went to the library and picked them out, read them, and still was convinced Chomsky, although more right than I had reason to believe when I had started, was nonetheless basically wrong. So another ten-page single-spaced handwritten letter went off *to* Chomsky, which within a week was answered by another ten-page single-spaced typewritten letter *from* Chomsky, with another bunch of sources. Well, at the end of this exchange – went about three or four times – I was completely convinced that I had basically not known what I was talking about. And it was *not* because of the force of his rhetoric, but it was because he was able to sort of show that, look, you can have a reasoned debate on this topic, and here's the documentary evidence, here's the historical record from primary sources. So, go ahead and try to argue against it. And that I think was an unbelievable insight. I used to think that politics was essentially like religion – you just sit there and hurl thunderbolts at one another – that the only thing

you could say about someone was that they were immoral, not that they were wrong, factually incorrect.[102]

Chomsky wrote over two thousand letters in 1989, according to his secretary,[103] and he reportedly spends twenty hours a week dealing with his correspondence.[104] A large part of this correspondence is undoubtedly related to linguistics, but the remainder may well be taken up with politics, of the kind described. This is another kind of public service intellectuals might provide, though few could equal Chomsky's capacity for work.

In fact, Chomsky is renowned for his work rate. His written output is awe-inspiring in itself – over twenty-five books in twenty-five years, to which we must add collections of interviews, his writings in linguistics and numberless articles. When we take account of his teaching responsibilities, his speaking tours – speaking perhaps several times a week – and his vast correspondence, it is easy to understand why Chomsky describes himself as a 'fanatic'. David Barsamian once asked, 'In response to questions about your prodigious work productivity, you say you are a "fanatic"? Do you like that about yourself?' Chomsky replied, 'I neither like it nor dislike it. I recognize it. It does require a degree of fanaticism even to be able to break out of the constant drumbeat of ideology and indoctrination and to gain the relevant information and organize it. Even that limited commitment requires a degree of fanaticism, and to pursue it beyond that, the constant travel, speaking, etc., sure, that's another form of fanaticism.'[105] Ferber notes that during the 1960s, legends grew up about Chomsky's workload among local activists:

> We had a theory even then that there were six Chomskys. There was the Chomsky who was the world's greatest linguist who wrote a book about linguistics every year. There was the Chomsky who wrote an article for the *New York Review* every couple of issues.... Then there was the Chomsky who spoke at a different anti-war rally every night. Then there was the Chomsky who was always at his home or at his office and was always ready to help. Then there was the Chomsky who was married and had three children and seemed to be a pretty serious person on that. We just couldn't believe it.... We really thought that there had to be twins at least.[106]

Chomsky's call for intellectuals to reorient themselves to serve popular movements touches on a deeper problem. Chomsky argues that 'The promise of past revolutions has been betrayed, in part, by the willingness of the intelligentsia to join or serve a new ruling class',[107] an expression of the 'disease of the intelligentsia'. Only if such elitist tendencies are overcome will possibilities open up for non-authoritarian solutions to our social problems. Chomsky suggested in the 1970s that efforts to organize scientists to refuse military work were of great significance, both in themselves, and also as an indication for the future.[108] Scientists and engineers, even as an organized group, would probably have little effect on the patterns of state investment and subsidy by themselves, he notes: their organized resistance would gain importance only if there was a mass movement to which it could contribute, and in which it could be absorbed 'as an important constituent element'.[109] Furthermore, Chomsky warns that 'No movement for social change can hope to succeed unless it makes the most advanced intellectual and technical achievements its own, and unless it is rooted in those strata of the population that are productive and creative in every domain.'[110] Chomsky comments,

> The 'system' looks overwhelmingly powerful when one watches Mayor Daley's police or the B-52s, but it has its weaknesses, and one such weakness is its 'personnel'. The same technical intelligentsia that some see as a potential elite of the post-industrial society might help to concentrate social energies in very different places, if they can overcome the élitism and arrogance and factionalism that have been the curse of the left.[111]

Chomsky's remarks on the special opportunities and responsibilities of the intelligentsia do not detract from his belief that it is ordinary people, those whose names do not enter history books, who create history. It is those organizers at the grassroots level who create social change and who enable others to rise to prominence as 'leaders' or 'spokespersons'. As we have just seen, Chomsky believes that organized resistance by scientists and other vital sectors of society will find significance only if there is a larger social current within which it can be absorbed. Chomsky's insistence that he is but a 'small participant' in a grassroots movement, and that his visibility is simply an expression of the strength of that movement, is all of a piece with his anarchist convictions, and his deep respect for ordinary people, the bulk of the population, who are invariably treated with contempt by the educated classes. When he is asked about his heroes, Chomsky demurs. He answers, 'I know that's not the question you're asking, but I'm purposely evading it. I know there are people who have said smart things, which is fine, it's not hard to say smart things.'[112] The real heroes are those who struggle. Chomsky cites Rousseau, who commented that those who had lost their freedom do nothing but boast incessantly of the peace and repose they enjoy in their chains.... But when I see the others sacrifice pleasures, repose, wealth, power, and life itself for the preservation of this sole good which is so disdained by those who have lost it; when I see animals born free and despising captivity break their heads against the bars of their prison; when I see multitudes of entirely naked savages scorn European voluptuousness and endure hunger, fire, the sword, and death to preserve only their independence, I feel that it does not behoove [sic] slaves to reason about freedom.[113]

For Chomsky, it is the example of ordinary people around the world, finding the courage to continue struggling in the face of terror and poverty, that is 'more inspiring than the writings of the sages'.[114] The existence of an instinct for freedom has not yet been proven, but, if it exists, Chomsky suggests, 'history teaches that it can be dulled, but has yet to be killed'.[115]

Chomsky notes that 'Traditionally the role of the intellectual, or at least his [sic] self-image, has been that of a dispassionate critic.'[116] 'The intellectual community used to be a kind of critical voice. That was its main function. Now it is losing that function and accepting the notion that its role is to carry out piecemeal social technology.'[117] Chomsky suggests that

The intellectual has, traditionally, been caught between the conflicting demands of truth and power. He [sic] would like to see himself as the man who seeks to discern the truth, to tell the truth as he sees it, to act – collectively where he can, alone where he must – to oppose injustice and oppression, to help bring a better social order into being. If he chooses this path he can expect to be a lonely creature, disregarded or reviled. If, on the other hand, he brings his talents to the service of power, he can achieve prestige and affluence. He may also succeed in persuading himself – perhaps, on occasion, with justice – that he can humanize the exercise of power by the 'significant classes'.[118]

It is impossible not to see something of Chomsky's own position in this passage. I am reminded of the five commandments of the Soviet intellectual, as reported in the Russian press in 1993:

1: Do not think.
2: If you think, do not speak.
3: If you think and speak, do not write.
4: If you think, speak and write, do not sign.
5: If you think, speak, write and sign, do not be surprised.[119]

Having thought, spoken, written, signed and indeed acted, Chomsky has not been surprised by the response. Despite everything, he has continued. Richard Falk comments, 'Over a period that now stretches across several decades, Chomsky has displayed an exemplary serious-ness of political and moral purpose that stands in happy contrast to the complacency and opportunism of so many of Chomsky's academic peers. To resist effectively on the US political scene is, first of all, to be neither seduced nor distracted. And it is, secondly, to keep going, not to give way to burnout or careerism.'[120] Chomsky is fond of Gramsci's motto, 'pessimism of the intellect, optimism of the will'. Few have embodied it as he has.

It would be presumptous to attempt a summary of Chomsky's contributions to the struggle for justice and peace. Perhaps a final image may be appropriate. Jay Parini ends a profile of Chomsky by telling the following anecdote. After a book-signing session in Vermont, Parini and Chomsky walked down the road and came to a crossing;

> the light was red, but – as is so often the case in Vermont – there was no traffic. I began, blithely, to cross the intersection, but realized suddenly that Chomsky had refused to walk against the light. Mildly embarrassed, I went back to wait with him at the curb until the light turned green. It struck me, later, that this was not an insignificant gesture on his part. He is a man profoundly committed to law, to order – to the notion of a world in which human freedom operates within a context of rationally agreed-upon limits.[121]

I am not sure this reflects very much of Chomsky's life. I prefer to end with another image of Chomsky, standing in another street, in another city, many years earlier, among thousands of other demonstrators, disrupting business as usual in the capital, while US warplanes pounded Indochina to pieces. This is another way of keeping the law, the reluctant activist endangering himself for others.

Notes

Abbreviations

501	*Year 501: The Conquest Continues* (1993)
AC	*After the Cataclysm: Postwar Indochina & the Reconstruction of Imperial Ideology (The Political Economy of Human Rights: Volume II)* (1979)
APNM	*American Power and the New Mandarins* (1969)
AWWA	*At War With Asia* (1971)
BB	*The Backroom Boys* (1973)
CA	*Noam Chomsky: Critical Assessments* (1994)
CD	*Chronicles of Dissent* (1992)
CR	*The Chomsky Reader* (1987)
CT	*The Culture of Terrorism* (1988)
CU	*The Chomsky Update* (1990)
DD	*Deterring Democracy* (1991)
FRS	*For Reasons of State* (1973)
FT	*The Fateful Triangle: The United States, Israel and the Palestinians* (1983)
HR	*'Human Rights' and American Foreign Policy* (1978)
KRL	*Keeping the Rabble in Line* (1994)
LL	*Letters from Lexington: Reflections on Propaganda* (1993)
LP	*Language and Politics* (1988)
LR	*Language and Responsibility* (1979)
MC	*Manufacturing Consent: The Political Economy of the Mass Media* (1988)
MCNCM	*Manufacturing Consent: Noam Chomsky and the Media, The companion book to the award-winning film by Peter Wintonick and Mark Achbar* (1994)
NI	*Necessary Illusions: Thought Control in Democratic Societies* (1989)
PE	*Pirates and Emperors: International Terrorism in the Real World* (1987)
PEHR	*The Political Economy of Human Rights* (two vols., 1979)
PI	*On Power and Ideology: The Managua Lectures* (1987)
PKF	*Problems of Knowledge and Freedom* (1972)

PME   *Peace in the Middle East? Reflections on Justice and Nation-*
                hood (1974)
RC   *Rethinking Camelot: JFK, the Vietnam War, and US Political*
                Culture (1993)
RP   *Radical Priorities* (1981)
TNCW   *Towards a New Cold War: Essays on the Current Crisis and*
                How We Got There (1982)
T T T   *Turning the Tide: US Intervention in Central America and*
                the Struggle for Peace (1985)
WCTWF   *The Washington Connection and Third World Fascism (The*
                Political Economy of Human Rights: Volume I) (1979)

Abbreviations of Journals and Newspapers

BG   *Boston Globe*
NYRB   *New York Review of Books*
NYT   *New York Times*
TLS   *Times Literary Supplement*
WP   *Washington Post*

Unless otherwise indicated, audio-tapes and transcripts of interviews and talks
are supplied by David Barsamian of Alternative Radio, 2129 Mapleton,
Boulder, CO 80304, USA. I conducted the interviews with Mike Ferber,
Norbert Hornstein and Louis Kampf, and the one interview with Noam
Chomsky not ascribed to others.

Introduction

1. Israel Shenker, 'A Linguistics Expert Believes that Academics Should also
be Activists', NYT, 27 October 1968, p. 64.
2. Auberon Waugh, 'From Oxymoron to Boiled Egg', *Independent* 26
March 1988. The 'oxymoron' of the title is, according to Waugh, the concept of
a 'libertarian socialist'.
3. John A. Garraty and Jerome L. Sternstein, eds., *Encyclopedia of American
Biography*, New York: Harper & Row 1974, p. 915.
4. Brian Morton, 'Chomsky Then and Now', *Nation*, 7 May 1988, p. 652.
5. Jim Merod, *The Political Responsibility of the Critic*, Ithaca, NY: Cornell
University Press 1987, p. 55.
6. Paul Robinson, *New York Times Book Review*, 25 February 1979, p. 3.
Chomsky himself is amused by the recurring use of this quotation. He remarks,
'That's the kind of quote that publishers like to take and put on books. But
that's only because they don't look at the context. If you go back and look at the
context of that remark, the sentence was: "arguably the most important
intellectual alive, how can he write such nonsense about international affairs
and foreign policy?" They don't put that sentence on the cover of a book. I
always get a kick out of it when I see that line quoted.' *Radical Philosophy*,
Autumn 1989, p. 35.

7. Robinson, *New York Times Book Review*, p. 3. Salkie misquotes this passage in CU, p. 221, n. 13.

8. David Warsh, 'On the Economic Significance of Noam Chomsky', BG, 29 September 1991, p. 33.

9. Chomsky comments, 'I doubt that these [citation indices] can even be close to true. If they were, they would be meaningless (consider that Marx, Lenin, Mao and Castro are listed high on citation indices in Western literature). Even if they were true and meaningful, they would be utterly irrelevant to any topic addressed here. Take a really important 20th-century figure: Bertrand Russell, who should be among the most cited, surely, if the ranking meant anything. Did his high ranking make his views on nuclear disarmament important? That's stressing exactly the wrong lessons' (MCNCM, p. 17).

10. LP, p. 628. Even in Israel. According to Chomsky, he was once asked to write regular columns in the Israeli *Labour Party Journal*. He comments, 'Positions that I maintain, which are essentially in terms of the international consensus, they're not a majority position in Israel, but they're part of the political spectrum, they're respectable positions. Here, it's considered outlandish.' LP, p. 696.

11. Christopher Hitchens, 'The Chorus and Cassandra', *Grand Street*, Winter 1984; reprinted in Hitchens, *Prepared for the Worst*, London: Hogarth Press 1990, p. 73.

12. C.P. Otero relates the story of a 'novelist who writes regularly for *The New York Times* and the *Washington Post*' who attempted to discover why the NYRB had stopped publishing Chomsky. The editors 'refused even to answer the phone'. Gore Vidal was asked to intercede, and did so. 'Silvers was willing to take his call, but told him he'd have to check with his lawyers before answering. When Vidal called back, Silvers told him that their lawyers had advised them not to say anything. He later checked with Barbara Epstein, who told that Silvers is constantly bombarded on this topic and is entirely paranoid about it.' LP, p. 73, n. 44.

13. Morton, 'Chomsky Then and Now'.

14. *New Statesman*, 21 January 1983, p. 25.

15. See p. 154.

16. Letter to Serge Thion, cited in Thion, *Vérité historique ou Vérité politique: le dossier de l'affaire Faurisson*, Paris: La Vieille Taupe 1980, p. 171.

17. Geoffrey Sampson, *Liberty and Language*, Oxford: Oxford University Press 1979, p. 5.

18. Ibid., p. 8.

19. Cited in Boyd Tonkin, 'Making a Difference', *City Limits* (London), 26 January–2 February 1989, p. 58. Sampson is not mentioned by name, but the reference is unmistakable.

20. Cited in CU, p. 38.

21. PKF, p. 44.

22. LR, p. 98, emphasis added.

23. FRS, p. 186.

24. Chomsky, *Reflections on Language*, London: Fontana 1976, pp. 133f, cited in Sampson, *Liberty and Language*, p. 30.

25. To indicate the general level of Sampson's arguments, we can turn to the opening pages of *Liberty and Language*, which is concerned, so its author

NOTES TO PAGES 5-9

informs us, 'with the ideas of a man who represents this scientistic pseudo-opposition to scientism more forcefully and influentially than anyone else in the contemporary world, and who bids fair to corner the forces opposed to scientism so completely as to render any genuine fight against scientism impossible of success' (pp. 3f). Scientism, that previously undetected danger to civilization as we know it, is 'the prejudice which holds that the scientific method applies to all possible subjects of human thought, or (what amounts to the same in practice) that matters which cannot be treated by the method of science are somehow unreal or unimportant' (p. 1). Equally startling revelations follow.

Just for the record, Chomsky's actual views on the scope of scientific method are that there are many areas of life which science is unlikely to penetrate: 'I think the Victorian novel tells us more about people than science ever will' (LP, p. 75). 'Science isn't the only thing in the world ... science is not the only way to come to an understanding of things' (LP, p. 465). For some appropriate commentary on Sampson's work and its reception in Britain, see reviews by David Lightfoot and Harry M. Bracken reproduced in CA.

26. Charles Glass, 'Beat the Devil', *Spectator*, 22 October 1988, p. 32.

27. Chomsky is referring here to his literary influences. CR, p. 4.

28. Transcript, interview by David Barsamian, 2 February 1990, MIT, Cambridge, MA, p. 7.

29. CR, p. 13.

30. Transcript, interview by David Barsamian, 2 February 1990, p. 4. Unless otherwise indicated, the information in the following paragraph draws on this interview.

31. Personal communication from Noam Chomsky, 12 October 1992.

32. Tape, 'At the Rowe Centre', Rowe, MA, 15–16 April 1989, tape 5, side A.

33. CR, p. 13.

34. Transcript, 'Reflections on the Gulf War', MIT, Cambridge, MA, 21 May 1991, p. 9.

35. LP, p. 394.

36. CR, p. 5f.

37. Ibid.

38. Ibid., p. 13.

39. LP, pp. 133, 697, 395.

40. CR, p. 11.

41. LP, p. 167.

42. CR, p. 13.

43. Transcript, interview by David Barsamian, 2 February 1990, p. 5.

44. Cited in Ron Grossman, 'Strong Words', *Chicago Tribune*, 1 January 1993, Tempo section, p. 1.

45. Tape, 'At the Rowe Centre', tape 2, side B.

46. CR, p. 11.

47. Cited in Tonkin, 'Making a Difference', p. 58.

48. LP, p. 167.

49. Ibid., p. 133.

50. Ibid.

51. CR, p. 10.

52. Transcript, interview by David Barsamian, 2 February 1990, p. 7.
53. LP, p. 693.
54. CR, p. 14.
55. Ibid.
56. Ibid., p. 13.
57. Chomsky, cited in John Horgan, 'Free Radical: A Word (or Two) about Linguist Noam Chomsky', *Scientific American*, May 1990, pp. 16f.
58. Transcript, interview by David Barsamian, MIT, Cambridge, 2 February 1990, p. 5.
59. CR, p. 12.
60. LP, p. 133.
61. Noam Chomsky, 'Nationalism and Conflict in Palestine', *Liberation* (New York), November 1969, p. 7.
62. CR, p. 9.
63. Ibid., p. 13f.
64. LP, p. 395.
65. CR, p. 6f.
66. Ibid., p. 7.
67. LP, p. 133.
68. Ibid., p. 119.
69. CR, p. 8.
70. LP, p. 167.
71. CR, p. 6.
72. Ibid., p. 8.
73. Ibid., p. 6.
74. Ibid., p. 8.
75. R.M.W. Dixon, 'The Emergence of Noam Chomsky', *Listener*, 21 May 1970, p. 691.
76. Tape, 'At the Rowe Centre', tape 3, side A. The revelation about the PhD is at the end of tape 2, side B.
77. CR, p. 8.
78. Ibid., pp. 15f.
79. Dixon, 'The Emergence of Noam Chomsky'.
80. LR, pp. 132f.
81. CR, p. 10
82. Ibid., p. 9
83. Ibid., p. 10.
84. LR, p. 134.
85. CR, p. 16.
86. LP, p. 133.
87. Ibid., p. 697.
88. Ibid., p. 133.
89. RP, p. 196.
90. APNM, pp. 10f.
91. Ibid., p. 257.
92. CR, pp. 54f.
93. Shenker, 'A Linguistics Expert'.
94. Martin Duberman, 'Immoral Imperialism', *New Republic*, 19 April 1969, p. 27.

95. Robert Sklar, 'The Intellectual Power Elite', *Nation*, 24 March 1969, reproduced in CA, Tome I, p. 60. The other reviews of APNM cited here are also collected in CA, Tome I.

96. Yorick Wilks, 'Weeping for a Nation', *Listener*, 30 October 1969, p. 604.

97. Duberman, 'Immoral Imperialism'.

98. TNCW, p. 81.

99. Sklar, 'Intellectual Power Elite'.

100. APNM, p. 283.

101. Marian Christy, 'My Natural Style is Irony', BG, 31 May 1989, p. 28.

102. Sklar, 'Intellectual Power Elite', in CA, p. 62.

103. LP, p. 129.

104. Parini, 'Noam is an Island', p. 39.

105. Ibid., p. 38.

106. LP, p. 154.

107. I may be wrong here. Chomsky told an interviewer, 'Some things are better described imprecisely. You want to express yourself with enough precision to yield understanding, to hit the right level of accuracy. Then the listener has to think for himself or herself' (BG, 31 May 1989, p. 28).

108. MCNCM, p. 10. Given Chomsky's misgivings about the use of the spoken word, I should perhaps explain my own extensive use of transcripts and tapes. Sometimes I have used such sources because these are the only sources available for some of Chomsky's thoughts and remarks. Sometimes I have used quotations to enliven the expression of Chomsky's ideas. As Carlos Otero has pointed out, using transcribed interviews does make Chomsky's ideas easier to digest. However, as Chomsky indicates, it also leads to a lack of nuance and a loss of documentation. The latter is particularly important because without the marshalling of evidence, Chomsky's work loses much of its ability to persuade and inform. As many commentators have pointed out, it is Chomsky's patient documentation and his control of the evidence that mark out his work as something special. However, in an introductory work such as this, which is an attempt to catch the broad sweep rather than a detailed assessment, the spoken word may perhaps be appropriate.

109. This has been done in the book *What Uncle Sam Really Wants*, eds. Arthur Naiman and Sandy Newman, Berkeley, CA: Odonian Press 1992.

110. Transcript, interview by David Barsamian, MIT, 2 February 1990, p. 9.

111. LP, p. 681. We should note that Chomsky does not allow others to edit his work: 'I don't even publish with publishers who require editing, because I know exactly what the editors do.' They standardize style. Chomsky observes, 'Well, I'd rather see people make grammatical errors, and say things the way they think' (Tape, 'At the Rowe Centre', tape 5, side A).

112. It is a curious fact that the main work on Chomsky as a thinker, John Lyons's *Chomsky* (London: Fontana 1970 or subsequent editions), barely mentions his political work. Dell Hymes, among others, criticized Lyons for this. Hymes later discovered that Lyons had only undertaken the book on the understanding that he need not assess Chomsky's political role, a subject which he did not feel prepared to treat. According to Hymes, the publisher at one point suggested an appendix on the latter topic, to be provided by someone else, 'but later dropped the idea' (CA p. 134n). The only other introductory work I am

aware of, Raphael Salkie's *The Chomsky Update* (London: Unwin Hyman 1990), is divided between Chomsky's linguistic and political writings.
113. PKF, p. 11.

1   The Propaganda Model

1. CR, p. vii.
2. Joseph Sobran, 'Hard to Place Phenomenon', *Washington Times*, 27 March 1991, G, p. 4.
3. Ibid.
4. The US government was seeking to prevent the *New York Times* from publishing extracts from the Pentagon's secret internal history of the Vietnam War. Chomsky resisted being called before a grand jury investigating the release of the documents by arguing that such an appearance would jeopardize both his rights under the First Amendment and his sources of information as a journalist and speaker on contemporary affairs (*Boston Herald Traveler*, 15 January 1972). He also argued that the government had illegally tapped his telephone. He was reprieved, along with Richard Falk and Ralph Stavins of the Institute for Policy Studies (NYT, 19 January 1972, p. 43). He later testified at the trial of the Pentagon analysts who had released the documents, arguing on behalf of the defendants that publication of the documents could not harm the national security of the United States (NYT, 7 April 1973, p. 16).
5. Cited in Anthony Lewis, 'Freedom of the Press – Anthony Lewis Distinguishes between Britain and America', *London Review of Books*, 26 November 1987, cited by Chomsky, NI, p. 2 and MC, p. 298. Herman and Chomsky also make it clear that they 'do not accept the view that freedom of expression must be defended in terms of instrumental terms, by virtue of its contribution to some higher good; rather, it is a value in itself' (MC, p. 298).
6. Freedom House Executive-Director Leonard Sussman, cited in MC, p. 170.
7. AC, p. 140.
8. There are some differences between Chomsky's approach and Edward Herman's approach to the Propaganda Model. See p. 174 n. 44.
9. NI, p. 13.
10. Ibid., p. 14.
11. Walter Lippmann, *Public Opinion*, London: Allen & Unwin 1932, p. 248, cited in DD, p. 367.
12. Similar exhortations and analyses can be found in the writings of other elite intellectuals: Alexander Bernays, Harold Lasswell and Reinhold Niebuhr, for example. See NI, pp. 16f.
13. Transcript, 'Noam Chomsky Meets the Washington Press', National Press Club, Washington, DC, 11 April 1989, p. 2.
14. Cited in Mark Hertsgaard, *On Bended Knee: The Press and the Reagan Presidency*, New York: Farrar, Straus, Giroux 1988, p. 84. A 'plurality' is a majority of those who expressed a preference.
15. NYT, 14 January 1986, cited in Hertsgaard, *On Bended Knee*. The inclusion of the trade unions as a perceived power centre, alongside corporations

and the federal government, is a sign of successful indoctrination, Chomsky suggests.

16. Transcript, 'Noam Chomsky Meets the Washington Press', p. 5.

17. NI, p. 10.

18. Transcript, 'Noam Chomsky Meets the Washington Press', p. 4.

19. MC, p. 299.

20. Chomsky, 'Introduction', in Cathy Perkus, ed., *Cointelpro: The FBI's Secret War on Political Freedom*, New York: Monad Press 1975, p. 10.

21. LP, p. 720.

22. See Perkus, *Cointelpro*, p. 16.

23. LR, p. 23.

24. Ibid., p. 24. Incidentally, according to Carlos Otero, when the Black community in Chicago wanted a white representative at Hampton's mass funeral, 'they asked Chomsky' (LP, p. 611).

25. NI, p. 189.

26. Ibid., p. 190.

27. MC, pp. 40f.

28. Ibid., p. 39.

29. Chomsky comments, 'Willingness to recognize the bare possibility of analysis of the media in terms of a propaganda model ... is so uncommon that the few existing cases perhaps merit a word of comment' (NI, p. 145).

30. NI, p. 146.

31. Ibid., pp. 146f.

32. Ibid., p. 382. I have confirmed this result.

33. The advanced student of Chomsky will note that as well as the main predictions about atrocities, the Propaganda Model makes what Chomsky calls 'second-order' and 'third-order' predictions. (The concept of 'orders of significance' comes from mathematics.) The second-order prediction of the model is that studies like PEHR will not be found within mainstream circles. No major investigation is needed here. The third-order predictions concern the reaction of mainstream intellectuals to a book about the media that investigates these topics. The prediction is that if a study of media performance appears that does not obey the accepted rules, and if it establishes unwelcome conclusions regarding media subservience to power, then there will be bitter condemnation from mainstream intellectuals. Chomsky goes further: 'In fact, one might draw an even sharper conclusion: exposure will be ignored in the case of constructive bloodbaths; it may be occasionally noted without interest in the case of benign bloodbaths; and it will lead to great indignation in the case of nefarious bloodbaths' (NI, p. 154). These predictions were fulfilled. When PEHR was published, Chomsky and Herman's work on media responses to constructive bloodbaths in Indonesia or Vietnam was ignored, their discussion of the benign bloodbath by Indonesia in East Timor was occasionally noticed in passing, but there was a tremendous wave of condemnation for Chomsky and Herman's discussion of media treatment of Cambodia. Chomsky notes that the sections in PEHR on media treatment of Cambodia 'elicited a huge literature of denunciation' (ibid., p. 155).

Notice the way that Chomsky uses the same material to draw out insights on a number of quite different levels of analysis in a highly compressed argument.

It is this kind of fast-moving critique, working on a series of ever-more abstract planes, that demands some mental agility from Chomsky's readers.

34. WCTWF, pp. 205–17.

35. AC, p. xiv.

36. WCTWF, p. 130.

37. AC, pp. 139f.

38. Tape of Noam Chomsky and Jan Myrdal speaking in Boston on 12 October 1979, provided by Caroline Bridgman-Rees.

39. To be strictly accurate, Chomsky alone was criticized for his alleged doubts. In the storm of denunciation that followed their writings on Cambodia, Herman was strangely exempt from criticism. His co-authorship of the works in question was ignored by most critics. This tends to suggest that the main motive for the criticism was the desire to attack Chomsky for other reasons.

40. Gitta Sereny, *New Statesman*, 17 July 1981, p. 17.

41. Leopold Labedz, 'Under Western Eyes: Chomsky Revisited', *Encounter*, July 1980, p. 34.

42. For overviews of the controversy, see also Christopher Hitchens, *Preparing for the Worst*, London: Hogarth Press 1990, pp. 68–72, and Edward Herman, 'Pol Pot, Faurisson and the Process of Derogation', in CA, pp. 599–615.

43. Chomsky and Herman, 'Distortions at Fourth Hand', *Nation*, 25 June 1977, p. 791; AC, p. 147.

44. Labedz, 'Under Western Eyes', p. 29. The phrase should read 'in *the* thousands'.

45. Lacouture's review, translated from the French, appeared as 'The Bloodiest Revolution', NYRB, 31 March 1977. Chomsky points out that the review, translated in record time, appeared in English before the book did, so that when he subsequently obtained Ponchaud's *Année Zero*, he was one of the few people in the United States actually to know what was in the book that everybody was discussing.

46. 'Cambodia: Corrections' appeared in NYRB, 26 May 1977, but not in the French journals which had originally carried Lacouture's review. Chomsky describes Lacouture's corrections as partial.

47. MCNCM, p. 107. Achbar stresses that these are only *index* entries, not column inches of actual stories. It seems safe to suggest that comparison of actual story lengths, together with placement and tone, would heighten the contrast in treatment.

48. Daniel Moynihan, *A Dangerous Place*, Boston: Little, Brown 1978, cited in DD, p. 200.

49. Incidentally, Chomsky does not exempt himself from this criticism. He once wrote, 'The atrocities in Timor and Cambodia under Pol Pot began at about the same time, but I published my first word about the former nineteen months after writing about Khmer Rouge atrocities' (NI, pp. 156f). Once he took up the issue, however, Chomsky became perhaps the most significant individual opponent of the Indonesian occupation, at one point testifying to the United Nations on the issue.

50. NI, p. 152.

51. Ibid.

2 The Culture of Terrorism

1. Chomsky has some harsh comments to make about *Nineteen Eighty Four*, in his view, a 'very shallow book' and a 'tenth-rate novel'. As a prediction of what would happen in England, it was poor. As a critique of Stalinism, it is inferior to many factual accounts of Stalinist terror. Furthermore, Chomsky suggests, it is 'trivial' to write about the Soviet Union, with its obvious forms of indoctrination. In contrast to this 'overrated' book, Chomsky suggests that Orwell did write 'one really great book', probably his least well-known book, one which influenced Chomsky a great deal – *Homage to Catalonia*. (LP, pp. 629f, 727, 630, 629). Reading *Homage to Catalonia* apparently helped to confirm Chomsky's attitudes in relation to the Spanish Civil War, though reading original materials on libertarian collectivization in Spain had apparently given him a more powerful experience of the war, some years before he came across Orwell's book (personal communication from Noam Chomsky, 5 October 1993).

For all of his criticism of Orwell's better known work, Chomsky acknowledges that Orwell was 'an honest man', who tried and often succeeded in 'extricating himself from the systems of thought control'. In these respects, Chomsky comments, Orwell was 'very unusual and very praiseworthy' (LP, p. 630). Indeed, Chomsky frequently refers to Orwell in his own writings, especially in relation to Orwellian inversions of meaning. Chomsky is also fond of invoking the 'memory hole' used in the Ministry of Truth to dispose of unwanted truths.

2. John Dolan, 'Introduction: Non-Orwellian Propaganda Systems', *Thoreau Quarterly*, vol. 16, nos 1, 2, Winter/Spring 1984.

3. TNCW, p. 14.

4. LR, p. 31.

5. CR, p. 224. Chomsky may have subsequently revised his opinion of Orwell. In a recent essay, he cites an unpublished introduction to *Animal Farm*, in which Orwell wrote that 'The sinister fact about literary censorship in England is that it is largely voluntary. Unpopular ideas can be silenced, and inconvenient facts kept dark, without any need for any official ban.' The desired outcome is attained in part by the 'general tacit agreement that "it wouldn't do" to mention that particular fact', in part as a consequence of media concentration in the hands of 'wealthy men who have every motive to be dishonest on certain important topics'. The result is that 'Anyone who challenges the prevailing orthodoxy finds himself silenced with surprising effectiveness' (Chomsky, MS, 'The Clinton Vision', 1993).

6. MC, p. xii.

7. T.W. Bohm, letter, *Spectator*, 11 April 1987; Chomsky, letter, 2 May 1987.

8. PE, p. 21.

9. TNCW, p. 92.

10. In this connection, it may be worth noting that Chomsky dismisses the supposedly 'left-wing' claim that Western freedoms are somehow illusory. A French critic suggested to Chomsky that an 'analyse approfondie' or 'deep analysis' of society demonstrated that the formal liberties of bourgeois democracy were 'not worth anything', and that alienation and servitude were

generated equally by the 'hard totalitarianism' of the Soviet bloc and by the 'soft totalitarianism' of the West. Chomsky responded that this 'analyse approfondie' was not only 'extremely superficial', but also 'helplessly misguided'. The totalitarianism of the Eastern bloc did not begin to approach the guarantee of freedom and rights that existed in the industrial democracies. Chomsky commented, 'It is obvious that the so-called "libertés formelles" represented an achievement of enormous significance.' The task for the present is to extend these achievements to new domains, not to denigrate and ignore them. (LP, p. 313).

11. WCTWF, pp. 66f. The latter quotation is taken by Chomsky and Herman from William McNeill, *The Rise of the West*, Chicago 1963, pp. 256f.

12. CR, p. 132.

13. TNCW, pp. 91f.

14. Ibid., p. 80.

15. Chomsky, '1984: Orwell's and Ours', *Thoreau Quarterly*, vol. 16, nos 1, 2, Winter/Spring 1984, p. 18.

16. CR, p. 132.

17. PI, p. 127.

18. NI, p. 48.

19. LP, p. 376. This is not to suggest that those at the liberal extreme in the mainstream are all consciously engaging in deceit. Some may be, but most are no doubt honestly expressing their points of view. Chomsky comments, 'I don't say they are lying. The more intelligent people are just lying, but the less intelligent believe it, and they believe it by a very simple and very familiar psychological mechanism.' It is easy to convince oneself that an immoral act is in fact moral if it is in one's interest. 'Everybody who is sufficiently honest knows that they do this all the time' (LP, p. 713).

20. CR, p. 132.

21. TNCW, p. 81.

22. CR, p. 126.

23. Cited in APNM, p. 240.

24. Chomsky, letter, *Listener*, 15 January 1970, p. 88.

25. Arthur Schlesinger, letter, *Listener*, 29 January 1970, p. 150.

26. Noam Chomsky, letter, *Listener*, 19 February 1970, p. 252.

27. LP, p. 622.

28. CR, p. 224.

29. Ibid.

30. Analyst, *The Pentagon Papers*, Gravel edition, vol. II, Boston: Beacon Press 1972, p. 22, cited in TNCW, p. 376n.

31. CR, p. 225.

32. Noam Chomsky, 'The Pentagon Papers as Propaganda and as History', in Noam Chomsky and Howard Zinn, eds., *The Pentagon Papers*, The Senator Gravel Edition, vol. V: Critical Essays, Boston: Beacon Press 1972, p. 195.

33. Ibid., p. 196.

34. CR, p. 225.

35. DD, pp. 317f. On the policy of attacking 'soft targets', see CT, pp. 43, 75–79, 208; NI, pp. 204f.

36. Ibid., p. 318.

37. Cited in DD, p. 321.

38. LP, p. 726.
39. Ibid., p. 620.
40. Ibid., p. 726
41. Ibid., p. 620, emphasis in the original.
42. Ibid., p. 727.
43. Ibid., p. 621.
44. There is an interesting difference of emphasis between the two Propaganda Model theorists. Herman, as befits an economist, stresses the corporate power of media enterprises and the mergers and other forms of economic concentration which have enhanced monopoly or oligopoly power. Chomsky, in contrast, tends to emphasize the individual surrender of each intellectual to the dominant ideology. There may be a difference of value judgement about the relative significance of the two factors in producing media conformity, or there may be a tactical difference over the most important message to present to intellectuals reading such critiques. The 'five filter' version of the Propaganda Model set out in MC could be described as the Herman/Chomsky model, as opposed to the Chomsky/Herman model. My remarks will be restricted to Chomsky's ideas, in so far as these can be disentangled from the Herman/Chomsky model.
45. MC, p. 14.
46. RP, p. 189.
47. James Curran and Jean Seaton, *Power without Responsibility: The Press and Broadcasting in Britain*, 2nd edn., London: Methuen 1985, p. 31, cited in MC, p. 14.
48. NI, pp. 7f.
49. Ibid., p. 8.
50. PI, p. 125.
51. MC, p. 16.
52. Ibid., p. 22.
53. Ibid., p. 26.
54. Ole R. Holsti and James N. Rosenau, *American Leadership in World Affairs*, Boston: Allen & Unwin nd, p. 174.
55. Cited in Finlay MacDonald, 'Don't Believe the Hype', *Listener* (New Zealand), 9 October 1993, p. 33.
56. TNCW, p. 94.
57. Cited in MacDonald, 'Don't Believe the Hype'. For more on conspiracy theories, see pp. 68–70.
58. TNCW, p. 14. A former student of Chomsky suggests that there are two versions of this analysis: 'I call it "crude Chomskyanism" and "subtle Chomskyanism". When Chomsky's really flying rhetorically, there's a crude edge to it, I think: people do things because they're bought off. I don't think that's true. I think he has a more subtle version, which is that the people you hear about do it for whatever reason, but the reason you hear about them is because it serves the purposes of those people who can afford to make these people heard' (telephone interview with Norbert Hornstein, Professor of Linguistics, University of Maryland, 22 April 1993). It seems to me that Chomsky's analysis in his writings focuses on a process of gradual accommodation rather than bribery, but it is interesting to hear different interpretations of the oral tradition.

59. Norman Finkelstein's exposé of Peters's book, *From Time Immemorial*, appeared in Edward Said and Christopher Hitchens, eds., *Blaming the Victims: Spurious Scholarship and the Palestinian Question*, London: Verso 1987, three years after it was completed. A condensed version was published in *In These Times*, 5 September 1984.

60. MC, p. 306. For some elements of society, there are even more direct dangers. We have already noted the case of Fred Hampton, a Black political organizer assassinated by the FBI. During the Vietnam War, even Chomsky was subjected to what he describes as 'threats of a fairly serious nature that were quite real by the late 1960s' (CR, p. 55).

61. TNCW, pp. 9f.

62. MC, p. 305.

63. Ibid.

64. Ibid.

65. WCTWF, p. 78.

66. PI, p. 125.

67. Transcript, 'Beyond the Reagan Era: Questions and Answers', Boulder, Colorado, 24 January 1988, p. 6.

68. Ibid., p. 5.

69. NYT, 31 December 1987.

70. 'Beyond the Reagan Era: Questions and Answers', emphasis in the original.

71. TNCW, p. 93.

72. Ibid.

73. LR, p. 108.

74. MC, p. 304.

75. NI, p. 11.

76. Herman and Chomsky, 'Propaganda Mill: The Media Churn out the Official Line', *The Progressive*, June 1988, p. 14.

77. MC, pp. 4f.

78. Tape, 'Media, Propaganda and Democracy', November 1988, Toronto, part 5, side B.

79. Ibid.

80. WCTWF, pp. 75f. Chomsky and Herman then quoted from a study entitled *The Sponsor*: 'Exciting "entertainment" provided the escape route – seemingly unrelated yet subtly supportive of what was being done ... the drama could have meaning only if viewers accepted, consciously or unconsciously, its underlying premise: that "we" faced enemies so evil and so clever that "the intricate means used to defeat them are necessary".'

81. Cited in RP, p. 213. Furthermore, Chomsky writes, 'The pernicious impact of the media goes beyond the restriction of information and opinion. In an important forthcoming essay, D.W. Smythe and H.H. Wilson observe that "the principal function of the commercially supported mass media in the United States is to market the output of the consumer goods industries and to train the population for loyalty to the American economic-political system." They quote a set of specifications given by major national advertisers to TV and radio writers, which states, in particular: "In general, the moral code of the characters in our dramas will be more or less synonymous with the moral code of the bulk of the American middle class, as it is commonly understood. . . . There will be no

material on any of our programs which could in any way further the concept of business as cold, ruthless and lacking in all sentiment or spiritual motivation." '

82. On the conventional usage of the term 'PC', Chomsky comments:

Suppose, for the sake of argument, we grant the accuracy of all the condemnations and the implicit claims about the golden age before the new orthodoxy established its iron grip. Still, one obvious question comes to mind. Why is it taken for granted, across the board, that to oppose racism and sexism, and to call for respect for other cultures, is a 'leftist' position – hence by implication, one that decent folk must abjure? The tacit assumption is not addressed. Its implications are not without interest. (LL, p. 115)

A typical Chomsky response, demanding some effort from the reader.

83. LP, p. 431. Some, like Matthew Rothschild of the *Progressive*, have criticized the Propaganda Model for this weakness. Chomsky responds, 'Let's go back to the General Motors case. Some economist is talking about General Motors's decisions. He talks about the general concern for increasing market share and profits, what happens if you build this kind of car and not that kind of car, concern over costs, etc. Suppose somebody came back and said, that's a conspiracy theory, because you didn't interview the executive to find out what happened in the director's meeting on such and such a day, who said this, etc. That would be a joke' (CD, p. 345).

84. John Corry, 'Is Television Unpatriotic or Simply Unmindful?', NYT, 12 May 1985, cited in MC, p. 171.

85. LP, p. 548.

86. NI, p. 146.

3 Intellectual Self-Defence

1. LP, p. 315.

2. Jay Parini, 'Noam is an Island', *Mother Jones*, October 1988, pp. 39f.

3. Ibid., p. 39.

4. LP, p. 561.

5. Interview with Michael Ferber, Professor of English, University of Maryland, New Hampshire, 28 April 1993.

6. CR, p. 49.

7. T T T, p. 247.

8. CR, p. 51.

9. NI, p. 134. See also MCNCM, pp. 108–12 for information about one of the individuals involved.

10. LP, p. 623.

11. Ibid.

12. Ibid., p. 392.

13. Ibid., p. 622. It does not follow, of course, that Chomsky is equating Stalinist or Nazi propaganda systems with the US media.

14. Cited in CT, p. 201.

15. TNCW, p. 14.

16. Transcript, 'International Terrorism: The Problem and the Remedy', Community Church of Boston, 8 February 1987, p. 7.

17. Cited in NI, p. 148. LaFeber put forward two other criticisms. He suggested that the Propaganda Model was undermined by the fact that some

escape its control, a damaging 'anomaly'. On that basis, Chomsky points out, 'an account of how *Pravda* works to "mobilize bias" would be undermined by the existence of dissidents'. The model only predicts that the media will produce propaganda. It does not offer any predictions on how successful that propaganda will be.

LaFeber also pointed to the existence of opposition to government policies expressed within the mass media. Chomsky responds that the existence of disagreements between different elite elements is entirely consistent with the Propaganda Model: 'The propaganda model does not assert that the media parrot the line of the current state managers in the manner of a totalitarian regime; rather, that the media reflect the consensus of powerful elites of the state–corporate nexus generally, including those who object to some aspect of government policy, typically on tactical grounds.' LaFeber was referring in particular to the widespread opposition to the continued funding of the Contras. Chomsky comments, 'a propaganda model is not refuted if the media provide a platform for powerful domestic elites that came to oppose the contra option for destroying Nicaragua; rather it is supported by this fact'. The Propaganda Model predicts that elite disagreements will generally be expressed in debate in the media, so long as the discussion assumes certain basic principles; for example, that the United States has the right to use force in pursuit of its ends, regardless of the law.

18. Ibid., p. 150.

19. MC, pp. 226f.

20. Herman and Chomsky, 'Propaganda Mill: The Media Churn Out the "Official Line"', *The Progressive*, June 1988, p. 15.

21. Ibid.

22. LaFeber, 'Chomsky's Challenges', in CA p. 321.

23. Seymour Melman, 'To Extricate America', *Catholic World*, November 1969, reproduced in CA, p. 83.

24. CD, p. 362.

25. LP, pp. 622f. At the same time, Chomsky does not 'say that it is impossible to create an intellectually interesting theory dealing with ideology and its social base'. It is even conceivable that such theoretical analysis could attain a level at which it would require special training and form, in principle, part of science. However, according to Chomsky, such a science and such training are not necessary for the ordinary person to remove the distorting prism imposed by the intelligentsia on social reality (LR, p. 5).

26. LR, p. 4.

27. Ibid., pp. 4f.

28. Ibid., p. 5.

29. Tape, 'Violence and Freedom', CSU: Fort Collins, CO, 10 April 1990, part 1, side A.

30. LP, p. 740.

31. Chomsky, interviewed by Rory Cox, *Propaganda Review* (San Francisco), no. 7, undated, p. 7.

32. Tape, 'Media, Propaganda and Democracy', November 1988, Toronto, part 3, side 2.

33. CR, p. 135. This is only a small part of the suppression of Arab peace offers by the US media. See FT, chapter 3, for the record up to 1983.

34. PE, p. 73. Chomsky gives a particular example of the relative glasnost in the local quality press, which demonstrates the possibilities for the honest reporter. The US press generally reproduces State Department propaganda, Chomsky notes. 'After one of these State Department handouts was published in the *Boston Globe* in 1978 or '79, I wrote to the editor of the Sunday edition of the *Globe*. And I told him, look, what you just published is simply a pack of lies, and I'll send you some documentation about it, and I think you ought to tell the truth, not just publish State Department lies, but publish the facts, which are obtainable from refugees, from church sources and others, about what's going there, which is a kind of genocide.' A local reporter was sent along, who dug into the story and 'dealt with it the way you deal with a story of corruption in the police department', which is to say, without ideological constraints. The end-result, including the unpublished transcript of a *New York Times* interview with a Portuguese priest from East Timor, was, in Chomsky's words, 'a very good article, the best article that appeared in the whole United States about the U.S.-backed invasion of Timor'. (Chomsky, '1984: Orwell's and Ours', *Thoreau Quarterly*, vol. 16, nos 1, 2, Winter/Spring 1984, pp. 23f.) Chomsky remarks that, while he has not studied the matter, 'my general impression is that local journalism has done a lot better than international journalism' (p. 22).

35. LP, pp. 628f.

36. Chomsky presents an interesting personal experience of the workings of the media: 'I once happened to be caught in Laos by accident . . . during a period when practically the whole Southeast Asia press corps was there. . . . I would say for three-quarters of the press, the way they got the news was (1) by going to the American embassy and (2) by trying to rip one another off in the bar at the hotel where they all hung out.' During this time, Nixon made a speech claiming that the number of North Vietnamese troops in Laos had increased from 50,000 to 67,000 in a major invasion. 'A couple of hours before the speech was heard in Laos, all the reporters had gone to the five o'clock briefing and the American military attaché had given them the same briefing he had been giving them for the last couple of years: 50,000 North Vietnamese troops. Now, every single reporter there knew that Nixon was lying. How could it be that 17,000 troops came in and the American military attaché in Laos never heard of it?' Only one reporter mentioned this lie, and then in a misleading fashion (see AWWA, p. 164). 'None of the others even reported it.' Chomsky then sought documentation for the 50,000 figure from the political officer of the American embassy. After checking the available reports, 'I discovered that, according to their own sources, there was one regiment of perhaps 2,500 North Vietnamese troops there. . . . The 50,000 were mostly an invention and the rest were old men carrying sacks of rice on their backs.' Chomsky also went to interview refugees from the Plain of Jars: 'I went out to the refugee camps which were about thirty kilometres outside of Vientiane and I spent ten or twenty hours there taking information. *One* reporter came with me – a stringer from the *Far Eastern Economic Review* – and, again, David Greenway went out one day on his own.' The rest of the US press corps didn't bother.

Chomsky also discovered 'that the minister of rural affairs was secretly a Pathet Lao supporter'. Chomsky interviewed him: 'the only thing he asked me to do was to identify him as an urban intellectual. So if you look at the article, the book, that I wrote about this afterwards, you'll notice there's a report there about an urban intellectual who's supporting the communist guerrillas for this and that reason' (AWWA, p. 150). Chomsky also, during his week in Vientiane, found and interviewed Pathet Lao guerrillas who were resting in the city. No US reporter ever found these people, who were readily available, for the simple reason that they were not looking for them: 'They've been sufficiently indoctrinated so that they don't know to look for it. I mean they're committed to the view that "We're there for noble motives to defend the people against the communists." And if that's your assumption, you don't look for these things. And you don't find them. Now that's what people have to break out of' ('1984, Orwell's and Ours', pp. 46ff).

37. MC, p. 304.

38. T T T, p. 239.

39. Transcript, 'Beyond the Reagan Era: Questions and Answers', Boulder, Colorado, 24 January 1988, p. 6.

40. Ibid.

41. Transcript, 'Noam Chomsky Meets the Washington Press', National Press Club, Washington, DC, 11 April 1989, p. 10.

42. Ibid.

43. Transcript, 'International Terrorism: The Problem and the Remedy', p. 3.

44. Transcript, 'Media Control in Democracy', Boston, MA, 9 November 1991, p. 6.

45. Excerpt from Chomsky, 'The Drift towards Global War', in *Studies in Political Economy*, Summer 1985, reproduced in MCNCM, p. 121.

46. T T T, p. 170.

47. CD, p. 380.

48. Transcript, 'Noam Chomsky Meets the Washington Press', p. 5.

49. Ibid.

50. Transcript, 'Media Control in Democracy', p. 7.

51. LP, pp. 742f.

52. Ibid., p. 717.

53. Ibid., p. 742.

54. CD, p. 243.

55. Staughton Lynd, 'Thoughts on Chomsky', *Liberation* (New York), February 1969, p. 33.

56. Parini, 'Noam is an Island', p. 38.

57. Bill Moyers, ed., *A World of Ideas: Conversations with Thoughtful Men and Women about American Life Today and the Ideas Shaping Our Future*, New York: Doubleday 1989, p. 55.

58. CR, p. 48. Chomsky has occasionally expressed less caution on this topic, so that one can find a degree of inconsistency in his writings. More interestingly, he points out that ruling elites must believe in the decency of the population, else why construct such a sophisticated system of deception and indoctrination?

59. CD, p. 355.

60. LP, p. 742.

61. Ibid.

62. Ibid.

63. Tape, 'At the Rowe Centre', Rowe, MA, 15–16 April 1989, tape 4, side A.

64. Ibid.
65. Interview with Louis Kampf, MIT, 22 April 1993.
66. CD, pp. 242f.
67. LP, p. 392.
68. T T T, p. 246.
69. Ibid.
70. Parini, 'Noam is an Island', pp. 39f.

4 Patterns of Intervention

1. Tape, 'Violence and Freedom', CSU/Fort Collins, CO, 10 April 1990, part 3, side B, emphasis in original.
2. CR, p. 36.
3. LP, p. 717.
4. APNM, p. 271.
5. LR, p. 6.
6. Ibid., p. 7.
7. Cited in TNCW, p. 91.
8. Ronald Steele, *Pax Americana*, New York: Viking 1967, cited in APNM, p. 168.
9. Cited in APNM, p. 30.
10. TNCW, p. 73.
11. Ibid., p. 74.
12. CT, p. 21.
13. Norman A. Graebner, *Cold War Diplomacy: 1945–60*, New York: D. Van Nostrand 1962, cited in TNCW, p. 110.
14. TNCW, p. 110. This analogy seems to have been prompted by a letter by a scientist in response to Lacouture's corrections in the Cambodia debate (see p. 30). Lacouture had acknowledged his crucial misreadings of Ponchaud's book (after they had been pointed out to him by Chomsky), but had then gone on to reaffirm his ultimate conclusion that the leaders of Cambodia were involved in systematic massacre and genocide. Chomsky wrote later: 'After Lacouture's corrections appeared, a letter was sent to the *New York Review* by a well-known scientist (Nobel Laureate) commenting that in his field, when conclusions are published based on certain evidence and it then turns out that the cited evidence is incorrect, the scientist does not retract the evidence while reiterating the conclusions – but evidently matter [sic] are different in journalism. The letter was not published' (AC, p. 378n).
15. Chomsky, *Knowledge of Language: Its Nature, Origin and Use*, New York: Praeger 1986, p. xxvii.
16. Hans Morgenthau, *New Republic*, 22 January 1977, cited in TNCW, p. 92.
17. TNCW, p. 93.
18. CR, p. 316.
19. Ibid.
20. T T T, p. 47
21. Ibid.
22. PI, p. 7.
23. CR, p. 318.

24. Lars Schoultz, *Comparative Politics*, January 1981, cited in T T T, p. 157.

25. Michael Klare and Cynthia Arnson, *Supplying Repression*, Washington, DC: Institute for Policy Studies, 1981, cited in T T T, p. 158, emphasis in original.

26. Table 1, WCTWF, p. 45. The ten countries were Brazil, Chile, Dominican Republic, Guatemala, Indonesia, Iran, Philippines, South Korea, Thailand and Uruguay.

27. Ibid., p. 44. The fact that military aid dropped 8 per cent after the coup is, say Chomsky and Herman, misleading, 'since the high rate of military aid under Allende reflected US support for the right-wing military in the interests of counter-revolution – economic aid to the civil society declined precipitously under Allende.' See p. 69 for some relevant remarks.

28. Ibid., p. 43.

29. Chomsky summarizes their conclusions in TNCW, p. 206. The table is found on p. 43 of WCTWF.

30. WCTWF, p. 3.

31. T T T, p. 158.

32. WCTWF, p. 44, emphasis in original.

33. T T T, pp. 158f.

34. Transcript, 'Beyond the Reagan Era: Questions and Answers', Boulder, Colorado, 24 January 1988, pp. 1f.

35. CT, pp. 175–83.

36. Transcript, 'Roots of US Interventionism', Lewis and Clark College, Portland, Oregon, 24 January 1989, p. 13. For an analysis coming out of the Christic Institute perspective, see Jonathan Marshall, Peter Dale Scott and Jane Hunter, *The Iran–Contra Connection: Secret Teams and Covert Operations in the Reagan Era*, Boston: South End Press 1987.

37. RC, p. 37.

38. Chomsky commented that while he was not opposed to further inquiry into a possible high-level conspiracy to kill Kennedy, he was doubtful that it would lead anywhere. 'If someone can come up with a credible reason why some high-level cabal might have sought to assassinate JFK, I'd be interested. So far, all attempts have failed, as I read the record' (letter, *Z magazine*, January 1993, p. 6). He made it clear that he was not challenging the idea that Kennedy was killed for intending to withdraw from Vietnam; it would be possible on his analysis to believe that the high-level conspirators mistook JFK's intentions (p. 5). He also made it clear that his remarks on Kennedy's policy-making had no implications for theories regarding the mafia or right-wing Cubans, or other such theories: 'They bear only on the thesis that Kennedy was killed in a high-level conspiracy followed by a cover-up of remarkable dimensions' (RC, p. 38).

39. Letter, *Z magazine*, January 1993, p. 6.

40. CD, p. 381.

41. Ibid., pp. 381f. Chomsky adds, 'For people who believe in conspiracies, there's one sitting there waiting for them. Here's one for your favourite conspiracy theorist. In case anybody misunderstands, I don't believe this for one moment, but it's the kind of thing that goes around. Just imagine the CIA deciding: How can we undermine and destroy all of these popular movements? Let's send them off on some crazy wild goose chase which is going to involve

them in extremely detailed analysis and microanalysis and discussion of things that don't matter. That'll shut them up' (from KRL, cited in MCNCM, p. 131).

Widespread fear and cynicism explain the demand for conspiracy theories. There is also the supply side of the problem. Chomsky points to a widespread feeling of impotence and isolation on the Left: 'If you really feel, Look, it's too hard to deal with real problems, there are a lot of ways to avoid doing so. One of them is to go off on wild goose chases that don't matter. Another is to get involved in academic cults that are very divorced from any reality and that provide a defence against dealing with the world as it actually is. There's plenty of that going on, including on the left' (ibid.).

Incidentally, Chomsky's example of President Bush the blood-drinking alien is by no means extreme, as a little research in the North American 'alternative media' will demonstrate.

42. The references that follow are to quotations that are also cited in TNCW, pp. 96f.

43. Memorandum E-A10, 19 October 1940, Council on Foreign Relations (CFR), *War – Peace Studies*, cited in L. Shoup and W. Minter, *Imperial Brain Trust*, New York: Monthly Review Press 1977, p. 130.

44. Isaiah Bowman, memorandum T-A21, 16 January 1942, CFR, *War – Peace Studies*, cited in Shoup and Minter, *Imperial Brain Trust*, p. 163.

45. Memorandum E-A10, 19 October 1940.

46. Norman Davis, minutes S-3 of the Security Subcommittee, Advisory Committee on Postwar Foreign Policy, 6 May 1942, cited in Shoup and Minter, *Imperial Brain Trust*.

47. Winfield Riefler, memorandum T-A14, 17 June 1941, CFR, *War – Peace Studies*, cited in Shoup and Minter, *Imperial Brain Trust*, p. 175.

48. TNCW, pp. 419f n.

49. Minutes summarizing PPS 51, April 1949, cited from a secondary source in DD, p. 51.

50. TNCW, p. 97.

51. T T T, p. 48.

52. Cited in T T T, p. 47.

53. *Pentagon Papers*, Gravel edition, book III, p. 627, cited in BB, p. 50.

54. Cited in BB, pp. 50f. Recall that Beijing was not recognized as the government of China by the United States until 1971, when it was voted into the United Nations, and took the permanent seat in the Security Council previously held by Taiwan.

55. Ibid., p. 51.

56. Cited in ibid.

57. The phrase belongs to Walt Rostow, a noted foreign policy commentator. See BB, p. 49, for discussion.

58. CR, p. 322.

59. PI, p. 34.

60. BB, p. 70.

61. APNM, p. 203.

62. Charles Glass, 'American Samizdat', *New Statesman*, 25 April 1980, reproduced in CA, p. 202.

63. MCNCM, pp. 154f. For documentation on the Dominican Republic, Greece, Guatemala and Timor, see TNCW; on Cambodia, AWWA; on Lebanon, FT.

64. Chomsky, 'Vietnam: How Government Became Wolves', NYRB, 15 June 1972, p. 30.

65. BB, p. 59.

66. Ibid., p. 189n. Chomsky refers to remarks by John McNaughton in the *Pentagon Papers*, Gravel edition, vol. IV, p. 47.

67. Chomsky, 'The Pentagon Papers as Propaganda and as History', in Chomsky and Howard Zinn, eds., *The Pentagon Papers: Critical Essays*, The Senator Gravel edition, vol. V. Boston: Beacon Press 1972, p. 196.

68. Ibid.

69. T T T, p. 72.

70. CR, p. 322.

71. Robert W. Tucker, *Nation or Empire? The Debate over American Foreign Policy*, Baltimore, MD: Johns Hopkins University Press, 1968, p. 117, cited in CR, p. 247.

72. Ibid., pp. 247f. It was US policy to reimpose French colonialism on Indochina after the Second World War. The considerable support for this effort apparently included the offer of nuclear weapons to France. Daniel Ellsberg gives some references for the nuclear offer from the public record in his 'Call to Mutiny', reproduced many times, for example in Joseph Gerson, ed., *The Deadly Connection: Nuclear War and US Intervention*, Cambridge, MA: American Friends Service Committee 1983. Michio Kaku and Daniel Axelrod give a full account of top-level discussion of the nuclear option from declassified sources in *To Win a Nuclear War*, London: Zed Books 1987, pp. 88–94.

73. For a brief discussion of US terrorism against Cuba, see NI, pp. 274f and the references given there.

74. Robert W. Tucker, *Nation or Empire? The Debate over American Foreign Policy*, Baltimore, MD: Johns Hopkins University Press 1968, p. 117, cited in CR, p. 248.

75. CR, p. 248. The advent of fascism in Brazil was much lauded by US policy-makers, while the elected government of Salvador Allende was subjected to a systematic campaign of destabilization.

76. Cited in CR, p. 251.

77. Communism, to be accurate, is the belief that society should be governed by the doctrine 'from each according to their ability, to each according to their need'.

78. TNCW, p. 8.

79. Cited in DD, p. 49.

80. Ibid.

81. 'US Policy toward Latin America', NSC 5432, 18 August 1954, cited in PI, pp. 19f. Note the crude Marxist terminology.

82. Ibid., p. 10.

83. CT, p. 67. The United States justified its actions, including the mining of Nicaraguan waters, by claiming 'self-defence'. Chomsky notes that the UN Charter permits self-defence only in the event of an armed attack so sudden and extreme that the need for action becomes 'instant, overwhelming, and leaving no choice of means, and no moment for deliberation', in the usual formula. This was hardly the case in Central America. The Charter also requires that such counter-actions be 'immediately reported to the Security Council' (Article 51), which the United States failed to do (T T T, pp. 90, 89). Naturally, the World Court decision was ignored by both policy-makers and the US mass media, as

was the Court's compensation order against Washington, still unpaid at the time of writing.
84. PE, p. 114.
85. Ibid., p. 115. See T T T, pp. 14–28, among other places for documentation of the US role, and further references.
86. LP, p. 508.
87. APNM, p. 34.
88. 501, p. 94.
89. Transcript, 'Unfinished Business: the US and Central America', San Francisco, 17 March 1991, pp. 1ff.
90. Ibid.
91. For some enlightening remarks by leading liberals, see DD, pp. 264–70.
92. PI, p. 12.
93. LP, p. 729.
94. Walter LaFeber, 'Chomsky's Challenges', *In These Times*, 29 August–2 September 1982, reproduced in CA, p. 320.

5 Rational Suicide

1. WP, 20 November 1991, cited in RC, pp. 16ff.
2. RC, p. 17. Daniel Moynihan's efforts to block the UN are described in his memoirs, *A Dangerous Place*, Boston: Little, Brown 1978.
3. DD, pp. 9f.
4. CD, p. 209.
5. DD, p. 20.
6. Ibid.
7. LP, p. 472.
8. TN, p. 26.
9. Chomsky, 'The United States: From Greece to El Salvador', in Noam Chomsky, Jonathan Steele and John Gittings, *Superpowers in Collision: The New Cold War of the 1980s*, 2nd edition, London: Penguin Books 1984, p. 30.
10. AWWA, p. 24.
11. CD, p. 209.
12. LP, p. 472.
13. TNCW, p. 192.
14. BB, p. 20.
15. Cited in 501, p. 67, emphasis added.
16. Cited in DD, p. 23.
17. 501, p. 65.
18. Chomsky, 'Marching in Place', MS, 1993.
19. Ibid.
20. Cited in T T T, pp. 207f.
21. See BB, pp. 80ff.
22. DD, p. 28.
23. Cited in DD, p. 98.
24. Cited in DD, p. 59.
25. TNCW, p. 22.

26. T T T, p. 208. Critics have asked how the military budget could be so significant if arms procurement accounts for perhaps 3 per cent of US GNP. Chomsky responds, 'The figures about percentages of GNP are almost totally meaningless. The point is that the corporate managers in advanced industry – this is true of electronics, computers, pharmaceuticals, etc. – expect that the government, meaning the public, will pick up the costly parts of the production process, the parts that are not profitable – research and development.... Furthermore, the public, through the Pentagon, provides a state-guaranteed market, which is available for waste production if commercial markets don't work. That is a gift to the corporate managers' (transcript, interview by David Barsamian on KGNU Public Radio, Boulder, Colorado, 13 December 1989, p. 5).

27. Cited in T T T, p. 209.

28. PI, p. 106.

29. Transcript, interview by David Barsamian on KGNU Public Radio, Boulder, Colorado, 13 December 1989, p. 5.

30. Transcript, 'Questions & Answers with Freshman Sociology', University of Wyoming at Laramie, 21 February 1989, p. 2.

31. RP, p. 220ff.

32. Transcript, 'Creeping Fascism', New York, 26 April 1992, p. 4.

33. 12 February 1949, cited in T T T, pp. 209f. I understand that this article was usually the first item in one of the political courses run by Chomsky and Kampf.

34. Transcript, 'Creeping Fascism', p. 4.

35. Cited in T T T, pp. 212f.

36. T T T, p. 190.

37. Ibid., pp. 203f.

38. Ibid., p. 206.

39. PI, p. 98.

40. TNCW, p. 194.

41. Though there are some changes in the form of the public subsidy, derived in part from the changing international scene: inefficiency is no longer tolerable now that serious competition exists in Japan and Western Europe. 'Furthermore, the cutting edge of industrial development is shifting to biology-based technology ... [which] cannot easily be hidden behind a Pentagon cover' (Chomsky, '"Mandate for Change", or Business as Usual', Z magazine, February 1993, pp. 36f).

42. PI, p. 104.

43. Chomsky, The Race to Destruction – Its Rational Basis, Nottingham: Spokesman 1986, p. 21.

44. APNM, p. 133.

45. Ibid. As Chomsky points out, this risk was taken in order to establish that the United States alone had the right to maintain missiles on the borders of a potential enemy. The United States had missiles on the Soviet border in Turkey which it refused to withdraw in return for the withdrawal of Soviet missiles in Cuba. See T T T, pp. 172f.

46. The Race to Destruction.

47. Ibid., p. 1.

48. LP, p. 715.

49. Title of an article by Chomsky in David Copp, ed., 'Nuclear Weapons, Deterrence and Disarmament', *Canadian Journal of Philosophy*, supplementary vol. 12 (1988). The text of the article is apparently identical to the pamphlet *The Race to Destruction*.

50. LP, p. 756.

51. Ibid.

52. Ibid., p. 757.

53. Transcript, 'Creeping Fascism', New York, 26 April 1992, p. 11.

54. RP, p. 223.

55. FRS, p. 184.

56. T T T, p. 230.

57. LP, p. 185.

58. Ibid.

59. TNCW, p. 86.

60. Ibid., p. 5.

61. LP, p. 698.

62. Ibid., p. 744.

63. PI, pp. 11ff. The state system is, in Chomsky's view, an artificial and unnatural social development: 'In its modern form it developed in Europe, and you can see how artificial it is by just looking at European history for the last hundreds of years, a history of massacre, violence, terror, destruction, most of which has to do with trying to impose a state system on a society to which it has very little relation.' With the European conquest of much of the world, the imposition of the state system, cutting across communities and interests and forcibly bringing together people with nothing in common, has led to constant warfare and struggle and oppression. Chomsky describes this worldwide phenomenon as 'the plague of European civilization'. In the modern era, the state has reached new heights of destructiveness and hypocrisy: 'It's a miracle that it has survived as long as it did. In Europe, for example, the wars went from the beginnings of the modern period up until 1945, when a stable system was established', because at that point the logic of state conflict had reached the point of mutual annihilation (LP, pp. 745, 762, 745).

6 Visions

1. Transcript, interview by David Barsamian on KGNU Public Radio, Boulder, Colorado, 13 December 1989, p. 5.

2. Christopher Coker, 'The Mandarin and the Commissar: The Political Thought of Noam Chomsky', in Sohan and Celia Modgil, eds., *Noam Chomsky: Consensus and Controversy*, Lewes: Falmer Press 1987, p. 276.

3. RP, pp. 222, 223. Written at a time when a significant part of the New Left was beginning to turn towards political confrontation as an end in itself. We may note that Chomsky generally avoids using the phrase 'the Left': 'I don't like terms like "right" and "left"; especially in the United States, I don't think they mean very much.' His own definition is interesting: 'if we mean by the left what it historically meant, that is, that component of the body politic which is concerned with defending human rights, increasing democracy, increasing

public control over the major decisions in the society, including democratiz-ation of the private economy, placing it under public, democratic control, workers' control of production, community control over their affairs – if we are talking about the left in that sense, that is, an extension of the movement towards popular democracy and popular control to new and other spheres, overcoming authority and repression and autocratic structures and so on, if that's what we mean by the left, there isn't much of it in the United States' (LP, p. 688). The term is used more loosely in general discussion, and that is the sense in which I use it. For Chomsky, however, 'the Left' consists of 'the authentic Left' – that spectrum of opinion which he believes honours the real values of socialism. This is a very small fraction of the groups and movements usually denoted by the term.

4. Ibid.

5. Ibid.

6. Cited in PKF, p. 51.

7. RP, p. 223.

8. Ibid., p. 222.

9. PKF, p. 51. Chomsky refers to Russell's pre-First World War stance. Later, Russell became markedly less sympathetic to anarchism.

10. Cited in FRS, p. 151.

11. Perhaps even problems of nonhuman freedom. Chomsky remarks:

I think there's a very difficult ethical problem there that we as a species have not really faced.... If you look over our history there are a lot of problems that didn't look like ethical problems for a long time, slavery for example. We went through all of human history with nobody thinking, or very few people thinking, that there was an ethical problem in slavery. In fact, it was often considered moral to have slaves.... It's part of moral progress to be able to face things that looked as if they weren't problems, and I have that kind of a feeling about the animal issue.... The question arises what right do you have to torture other species for your own good. It's true it's a tricky question. I don't know what the answer is. I think it's a good thing that these questions are being raised.... The issues are hard.... A lot of these things are about trying to explore your own moral intuitions and if you've never explored them, you don't know what they are, you know. These are things that you've got to come to grips with by struggling over them. Abortion's a similar case. (Tape, 'At the Rowe Centre', Rowe, MA, 15–16 April 1989, tape 5, side B)

Michael Albert raised the issue in a 1993 interview with Chomsky. Albert asked whether Chomsky was a vegetarian. Their conversation went as follows:

NC: I'm not, but I think it's a serious question. If you want my guess, my guess would be...
MA: (breaking in): 'A hundred years from now everyone will.'
NC: Yeah, I think so. I mean, I don't know if it's a hundred years.
(Tape, 'Oppression and Liberation', Z magazine January 1993, side A)

12. CR, p. 29.

13. George Woodcock, Anarchism and Anarchists, Kingston: Quarry Press 1992, pp. 224, 225, 228, emphases in original.

14. LP, p. 395.

15. FRS, p. 162, CR, p. 31. This is an extraordinarily mild reference to Marx's role in the destruction of the First International. It would be difficult to find such an unsectarian remark in the works of any other anarchist of note. Chomsky also notes that Marx's 'personal behaviour (not to be confused with his thought) often left much to be desired, to put it mildly' (LP, p. 396).

16. LP, p. 177.

17. FRS, p. 155. Chomsky adds, 'It would be a grotesque error to say that Stalin was simply the realization of Leninist principles or anything like that', though at the same time there were aspects of the Leninist tradition 'which laid the groundwork for Stalin' (LP, p. 141).

18. LR, p. 74.

19. CR, pp. 29f.

20. Cited in FRS, pp. 155ff. Four pages earlier, Chomsky cites Rocker: 'For the anarchist, freedom is not an abstract philosophical concept, but the vital concrete possibility for every human being to bring to full development all the powers, capacities, and talents with which nature has endowed him [sic], and turn them to social account.'

21. For some comments on these issues and on the alleged contradiction between equality and freedom, see Chomsky, 'Equality: Language Development, Human Intelligence, and Social Organization', in CR.

22. FRS, p. 156.

23. Cited in FRS, p. 180. Chomsky notes the connection between such ideas and the notion of 'alienation' one finds in the early Marx.

24. PI, p. 116. According to Chomsky, classical liberal ideals have been 'perverted into an ideology to sustain the emerging social order' (FRS, p. 156). Since the 1930s, Chomsky notes, the term 'liberalism' has come to mean 'a commitment to the use of state power for welfare purposes' (LP, p. 656), rather than the restriction of state power. Chomsky also notes that the terms 'liberal' and 'conservative' have switched meanings. Perhaps surprisingly, Chomsky regards himself as a conservative: 'Mark Hatfield might qualify in the Senate. I'm another one, incidentally, in essential respects' (transcript, 'United States International and Security Policy: The "Right Turn" in Historical Perspective', University of Colorado, Boulder, 22 October 1986, p. 1). He comments, 'A modern conservative, like Taft, wants to cut back state power, cut back state intervention in the economy – the same as someone like Mark Hatfield – to preserve the Enlightenment ideals of freedom of expression, freedom from state violence, of law-abiding states, etc.' (LP, p. 656).

25. RP, p. 60.

26. DD, p. 371.

27. Anthony Crosland, cited in PKF, p. 52.

28. Cited in CR, p. 191.

29. FRS, p. 157.

30. Auberon Waugh, 'From Oxymoron to Boiled Egg', *Independent*, 26 March 1988. The reference to a boiled egg comes in the final two sentences of Waugh's review: 'To do him justice, Chomsky still thinks of himself as a democrat. He might just as well think of himself as a boiled egg.'

31. CR, p. 23. Some tendencies in modern anarchism favour a withdrawal from technology, industrialism and sometimes even from 'civilization'. Chomsky is unsympathetic to such a position, in part because of its irrelevance

to the actual conditions of contemporary life: 'Something's got to happen to the
5 billion people in the world. They're not going to survive in the Stone Age.' He
continues, 'suppose it turned out that the Kalahari Bushmen were living in an
absolute utopia. That's not true, but suppose it turned out to be true ... that
wouldn't tell us anything about this world ... if you want to be related to the
world in which people live, you have to start with the existence of that world,
and ask how it can be changed' ('A Brief Interview with Noam Chomsky on
Anarchy, Civilization & Technology', *Anarchy: A Journal of Desire Armed*,
Summer 1991, p. 27). For Chomsky, 'Industrialism is far from obsolete. The
vast majority of the human race has not even entered the industrial era, or has
barely entered it, and in the advanced industrial societies the production of
useful goods poses real and imminent problems' (LP, p. 391).

32. RP, p. 248.
33. FRS, p. 161.
34. LP, p. 168.
35. Ibid.
36. RP, p. 249.
37. Ibid., p. 224
38. CR, p. 31.
39. RP, p. 249.
40. Ibid.
41. Ibid., p. 240.
42. Ibid., p. 249.
43. Ibid., p. 247.
44. FRS, p. 142.
45. CR, p. 32.
46. LP, p. 162.
47. RP, p. 239.
48. Joshua Cohen and Joel Rogers, 'Knowledge, Morality and Hope: The
Social Thought of Noam Chomsky', *New Left Review*, no. 187, May/June
1991, p. 14.
49. RP, p. 250.
50. Ibid. Cohen and Rogers also suggest that 'specialized agencies for
administration and enforcement' of the terms of order are necessary in large,
complex associations, and this tends to undermine the anarchist case. They
recognize the danger that such agencies 'would engender a concentration of
power, and that such a concentration would produce greater threats to human
freedom than those resulting from the absence of specialized political arrangements' (p. 16). They regard this as an empirical issue 'and one about which we
can only hope some day to have data'. It is difficult to evaluate this analysis,
given the high level of generality at which it is pitched. I suspect that Chomsky
would not disagree with Cohen and Rogers on the possible need for
administrative and enforcement agencies – the debate would be over the nature
and powers of such agencies, and the structures and procedures needed to
maintain accountability and direct control. There is a wide range of conceivable
enforcement agencies, ranging from Greenpeace to the Gestapo. Some more
concrete proposals are needed for any more fine-grained analysis.
51. RP, p. 251.
52. Ibid., p. 225.

53. FRS, p. 162.

54. RP, p. 246.

55. APNM, p. 63.

56. RP, p. 260.

57. Bracken, 'Extracts from Round Table on the Concept of Human Nature in Chomsky', in CA, p. 279.

58. LP, p. 147. For more on the innate capacity of the mind for 'moral development', see p. 193 n. 16.

59. LP, p. 246, emphasis added.

60. Ibid., pp. 385f.

61. Ibid., p. 597. There is a certain amount of resistance to the idea of a 'human nature' in left-liberal circles, especially the idea that talents and aptitudes are genetically determined and vary between people. Chomsky argues that this should be a 'matter for delight rather than a condition to be abhorred'. 'Those who assume otherwise must be adopting the tacit premise that people's rights or social reward are somehow contingent on their abilities' (CR, p. 199).

In the particular case of racial difference, Chomsky argues, it is possible that, for example, Jews have a genetically determined tendency 'towards usury (like squirrels bred to collect too many nuts) or a drive towards antisocial conspiracy and domination, and so on' (FRS, p. 144). It is also possible that there is some correlation between race and intelligence. But in a non-racist society, these differences – if shown to exist – would be of no significance. 'The mean IQ of individuals of a certain racial background is irrelevant to the situation of a particular individual, who is what he [sic] is' (ibid., p. 147). The desire of some in left-liberal circles to deny that these racial differences might exist is in part a rejection of racism. In part, it may also be due to the idea that rights and rewards should accrue to ability and intelligence, a disturbing and elitist doctrine.

62. Ibid., p. 245.

63. Chomsky points out that 'People have been trying to solve the problem of free will for thousands of years, and they've made zero progress. They don't even have *bad* ideas about how to answer the question. My hunch – and it's no more than a guess – is that the answer to the riddle of free will lies in the domain of potential science that the human mind can never master because of the limitations of its genetic structure.' Similarly the aesthetic sense, and, according to Chomsky, all other human abilities. Another likely candidate for impenetrability is literary theory: 'ever since the ancient Greeks people have been trying to find general principles on which to base literary criticism, but, while I'm far from being an authority in this field, I'm under the impression that no one has yet succeeded in establishing such principles. Very much as in other human sciences' (LP, pp. 415, 416; LR, pp. 56f).

Chomsky notes that 'Organisms are good at some things, bad at others – these properties go together.' In order to be good in one area, an organism must specialize at the cost of other abilities – if it is to be good at swimming, it will have to sacrifice excellence in flight. The same is true of mental life, Chomsky suggests. 'If you're capable of solving problems in certain domains, it's because of specific adaptations, highly specific genetic instructions which are going to block access to other domains. If humans are part of the physical world, as certainly we can assume, and if humans are very good at certain tasks, as they are in acquiring language or (at another level of inquiry) constructing quantum theory, then the very intellectual structures that permit them to succeed in these domains are going to lead them to fail constantly in domains that don't happen to be ordered or constructed in a way that corresponds to their intelligence. It is reasonable to suppose that the history of successful science somehow reflects the nature of human intelligence.' Our knowledge has grown in those areas which we are able to analyse and understand, and not in others, and this indicates something about the structure of our mental capacities.

The process of developing knowledge is highly complex. Chomsky points out that all theories are 'vastly underdetermined by evidence'. The whole point of having a theory is that it explains much more than the limited number of circumstances which are used to test it. The concept of gravity is based on a rather limited number of observations in relation to the entire universe, but is none the less regarded as a universal principle. Chomsky argues that 'what we find is that certain moves from evidence to theory are regarded as sensible while other moves are regarded as ridiculous. This means that we must be designed specifically to map our current problem situations into a certain small sub-class of possible theories. The whole history of science is an indication of this. But, of course, the very same constraint that leads to the choice of certain theories and the rejection of others is an initial constraint on the nature of our intelligence. And it may be that it leads us in the wrong directions. There's no guarantee that the world is designed so that it will conform to the structure of our intelligence. It's sort of a miracle if it ever happens. . . . It's just blind luck if the structure of our intelligence and the nature of the world tend to correspond in some domain' (LP, pp. 466, 467). There is an important codicil to this view of human intelligence: 'Notice that these quite natural views on the scope and limits of knowledge set no finite limits on human progress. The integers form an infinite set, but they do not exhaust the real numbers. Similarly, humans may develop their capacities without limit, but never escaping certain objective bounds set by their biological nature. I suspect that there is no cognitive domain to which such observations are not appropriate' (Chomsky, *Reflections on Language*, London: Fontana 1975, p. 124).

These ideas are together perhaps the most extreme example of Chomsky's ability to stand outside conventional thought and examine the human race from a Martian point of view. The level of abstraction involved makes it difficult to achieve such a perspective.

64. LP, p. 773.
65. CR, p. 192.
66. LP, p. 144.
67. RP, p. 224. Cohen and Rogers have registered their doubts as to the ability of an anarchist society to 'encourage the formation of a sense of justice comprehensive enough to include all members of the order'. In particular, they suggest that investing power in organic local groups, such as neighbourhoods and workplaces, may foster parochialism and that 'One of the virtues of less organic and more "alienated" political forms that are abstracted from everyday life – political parties, territorially defined representative bodies, and special-ized organizations for making and enforcing collective decisions – is that they plausibly encourage the members of society to regard one another as equal *citizens*, deserving of justice whatever the particulars of their aspirations, class situation, or group affiliations.' Cohen and Rogers produce no evidence to

suggest that political parties and the nation-state in themselves encourage individual members of society to regard one another as equal citizens, and I suspect that Chomsky himself would be rather sceptical, especially in view of his belief that political parties are essentially expressions of class interests (RP, p. 250). Certainly, his remarks on the Middle East would suggest some scepticism towards the Cohen–Rogers thesis. The Arab–Israeli conflict has, in Chomsky's view, been 'a perfect example of the utility of anarchism, really ... there couldn't be a more dramatic example of the absurdity of people organizing themselves into state systems for the purposes of mutual destruction' (LP, pp. 193f). 'There couldn't be a better argument for anarchism' (ibid., p. 195). The nation-state has tended to promote destructive rather than constructive tendencies in society.

It is also Chomsky's conviction that citizenship and other rights have been the product of popular struggle *against* authoritarianism, and can only be safeguarded by the willingness of ordinary people to defend their rights. The question is whether this willingness is best fostered by community and workplace organizations or by more alienated social forms.

68. To which the standard counterargument is that concentrating power into a coercive apparatus only strengthens ugly tendencies in human nature, and enables anti-social elements to create more harm than if power were dispersed throughout society.

69. FRS, pp. 154f.

70. PKF, p. 51.

71. RP, p. 260.

72. T T T, p. 241.

73. Transcript, 'Questions and Answers with Freshman Sociology', University of Wyoming at Laramie, 21 February 1989, p. 6.

7 Strategies

1. Mike Ferber, interviewed at the University of Maryland, New Hampshire, 28 April 1993.

2. Finkel, unpublished review commissioned by the *Nation* in Fall 1987, CA, pp. 464, 468.

3. CR, p. 50.

4. Ibid.

5. Chomsky, Paul Lauter and Florence Howe, 'Reflections on a Political Trial', in *Trials of the Resistance*, New York: New York Review of Books 1970, p. 91.

6. Chomsky, letter, *New York Review of Books*, 27 March 1969, p. 45.

7. LP, p. 86.

8. Ibid., p. 164.

9. Ibid., p. 188.

10. RP, p. 252.

11. We may note Chomsky's suggestion that a centralized standing army with high-technology weaponry might not be the most effective form of defence for the revolutionary territory: its best method of defence might be 'its political appeal to the working class in the countries that were part of the attack'. If a

conventional military force were needed for defence, 'we can be fairly sure that that would contribute to the possible failure or at least decline of the revolutionary force...' (RP, p. 253).

12. Fons Elders, ed., *Reflexive Water: The Basic Concerns of Mankind*, London: Souvenir Press 1974, p. 186.

13. LR, p. 80.

14. Elders, *Reflexive Water*, p. 186.

15. Ibid., p. 185.

16. Chomsky observes that 'just as people somehow can construct an extraordinarily rich system of knowledge of language on the basis of rather limited and degenerate experience, similarly, people develop implicit systems of moral evaluation, which are more or less uniform from person to person ... over quite a substantial range we tend to make comparable judgements, and we do it, it would appear, in quite intricate and delicate ways involving new cases and agreement often about new cases, and so on, and we do this on the basis of a very limited environmental context available to us' (LP, pp. 240f). Even at the outer limits, Chomsky finds evidence of an innate moral sense: even the Nazis did not boast that it was simply fun to kill Jews. They constructed elaborate justifications involving the defence of civilization and the highest values of culture, and so on – 'What they said was it's highly moral to kill Jews ...' (transcript, 'Beyond the Reagan Era: Questions and Answers', Boulder, Colorado, 24 January 1988, p. 8). On the modular view of the mind, the moral capacity is one of the many interacting higher order functions of the brain. For some comments on this subject, see Joshua Cohen and Carl Rogers, 'Knowledge, Morality and Hope: The Social Thought of Noam Chomsky', *New Left Review*, no. 187, May/June 1991.

17. CR, p. 32.

18. LP, p. 740.

19. Ibid., p. 748.

20. Ibid., p. 765.

21. Ibid., p. 766.

22. RP, p. 222.

23. Ibid., p. 223.

24. LP, p. 188.

25. Cited in FRS, p. 157.

26. Cited in FRS, p. 162.

27. Chomsky, 'The Soviet Union versus Socialism', *Our Generation*, No. 17:2, p. 50.

28. Ibid.

29. RP, pp. 221f.

30. Ibid., p. 239.

31. Ibid.

32. CR, p. 51.

33. LP, p. 176.

34. Ibid.

35. Ibid.

36. RP, p. 238.

37. PI, pp. 134f.

38. RP, p. 239.

39. Chomsky, 'Knowledge and Power: Intellectuals and the Welfare–Warfare State', in Priscilla Long, ed., *The New Left*, Boston: Porter Sargent 1970, p. 192.

40. PKF, p. 63.

41. CR, p. 31.

42. According to Chomsky, his own practice is to vote for the 'lower level things. Like it usually matters who's on the school committee. That you can have some influence over' (transcript, 'Creeping Fascism', New York, 26 April 1992, p. 14).

43. 'American Dissident', *New Statesman and Society*, 3 June 1994, p. 22.

44. LP, p. 763.

45. Transcript, 'Beyond the Reagan Era: Questions and Answers', p. 3.

46. TNCW, p. 5.

47. LP, p. 763.

48. PI, p. 116.

49. T T T, p. 221.

50. CT, p. 257.

51. T T T, p. 226. During the Vietnam War, Chomsky pointed out that the anti-war activities of US unions were poorly reported and commented, 'Whatever criticisms one may make of the unions, they are still the most democratic institutions in the United States, and might recover their position as a leading force for decency and social change' (RP, p. 238). Chomsky has made criticisms of the unions. John Horgan reports that during a day with Chomsky, 'I watched him tell a group at Harvard University how modern labor unions are more concerned with maintaining their own power than with representing workers. His audience? Union organizers, naturally. "I'm not interested in giving people A's for doing things right," Chomsky informs me later' ('Free Radical, A Word (or Two) about Linguist Noam Chomsky', *Scientific American*, May 1990, p. 16).

52. PI, p. 118.

53. LP, p. 600.

54. Ibid., p. 648.

55. Ibid.

56. Ibid., pp. 648f.

57. Ibid., p. 649.

58. APNM, pp. 309f.

59. T T T, p. 252.

60. Ibid.

61. Ibid.

62. BB, p. 43.

63. FRS, p. 80.

64. BB, p. 43.

65. APNM, p. 311.

66. Cited in Chomsky, 'The Menace of Liberal Scholarship', NYRB, 2 January 1969, p. 37.

67. Ibid.

68. The phrase is used in FRS, p. 73.

69. Chomsky, 'The Meaning of Vietnam', NYRB, 12 June 1975, pp. 31f.

70. T T T, p. 248.
71. Chomsky, *The Responsibility of Intellectuals*, New York: The Inter-University Committee for Debate on Foreign Policy nd, p. 12.
72. BG, 17 October 1965, p. 1.
73. Transcript, 'Noam Chomsky Meets the Washington Press', National Press Club, Washington, DC, 11 April 1989, p. 7.
74. Ibid.
75. The demonstration is discussed in 'On Resistance' in APNM.
76. Chomsky, 'Mayday: The Case for Civil Disobedience', NRYB, 17 June 1971, p. 19.
77. Benjamin Spock and Mary Morgan, *Spock on Spock: A Memoir of Growing Up with the Century*, New York: Pantheon 1989, p. 192.
78. Cited in Stewart Burns, *Social Movements of the 1960s: Searching for Democracy*, Boston: Twayne Publishers 1990, p. 113.
79. 'Hanscom Field Protesters Fined', *Boston Herald Traveler*, 25 August 1971.
80. NYT, 18 April 1972, p. 21.
81. '12 in Mass. Nix Tax in Viet Protest', *Boston Herald Traveler*, 10 April 1966.
82. BG, 25 March 1967, p. 5.
83. Interview, Kampf, 22 April 1993, MIT, Cambridge, MA. RESIST still exists, at the time of writing, as a socialist fund-raising body.
84. Louis Kampf, another key figure in RESIST, recalls that Chomsky was generally the 'voice of sweet reason' at RESIST meetings. He gives an example of Chomsky's creative approach to conflict resolution. At a RESIST meeting in New York, a hostile group of draft resisters came to demand control of RESIST's finances – apparently opposed to the 'diversion' of money to draft counselling and advisory groups. After some acrimonious debate, Chomsky suggested that a representative of the group come to the RESIST office in Boston the next day and examine their files, and decide which groups should not have been given money. When the files had been inspected, the resisters saw that money was being passed on to Black groups in Mississippi who wanted to develop anti-draft work and so on, and they withdrew their objections. Kampf notes that everyone else at the meeting was just angry – Chomsky was the only one with a constructive proposal (Kampf, interview, MIT, 22 April 1993).
85. Resist Newsletter no. 7, 8 March 1968. Given this kind of evidence, it does seem extraordinarily incompetent of the FBI not to have indicted Chomsky for his draft resistance support work.
86. Mike Ferber, interview, 23 April 1993.
87. Jonathan Allen, ed., *March 4: Scientists, Students and Society*, Cambridge, MA and London: MIT Press nd, p. xi.
88. Louis Kampf, interview, 22 April 1993.
89. RP, p. 229. For an account of the research strike, see Allen, *March 4*. Chomsky was, as one would expect, an important figure in the debate.
90. Chomsky and others, letter, NYRB, 4 October 1973.
91. APNM. This is the only dedication in any of Chomsky's political books, apart from MC, dedicated to the memory of Alex Carey, a fellow analyst of the propaganda system.

92. Robert L. Levey, 'The Revolt of Noam Chomsky', BG, 27 February 1968.

93. Transcript, 'Questions and Answers with Community Activists', University Common Ministry, Laramie, Wyoming, 20 February 1989, p. 1. The 'Tet Offensive' was a massive uprising by Vietnamese resistance forces on 31 January 1968, which persuaded large sections of the US corporate elite that the costs of subjugating Vietnam outweighed any possible future benefits and that the war should therefore be terminated.

94. TNCW, p. 150. Note that according to opinion polls, popular opposition to the war jumped dramatically during 1971. Chomsky cites Harris polls showing that 65 per cent of the population thought the war was immoral in October 1971, compared to 47 per cent in January. FRS, pp. 52f.

95. T T T, p. 246, citing John Rielly, *Foreign Policy*, Spring 1983.

96. Bill Moyers, ed., *A World of Ideas: Conversations with Thoughtful Men and Women about American Life Today and the Ideas Shaping Our Future*, New York: Doubleday, p. 56.

97. Chomsky, letter, *Commentary*, 48.4, October 1969, p. 20.

98. Moyers, *A World of Ideas*.

99. We may separate two dimensions of effectiveness (doubtless there are others): the effects on policy-makers and the effects on the general public. Chomsky noted, 'These do not necessarily correlate. For example, it is possible that some action might lead to a decision to restrict American military involvement, and at the same time to increased public support for this involvement' (FRS, p. 78). The priority in any conflict of goals, he argued, should be to restrict actual human suffering, rather than potential gains in the future.

100. T T T, p. 252. Chomsky suggests that civil disobedience must be preceded by work to prepare the ground in people's mind, to enable them to understand the action that is taken. It must also be preceded by a careful judgement of the likely consequences of the action proposed on suffering people and on the building of a movement for social change. It can easily be the case that an action which seems right in itself will entrench jingoistic attitudes. Furthermore, and this may well be a new contribution to the debate, Chomsky argues that if there has been no prior evaluation of the consequences of an action, then that action, however nonviolent in form, is profoundly immoral. Chomsky is insistent that the proper test is the likely consequences for other suffering people, not for oneself or one's conscience or one's relationship with God: 'if it is undertaken because it is one's duty to God, then its moral value is nil, maybe negative, on a par with investing in the stock market' (personal communication, 5 November 1993).

101. LP, p. 188.

102. Ibid.

103. Ibid., p. 447.

104. T T T, p. 249.

105. RP, p. 223.

106. Transcript, 'Pearl Harbor', 16 November 1991, p. 8. Chomsky is referring to the media in particular. For some reason this sentence is not included in the version of this transcript in CD.

107. Transcript, 'Roots of US Intervention', Lewis & Clark College, Portland, Oregon, 24 January 1989, pp. 11ff.

108. Ibid. p. 8.

109. RP, p. 204. The search for confrontations can also be a 'manipulative and coercive tactic', attempting to 'bring people to a certain degree of commitment, not by having it grow out of their own understanding and experience in the realities of the world, but as the result of a situation which often does not reflect the realities of society'.

110. Ibid., pp. 205f.

111. APNM, p. 315.

112. Ibid.

113. PI, p. 111.

114. LP, p. 763.

115. CR, p. 50.

116. T T T, p. 253.

117. Ibid., p. 251. The problems of separatism and subcultures arise particularly in relation to what could be called 'caste oppression'. Chomsky noted in 1971 that 'Many young radical activists tend to be somewhat contemptuous of "conscience radicalism" that grows out of concern for the suffering of others: Vietnamese, oppressed minorities, exploited workers, for example. They argue, perhaps with justice, that a serious and sustained commitment to radical social change will in general develop only as a response to "one's own oppression" – often, therefore, caste rather than class oppression, as women, students in authoritarian schools, victims of repressive life styles and cultural patterns, and so on.' Chomsky responded that much of this kind of oppression could be eliminated without challenging the distribution of power substantially: 'As a rational system of exploitation, capitalism has no inherent need for racist and sexist practices and should be quite ready to tolerate a levelling of all individuals into interchangeable parts of the production process or equivalent units of individual consumption, without invidious distinctions of race or sex or ethnic origin' (RP, p. 236). At the same time, he recognized that such struggles might not be easily contained by the authorities, and could lead on directly 'to a significant challenge to authoritarian institutions, to centralized control, and to coercive industrial as well as cultural patterns' (ibid., p. 241).

As far as 'acceptance without awareness of the doctrines of the state religion' goes, Chomsky has repeatedly remarked that popular opposition movements are often trapped within the propaganda framework, without being aware of their contribution to state propaganda. For example, Chomsky commented in 1988, 'take *New England Peacework*, which is a Quaker-based journal and a very good journal for the local peace movement. Right now it's devoting page after page to a debate which is essentially determined by the [government] Office of Public Diplomacy and they don't recognize it. There's a debate going on every issue, with half the issue devoted to it, about whether the left, so-called, took exactly the right position with regard to Cambodia in the late 1970s. The fact of the matter is that the left, such as it is, barely existing, took approximately the position that was taken by virtually all competent authorities, State Department intelligence, Cambodia scholarship, etc. At the same time the left and the peace movement were avoiding major atrocities elsewhere. Nevertheless, there's no debate going on about, let's say, the failure to respond to East Timor, or the failure of the left to respond to the US bombing of Cambodia in the early 1970s, which probably killed tens if not hundreds of thousands of people, or the failure of the left to respond to the growing and already quite horrifying crisis in Central America' (CD, p. 154). The agenda is set by elite interests and is followed unconsciously by the peace movement.

Chomsky acknowledges that the agenda is, to an extent, always set by those who hold power. The question is whether one is aware of one's position or not. In the case of Vietnam, Chomsky notes, 'There is no more striking example of the extraordinary power of the American system of thought control than the debate that took place over North Vietnamese aggression and whether the US had the right under international law to combat it in "collective self-defence against armed attack". Learned tomes were written advocating the opposing positions, and in less exalted terms, the debate was pursued in the public arena opened by the peace movement. The debate was a magnificent reflection of the system of thought control, as well as a contribution to it, since as long as the debate is focused on the question of whether the Vietnamese are guilty of aggression in Vietnam, there can be no discussion of whether the US aggression against South Vietnam was indeed what it plainly was.' Chomsky comments, 'As one who took part in this debate, with complete consciousness of what was happening, I can only report the recognition that opponents of state violence were trapped, enmeshed in a propaganda system of awesome effectiveness.... It was necessary, throughout, to enter the arena of debate on the terms set by the state and the elite opinion that loyally serves it, however one might understand that by doing so, one is making a further contribution to the system of indoctrination. The alternative is to tell the truth, which would be equivalent to speaking in some foreign tongue' (PE, pp. 36f).

118. LP, p. 173.

119. Transcript, interview by David Barsamian, Cambridge, MA, 18 November 1990, p. 8.

8   The Function of the University

1. Cited in FRS, p. 86. It should not be necessary to point out that the 'spiritual' element referred to has nothing to do with religious belief. Chomsky has made it clear that in his view, 'irrational belief is a dangerous phenomenon', and he tries consciously to avoid it. At the same time, he observes, 'I certainly recognize that it's a major phenomenon for people in general, and you can understand why it would be. It does, apparently, provide personal sustenance, but also bonds of association and solidarity and a means for expressing elements of one's personality that are often very valuable elements. To many people it does that. In my view, there's nothing wrong with that' (LP, p. 773).

2. FRS, p. 86.

3. Ibid., p. 87.

4. RP, p. 241.

5. Ibid., p. 199.

6. Ibid., p. 185.

7. Ibid.

8. Noam Chomsky's contribution to the MIT Commission on Education, 11 November 1969, original transcript, folder 'Noam Chomsky, 11 November 1969', box 2, Collection ACS6, the Institute Archives, MIT Libraries,

Cambridge, MA, pp. 2f. Chomsky notes that even after a very brief period of absorption by dominant institutions, young people tend to lose much of their independence of thought. In the late 1970s, for example, Chomsky's own university, the Massachusetts Institute of Technology, held a referendum on the proposal effectively to turn a third of the Nuclear Engineering Department over to the government of Iran for the training of a large number of Iranian nuclear engineers. Students were approximately four to one against such a move, while faculty members were approximately four to one in favour. Only a few years separated the two communities. Chomsky concluded that, somehow, 'incorporation into the institution has a tremendous effect on determining attitudes towards such matters, and the natural – I give my own value judgments, I can't help that – the natural and instinctive commitment to justice and truth and decency that one finds in a mind that hasn't yet been corrupted by its institutional commitments very rapidly attenuates when those institutional commitments take over' (LP, p. 249).

9. RP, p. 186.
10. FRS, p. 189, n. 16.
11. Ibid., p. 93.
12. George Kennan, quoted in NYT, 4 December 1968, cited in FRS, p. 93.
13. LP, p. 250.
14. Ibid., p. 161.
15. FRS, p. 14. Another weapon in the war on student activism has been the ideology of youthful hedonism. Chomsky observes, 'my feeling is that there has been a major effort, a concentrated major effort, especially directed against the youth, since about 1970, to try to convince people that they're hedonists. And narcissists.' While such tendencies always exist, other tendencies, emphasizing solidarity and compassion, and so on, also exist, but these have been driven out of popular culture by the cult of narcissism. Chomsky suggests that 'the net effect of this propaganda campaign has probably been to convince young people that if they are not narcissists, they're weird. So even if they have feelings of concern and sympathy, they had better suppress them because that's not what their generation is. And I think that has been successful.' The propaganda is presented as a description of the younger generation, but is, in Chomsky's view, 'an attempt at persuasion and inducement'. Not that there is necessarily a conscious conspiracy to implant these attitudes – like the Propaganda Model in general, this campaign is simply the outcome of shared interests converging in a certain direction (LP, p. 440).
16. LP, p. 535.
17. RP, p. 200.
18. Chomsky, interviewed by Alistair Clayre, 'Dissenting Intellectuals in America', *Listener*, 13 March 1969, p. 335.
19. Ibid.
20. RP, p. 201.
21. Noam Chomsky's contribution to the MIT Commission on Education, p. 5.
22. Ibid.
23. Ibid., pp. 5f.
24. Clayre, 'Dissenting Intellectuals in America', p. 336.
25. RP, p. 203.

26. Ibid., p. 204.
27. LP, p. 139.
28. Ibid., p. 247.
29. Ibid., p. 248.
30. Ibid.
31. Ibid., p. 139.
32. Ibid., p. 247.
33. FRS, p. 98.
34. CR, p. 47.
35. Ibid.
36. FRS, p. 101.
37. Ibid., p. 99.
38. PKF, p. 59.
39. FRS, p. 99.
40. Chomsky, 'The Faurisson Affair: His Right to Say it', *Nation*, 28 February 1981, p. 233.
41. References and rebuttals by Chomsky to some of the French attacks can be found in Chomsky's *Réponses inédites à mes détracteurs parisiens*, Paris: Spartacus nd. For a sample of the English-language campaign against Chomsky, see Lucy Davidovich, 'Lies about the Holocaust', *Commentary*, December 1980; Nadine Fresco, 'The Denial of the Dead', *Dissent*, Fall 1981, and Pierre Vidal-Naquet, 'Paper Eichmann?', *Democracy*, April 1981. Vidal-Naquet updated his essay with yet more falsehoods in 1987, which can be found in his *Assassins of Memory: Essays on the Denial of the Holocaust*, New York: Columbia University Press 1992, pp. 72ff. For exchanges in the British press, see the *Times Higher Education Supplement*, 7 November 1980; 12 December 1980; 6 March 1981; 27 March 1981; and in the *New Statesman*, 10 April 1981; 17 July 1981; 14 August 1981; 11 September 1981. For Chomsky's response to Davidovich et al., see AC, Chapter 6; NI, Appendix V, section 5; MC, Chapter 6, section 6.2.8. The record is reviewed by Christopher Hitchens, in *Grand Street*, Autumn 1985 (reprinted in *Prepared for the Worst*, London: Hogarth Press 1990, pp. 68–72), and by Brian Morton, 'Chomsky Then and Now', *Nation*, 7 May 1988.
42. Cited in LP, p. 316.
43. Martin Peretz, 'Washington Diarist', *The New Republic*, 3 January 1981.
44. Werner Cohn, *The Hidden Alliances of Noam Chomsky*, New York: Americans for a Safe Israel 1988, pp. 1, 33. When a restatement of Cohn's case appeared in a Canadian Jewish journal, Chomsky responded in a letter (reproduced below). His letter is typically restrained and ironic, a difficult feat under the circumstances.

Editor
Outlook
6184 Ash St., #3
Vancouver BC V5Z3G9

June 1, 1989

Dear Sir:

Observing the performances of Werner Cohn is a curious experience. An occasional phrase has a relation to reality, but it takes an effort to imagine what may lie behind the discourse.

In *Outlook*, May, Cohn presents a fevered account of a second existence that he has conjured up for me, in France, where I pursue my secret life as a neo-Nazi, hoping that no one outside of Paris will notice. He gives two proofs. The first is what he calls his 'most crucial source': 'a joint article by Chomsky and his friend Pierre Guillaume, "Une mise au point",' in Guillaume's book *Droit et Histoire*. The second is that 'Chomsky could have published the French version of his *Political Economy of Human Rights* (written with Edward Herman) with a commercial publisher, but, in order to show solidarity with VT [*Vieille Taupe*], Chomsky insisted on publishing the book with it.'

Since I never wrote a 'joint article' with Guillaume, I was curious, and after a search, found the book in question. Indeed, it contains the chapter 'Une mise au point', written in first-person singular by Guillaume, with no hint of any collaboration with me. I am mentioned in it, and fragments of a letter of mine are quoted in which I discuss changes in the U.S. intellectual climate since the 1960s (with typical veracity, Cohn describes this as my 'comments on Guillaume's version of the Chomsky–VT relationship', which is nowhere mentioned). By Cohn's intriguing logic, I am also the co-author of his various diatribes – perhaps in my third life, which he will expose in the next instalment.

Cohn asserts that I found 'nothing to correct in Guillaume's' account. He has not the slightest idea what my reaction to the article is. Recall that this 'joint article' is his 'crucial source.'

Let us turn to his second decisive piece of evidence. When I learned of Cohn's fairy tales about the French translation of the book of Herman and mine, I was intrigued. Of course, it is obvious even without further inquiry that his claims are outlandish. There is no possible way that he could know of my intentions (and those of my co-author, Edward Herman, who somehow seems to have disappeared from the tale; perhaps I invented him as a cover). But we need not speculate on Cohn's mystical ability to read minds.

Standard procedure is to leave translations in the hands of the publisher. I make no attempt to keep track of the innumerable translations of books of mine in foreign languages. Curious about Cohn's allegations, I contacted the publisher, who checked their files and located the contract for the French translation – with Albin-Michel, a mainstream commercial publisher, to my knowledge. They did not know whether the translation had appeared, never having received a copy. The same is true of my co-author and of me.

Note that these are the examples that Cohn selects as the decisive proof of his theses. A rational person will draw the obvious conclusions about the rest.

Cohn makes two further claims. He says that in defending the right of freedom of expression in the case of Robert Faurisson, I have always 'indicated' that my ' "diametrically opposed" view was more a matter of opinion than of scientific knowledge' (a statement that he appears to attribute to Guillaume); and I have always defended freedom of expression 'in terms that are absolutely incapable of hurting Faurrison [sic].' Consider these allegations.

In Cohn's 'crucial source,' cited above, Guillaume quotes my statement that 'there are no rational grounds that allow any doubt about the existence of gas chambers.' Thus Cohn is refuted by his own 'crucial source.' In my own writings, from the earliest until the present, the conclusions of standard

Holocaust studies are taken simply as established fact, as Cohn knows perfectly well. In the introduction to my first collection of political essays, 20 years ago, I add that we have lost our humanity if we are even willing to enter into debate over the Nazi crimes with those who deny or defend them. The only particle of truth in Cohn's absurd charge is that I never use the phrase 'scientific knowledge' in dealing with any questions of history; my book with Herman, for example, which is neither science nor mere opinion.

Turning to Cohn's second point, it is taken for granted by civil libertarians that defense of freedom of expression is independent of the views expressed. Thus when I sign petitions (and go far beyond that) in the case of Soviet dissidents, some of whom have absolutely horrendous views, I never allude to this fact in the slightest way. In signing petitions supporting Salman Rushdie, I make no comment about whether his book slanders Muslims. I have no doubt that this practice enrages mullahs in Qom and commissars in the Kremlin as much as it does Werner Cohn, and for the same reasons. Where no civil liberties issues arise, I have been quite explicit about the fact that the views of Faurisson and others are diametrically opposed to my own firm conclusions about the facts, as in the statement quoted in Cohn's 'crucial source.'

The remainder of Cohn's ranting has to do with the alleged views of others, and fanciful comments about France. His conceptions on these matters are, naturally, of no concern to me.

That Cohn is a pathological liar is demonstrated by the very examples that he selects. Knowing nothing about him, and caring less, I am in no position to comment further on what may lie behind this odd and pathetic behavior.

Sincerely yours,

Noam Chomsky

45. Brian Morton, 'Chomsky, Then and Now', *Nation*, 7 May 1988, p. 648.

46. APNM, p. 11.

47. PME, pp. 57f.

48. AWWA, p. 239.

49. Cited in Jay Parini, 'Noam is an Island', *Mother Jones*, October 1988, pp. 40f. The 'Stalinist doctrine' in question is the idea, associated with Zhdanov, that objectionable ideas should be suppressed by the state, something shared with fascist ideology, and by those who supported the decision against Faurisson.

50. CD, p. 350. Chomsky points out that the gypsies continue to suffer persecution on a grand scale.

51. Chomsky's contribution to the MIT Commission on Education, p. 10.

52. Israel Shenker, 'A Linguistics Expert Believes that Academics Should also be Activists', NYT, 27 October 1968, p. 64.

53. Clayre, 'Dissenting Intellectuals', pp. 335ff.

54. Louis Kampf, interview, MIT, 22 April 1993.

55. Norbert Hornstein, telephone interview, 22 April 1993.

56. Ibid. Hornstein also comments, 'Chomsky, I think, raised the footnote into a level of high art, and I think for the right reasons.'

57. Such activities were sometimes described by uncomprehending academics as 'off campus riots', preferable to on-campus rioting. (FRS, p. 93).

58. FRS, p. 87.
59. Chomsky, 'Knowledge and Power', in Priscilla Long, ed., *The New Left*, Boston: Porter Sargent 1970, p. 190.
60. RP, p. 201.
61. Ibid. For Chomsky, repression was not the only block to more objective and serious work. 'It should be recognized that, in any field, there is resistance to innovation on the part of those who have achieved a certain status and prestige. This natural resistance, easy to document, provides a kind of base line in terms of which one must assess the actual political repression that exists in the universities' (RP, p. 229).
62. Clayre, 'Dissenting Intellectuals', p. 334.
63. Ibid., p. 336.
64. Ibid., p. 334. There were, however, complaints from alumni and fellow staff members, and petty manoeuvrings. No department would give credits for the courses Kampf and Chomsky gave, which meant that students would have to 'audit' them as extras, in addition to their other course work.
65. Fons Elders, ed., *Reflexive Water: The Basic Concerns of Mankind*, London: Souvenir Press 1974, p. 194.
66. Ibid., pp. 194ff.
67. Transcript, 'International Terrorism: The Problem and the Remedy', Community Church of Boston, 8 February 1987, p. 7.
68. Ibid.
69. Chomsky, *The Responsibility of Intellectuals*, New York: The Inter-University Committee for Debate on Foreign Policy nd, p. 17.
70. Shenker, 'A Linguist Expert'.
71. Ibid.
72. LP, p. 98.
73. Ibid., pp. 98f.
74. Parini, 'Noam is an Island', p. 38.
75. LP, p. 396.
76. Chomsky's contribution to the MIT Commission on Education, pp. 63ff.
77. Ibid., p. 70.
78. Ibid.
79. Ibid., p. 69.
80. FRS, p. 100.
81. RP, p. 234.
82. FRS, p. 90.
83. Chomsky, 'The Menace of Liberal Scholarship', p. 38.
84. Boyd Tonkin, 'Making a Difference', *City Limits* (London), 26 January–2 February 1989, p. 58.
85. Chomsky, 'Towards a Humanistic Conception of Education', in Walter Feinberg and Henry Rosemount, eds., *Work, Technology, and Education: Dissenting Essays in the Intellectual Foundations of American Education*, Chicago and London: University of Illinois Press 1975, p. 219.
86. Ibid.
87. Note that Chomsky does not claim that his political writings are 'scientific'. He describes his political writings as 'neither science nor mere opinion'. (See p. 201, n. 44 above.)

88. APNM, p. 253.
89. CR, p. 30.
90. See p. 86.
91. Transcript, 'Questions and Answers with Freshman Sociology', University of Wyoming at Laramie, 21 February 1989, p. 2.
92. RP, p. 228.
93. Cited in FRS, p. 102. The Port Huron Statement has recently been republished (Chicago: Charles H. Kerr Publishing Company 1990).
94. CR, p. viii.
95. Chomsky, 'Knowledge and Power', in Long, *The New Left*, p. 193.
96. Ibid.
97. Shenker, 'A Linguist Expert', p. 64.
98. Cited in Dorothy Nelkin, *The University and Military Research: Moral Politics at MIT*, Ithaca and London: Cornell University Press 1972, p. 163.

9   The Responsibility of Intellectuals

1. Gwyn Williams, 'Walking Naked', *New Society*, 6 November 1969, reproduced in CA p. 79.
2. APNM, p. 257.
3. Ibid., p. 256.
4. TNCW, p. 8.
5. Ibid., pp. 8f.
6. Ibid., p. 9, emphasis added.
7. T T T, p. 2. When such remarks are passed through the distorting prism of US ideology, we find some strange responses emerging. Thus the respected commentator Christopher Coker asks rhetorically of Chomsky's work, 'Can all the terror of the Third World be laid entirely at the door of the United States?' (Christopher Coker, 'The Mandarin and the Commissar: The Political Thought of Noam Chomsky', in Sohan and Celia Modgil, eds., *Noam Chomsky, Consensus and Controversy*, Lewes: The Falmer Press 1987, p. 273).
8. LP, p. 369.
9. Ibid., p. 370.
10. Ibid., pp. 371f. He adds, 'These are, of course, transitory and sometimes personal judgments.'
11. Ibid., pp. 766f.
12. Ibid., pp. 178f.
13. Ibid., p. 286.
14. Richard Higgins, BG, 4 September 1988, p. 73.
15. PI, p. 51.
16. Ibid.
17. LP, p. 446.
18. *Facts on File Yearbook 1973: The Index of World Events*, New York: Facts on File Inc. 1974, p. 536. According to Chomsky, his political writings were banned in the Soviet Union, and Soviet advisers attempted to persuade Third World countries to follow suit (PE, p. 152).
19. Tape, 'Media, Propaganda and Democracy', Toronto, November 1988, tape 2, side B. This is, to my knowledge, the only time Chomsky has publicly

drawn attention to this aspect of his activism, though one can find several letters from him on behalf of people in the Eastern bloc in the *New York Review of Books*, and the *New York Times*. For example, on 28 November 1974 and again on 11 December 1975, Chomsky wrote to the NYRB on behalf of Dr Karel Curlik, a Czech academic who had worked with Chomsky at MIT, and who was suffering some persecution. On 18 February 1982, we find a letter in the NYRB supporting Andrzej Grzegorczyk, a Polish logician who had written that international law should encourage people to help others in time of disaster and had suffered for his temerity.

20. LP, p. 369.

21. Ibid.

22. Chomsky, letter, 'Vietnam, the Cold War and Other Matters', *Commentary*, 48, 4 October 1969, p. 20. The Catonsville Nine and the Milwaukee Fourteen were groups of anti-war protesters who burned draft board files in protest against the Vietnam War.

23. RP, p. 205.

24. TNCW, p. 67.

25. CR, p. 188.

26. Ibid.

27. 501, p. 109.

28. For some comments on these topics, which take up a growing share of Chomsky's writings, see 501, Chapter 4.

29. For example, see Chomsky's discussion of B.F. Skinner's behaviourism and Robert Herrnstein's justification for a stable hereditary meritocracy in 'Psychology and Ideology', in FRS, and his analysis of apologetics for inequality in 'Equality: Language Development, Human Intelligence, and Social Organization', in CR.

30. PI, p. 53.

31. APNM, p. 62.

32. LP, p. 659.

33. Ibid., p. 372.

34. Ibid., p. 595.

35. Chomsky later described one of the main arguments in APNM as the proposition that 'Bolshevism and American liberalism are basically manifestations of the same thing.' He conceded that he might not have presented the argument clearly enough: 'Now, that was kind of abstract and I don't think that many people knew what I was talking about, really, and I probably didn't do it right and so on, and I'd agree with all that . . .' (LP, p. 181).

36. Cited in APNM, p. 62.

37. Ibid. Bell's most important book, *The End of Ideology*, is discussed at length in APNM.

38. LP, p. 184.

39. Ibid., p. 599.

40. TNCW, p. 63 (emphasis in original). Chomsky's authority is Maurice Brinton, in *The Bolsheviks and Workers' Control*, London: Solidarity 1972. Brinton refers to V.I. Lenin, *Selected Works*, vol. VII, pp. 332–3, 340–42.

41. Cited in TNCW, p. 64.

42. Ibid.

43. Chomsky, 'Knowledge and Power: Intellectuals in the Welfare–Warfare

State', in Priscilla Long, ed., *The New Left: A Collection of Essays*, Boston: Porter Sargent 1970, pp. 175ff.

44. CR, pp. 20, 21.

45. *Guardian* (London), 23 November 1992, G2, p. 11.

46. LP, p. 598.

47. Chomsky comments, 'My suspicion is that plenty of people in the crafts, or mechanics probably do as much if not more intellectual work as people in universities.' Much of the work done in universities is, in his view, 'clerical work', and clerical work is no more difficult than repairing car engines. 'In fact,' Chomsky points out, 'I think the opposite. I can *do* clerical work, but I can never figure out how to fix an automobile engine' (Tape, 'At the Rowe Centre', Rowe, Massachusetts, 15–16 April 1989, tape 5, side A).

48. Ibid.

49. Ibid. Chomsky wrote in 1980 that French intellectual life had been turned into something 'cheap and meretricious' by the 'star' system: 'Thus we go from one absurdity to another – Stalinism, existentialism, structuralism, Lacan, Derrida – some of them obscene (Stalinism), some simply infantile and ridiculous (Lacan and Derrida). What is striking, however, is the pomposity and self-importance, at each stage' (letter to C.P. Otero, 30 June 1980, cited in LP, p. 311). Chomsky also refers to the 'peculiar and Dadaist character of certain currents of intellectual life in postwar France which turns rational discourse into a bizarre and incomprehensible pastime' (LP, p. 309).

Chomsky commented in 1989, 'In the case of Lacan, for example, it's going to sound unkind – my frank opinion is that he was a conscious charlatan, and was simply playing games with the Paris intellectual community to see how much absurdity he could produce and still be taken seriously. I mean that quite literally. I knew him' ('Noam Chomsky: an Interview', *Radical Philosophy*, August 1989, p. 32).

As for Foucault, whom he had debated, Chomsky told James Miller, 'I'd never met anyone who was so totally amoral.... Usually when you talk to someone, you take for granted that you share some moral territory. Usually what you find is self-justification in terms of shared moral criteria; in that case, you can have an argument, you can pursue it, you can find out what's right and what's wrong about the position. With him, though, I felt like I was talking to someone who didn't inhabit the same moral universe. I mean, I liked him personally. It's just that I couldn't make sense of him. It's as if he was from a different species or something' (James Miller, *The Passion of Michel Foucault*, New York: Simon & Schuster 1993, pp. 201, 203).

However, Chomsky concedes that some important work has been done within the 'postmodernist' framework. It is difficult to tease out the simple interesting points, 'but there are things there, there's even progress there'. He suggests that one of the reasons for the needless complexity of terminology is 'that it's extremely hard to have good ideas. There are very few of them around.' In the sciences, it is sometimes possible, generally on a small scale. 'Outside the natural sciences,' Chomsky suggests, 'it's extremely hard to do even *that*. There just isn't that much that's complicated that's at all understood outside of the core natural sciences. I mean, everything else is either too hard for us to understand, or pretty easy.' This leads some to mask the shallowness of their ideas in complex, perhaps meaningless terminology. Chomsky claims not to understand the term 'deconstruction' (CD, p. 362) (or indeed, in another framework, 'dialectical materialism'). He offers two possible explanations: 'Either I'm missing a gene, like tone-deafness, which is conceivable, or it's a way of disguising maybe interesting ideas in an incomprehensible framework for reasons which ultimately turn out to be careerist' (Tape, 'Dissidence in the US', *Z magazine*, side A).

50. Transcript, 'Questions and Answers with Community Activists', University Common Ministry, Laramie, Wyoming, 20 February 1989, p. 1.

51. 'There is, after all, a social requirement to prevent heresy. Institutions have to defend themselves somehow. If you can't do it by burning people at the stake or sending them to inquisitions, you have to find other ways' (Transcript, 'Questions and Answers with Community Activists', p. 2). Chomsky suggests that 'In this respect there's been a very sharp decline since the Middle Ages.' 'Medieval theology was an honest intellectual atmosphere: if people had heretical arguments you had to pay attention to them, think about them, find answers to them. We've degenerated far below that in modern culture.' Now, all that is required is to identify arguments as heretical – 'and that's the end of the discussion': 'this is another sign of the dramatic decline of the intelligentsia as they become the commissars for external power, state or private' (LP, p. 682).

52. LP, p. 599.

53. Ibid., p. 765.

54. Ibid., p. 674.

55. Ibid., pp. 73fn.

56. Bruce Andrews, *Public Constraint and American Policy in Vietnam*, Sage Publications, International Studies Series, vol. 4, 1976, cited in TNCW, p. 89.

57. T T T, p. 246, citing figures from John Rielly, *Foreign Policy*, Spring 1983, and Charles Kadushin, *The American Intellectual Elite*, Boston: Little, Brown Co. 1974. We should note that this greater scepticism and distrust need not lead in the direction of socialist politics. It is also the basis for fascists and other charismatics to mobilize mass support. 'It would be romantic to suppose that the lesser level of indoctrination on the part of the less educated part of the population leads to some sort of revolutionary spirit or progressive impulse or whatever' (LP, p. 765).

58. Ibid.

59. Cited in RP, p. 162.

60. Cited in RP, p. 161. One of the Trilateral analysts recalls, perhaps with a trace of nostalgia, that before the rabble became agitated, 'Truman had been able to govern the country with the cooperation of a relatively small number of Wall Street lawyers and bankers' (Samuel Huntington, cited in TNCW, p. 68).

61. Cited in DD, p. 358.

62. LP, p. 362.

63. Ibid.

64. CR, p. 52.

65. T T T, p. 224.

66. Transcript, 'Beyond the Reagan Era: Questions and Answers', Boulder, Colorado, 24 January 1988, p. 3.

67. There are other contrasts between these two periods: 'Kennedy's brinkmanship and nuclear adventurism aroused much admiration, while Reagan's rhetoric – which [fell] far short of Kennedy's actions – has, in contrast, provided a major impetus for an international disarmament movement' (T T T, p. 245). On the popular side of history, Chomsky points out that the solidarity movements of the 1980s went far beyond 'signing statements or even spending a night in jail, as Thoreau did': 'For the first time ever, thousands of North Americans participated directly, actually involved themselves in the lives and the suffering of the usual victims.' Nothing of this kind happened during the Indochina Wars (Transcript, 'Unfinished Business: The US and Central America', San Francisco, 17 March 1991, p. 1).

68. Transcript, 'Creeping Fascism', 26 April 1992, p. 15.

69. Cited in 501, p. 94.

70. APNM, p. 249.

71. Chomsky, 'Introduction', *The Conspiracy*, New York: Dell Publishing Company 1969, p. 19.

72. CR, p. 136.

73. According to the publishing house Pantheon Books, *American Power and the New Mandarins*, Chomsky's first book, sold 43,000 copies in the United States when it was published in 1969. *The Chomsky Reader*, published in 1987, sold 55,000 copies in the United States.

74. Herman reports an amusing instance: 'In a review of *The Chomsky Reader* in the *Los Angeles Times Book Review*, 30 August 1987, Steve Wasserman says that "Quite simply, Chomsky has become a pariah". Chomsky informs me that Wasserman, in his capacity of editor of the *Los Angeles Times*'s "Opinion", frequently solicited Chomsky to contribute to Opinion in the early 1980s, which was a new development, at a time when, according to Wasserman, Chomsky had become a pariah' (CA, p. 610, n. 6).

75. LP, p. 685.

76. Ibid., p. 737.

77. Bill Moyers, ed., *A World of Ideas: Conversations with Thoughtful Men and Women about American Life Today and the Ideas Shaping our Future*, New York: Doubleday 1989, p. 57. There are many intriguing parallels between Chomsky's political and linguistic careers. One of them is the way he has had to soften his message in different areas. John Lyons reports: 'Chomsky tells me that he is not himself aware of any change in his attitude over the years with respect to the role of simplicity measures and intuition. He thinks that some confusion may have been caused by the fact that *Syntactic Structures* was "a rather watered-down version of earlier work (at that time unpublished)" and that, for this reason, it "emphasized weak rather than strong generative capacity".' Lyons comments, 'One can only wonder whether Chomsky's work would have had the effect that it did within linguistics if *Syntactic Structures* had not been "watered down"' (cited in Dell Hymes, 'Review of Lyons', reproduced in CA, pp. 127f).

78. Boyd Tonkin, 'Making a Difference', *City Limits* (London), 26 January–2 February 1989.

79. LP, p. 688.

80. PE, p. 37. See also pp. 197f, n. 117.

81. Chomsky makes some terminological compromises in his writings, for

example his adoption of conventional usage in referring to the United States as 'America', or his use of the common phrase 'the Arab world' (see CD, p. 258). One interesting 'compromise' concerns the general framework of discussion of foreign policy in terms of 'us' and 'them'. This glosses over the fact that there are certain important disparities among 'us', and conceals the way that the costs and benefits of empire are distributed among different groups in society: 'it is far from clear that "we" benefit materially from the national commitment to "maintain this position of disparity" by force, a commitment that entails global confrontation with the constant threat of nuclear war, an economy driven by military production, loss of jobs to regions where US-supported thugs ensure low wages and miserable living standards, almost 60,000 soldiers killed in an attempt to enforce "our" will in Indochina, and so on' (T T T, p. 49). 'The idea that "we" confront "them" is a staple of the ideological system, one that has as much merit as the tenets of other religious cults. With this cautionary note, I will nevertheless continue to use these misleading formulations, thus adopting – with some misgivings – one of the conventional devices employed to prevent understanding of the world in which we live' (ibid.). One reason for adopting this framework is to convey the understanding that 'we', the people, have a responsibility for what is done to 'them' by our governments.

Chomsky also tends to prefer 'ruling elites' over 'ruling classes' (although he does not avoid the latter completely). He explains, 'As soon as you say the word *class*, everybody falls down dead. They think, "There's some Marxist raving again."' He also points out that there is a problem in trying to allocate Harvard professors and the editors of the *New York Times* to the ruling *class*. It is more accurate to speak of 'elites' or 'dominant sectors' or 'the establishment' (PFRM, pp. 69f).

Chomsky notes that it is difficult to 'find a way between intelligibility and avoidance of unwanted innuendo and propaganda' (personal communication, 12 October 1992).

82. TNCW, p. 89.
83. CR, p. 33.
84. Ibid., p. 36.
85. LP, p. 728.
86. NI, p. 379, n. 59.
87. LP, p. 370. For example, if people with privilege participate in civil disobedience, the danger of state violence to crush protest 'is considerably lessened (in the US; not everywhere), and the effectiveness of the action may also be enhanced.'
88. Tape, 'Thinking in the US', Z *magazine*, 1993, side B.
89. Robert Makin, 'Noam Chomsky', *Downtown* (New York), No. 329, 29 September–13 October 1993, p. 12.
90. Tape, 'Thinking in the US', side B.
91. LP, p. 775.
92. Tape, 'Violence and Freedom', CSU/Fort Collins, CO, 10 April 1990, tape 4, side B. Chomsky names three of the others who are willing to speak to groups: John Stockwell, Alex Cockburn and Dan Ellsberg.
93. MCNCM, p. 21. For a more nuanced view of postmodernism, see pp. 206f, n. 49.
94. LP, p. 774.

95. Ibid.
96. John Horgan, 'Free Radical: A Word (or Two) about Linguist Noam Chomsky', *Scientific American*, May 1990, p. 17.
97. LP, p. 389.
98. CR, pp. 18f.
99. LP, p. 389.
100. Ibid., p. 779. I am in no position to evaluate this suggestion.
101. MCNCM, p. 203.
102. Norbert Hornstein, telephone interview, 22 April 1993. Falk notes that, 'Every other prominent commentator on public affairs, whether considered as comparison or contrast with Chomsky, has relied upon the quality of his reasoning or on the mobilizing force of moral argumentation without attempting to contest the experts at the level of factual inference. Especially when dealing with contemporary history (Vietnam, Palestinian–Israeli conflict, Central America), Chomsky's critical claim rests on his superior mastery of the facts from which his political interpretation and moral condemnation flows almost inevitably' (CA, p. 584). In other words, Chomsky sticks to reality. Earlier we noted his dislike of the concept of 'radical scholarship' and his preference for 'objective scholarship'. 'Objective scholarship' could be translated as 'telling the truth'.

Underneath this terminological quibble, there may be some intriguing issues. One of Orwell's themes was the growing tendency in much of modern political discourse to denigrate the very idea of objectivity. A common view is that there is no such thing as objectivity, only different interpretations based on one's personal commitments. The implication is that one does not choose between two analyses of a particular event on the basis of the quality of the evidence presented, but on the basis of the alignment of the authors and the political objective of the argument. For those on the Left, the retreat to 'radicalism' may, in this case, be a tacit admission that 'reality' favours the dominant ideology, that the 'facts' substantiate the official version of events, and therefore the only response is to replace 'objectivity' with 'radicalism'.

To speculate further, this line of thought may be related, rightly or wrongly, to a growing sense of scepticism about 'objective reality' itself. Chomsky has indicated that on this issue he tends to follow those 'seventeenth-century thinkers who reacted to the skeptical crisis of the times by recognizing that there are no absolutely certain grounds for knowledge, but that we do, nevertheless, have ways to gain a reliable understanding of the world and to improve that understanding and to apply it – essentially the position of the working scientist today'. 'Similarly, in normal life a reasonable person relies on the natural beliefs of common sense while recognizing that they may be parochial or misguided, and hoping to refine or alter them as understanding progresses' (DD, p. 351). On the political level, one of Chomsky's contributions may be precisely to reaffirm the importance of rationality and objectivity as the basis of debate. If so, he has done this as much by example as by explicit argument.

Chomsky's 'uninflected rationalism', as one commentator has described it, is best summed up in his comment, 'There are no arguments that I know of for irrationality' (CR, p. 22).
103. Horgan, 'Free Radical', p. 17. This is a considerable understatement according to Chomsky (personal communication, 16 February 1995).

104. According to Alexander Cockburn, CD, p. x.
105. LP, p. 775.
106. Mike Ferber, interview, 27 April 1993.
107. RP, p. 235.
108. Chomsky discusses this possibility with reference to the US Anti-Ballistic Missile system. RP, pp. 202f.
109. RP, p. 243.
110. Ibid., p. 235.
111. Chomsky, 'The Menace of Liberal Scholarship', NYRB, 2 January 1969, p. 38. On the issue of sectarianism, in 1971, Chomsky urged 'sympathetic and fraternal disagreement and, where possible, cooperation among those who have rather different ideas about what are, after all, rather obscure and poorly understood matters' (RP, p. 239).
112. LP, p. 774. It is not difficult to detect the major intellectual influences in Chomsky's writings. His references to Rocker, Bakunin and the anarchist milieu of New York in the 1940s form one part of his background. Bertrand Russell is clearly a very important figure. Chomsky has also acknowledged the influence of Dwight MacDonald (in his anarcho-pacifist period): 'In 1945–46 Dwight MacDonald's *Politics* came out, which was a real eye opener' (CD, p. 360). The extent of MacDonald's influence may be judged by examination of his *The Responsibility of Peoples, and Other Essays in Political Criticism*, London: Victor Gollancz 1957. Particularly relevant are 'The Responsibility of Intellectuals' and 'Totalitarian Liberalism'. Chomsky also began reading I.F. Stone very early on, in 1940. Stone was then a reporter on the Philadelphia *Record*, Philadelphia of course being Chomsky's home town. Naturally, Chomsky subscribed to the famous *Weekly* from the beginning in January 1953 (Chomsky, interview, MIT, 25 March 1993). There are many other influences which can be detected. One of the most important intellectual figures in Chomsky's life is something of a mystery – Zellig Harris, Chomsky's mentor at university, did not publish on political issues and so we cannot trace the effect of his thought on Chomsky.
113. Cited in FRS, p. 172.
114. LP, p. 773.
115. DD, p. 401.
116. APNM, p. 251.
117. LP, p. 138.
118. Chomsky, 'Knowledge and Power', in Long, *The New Left*, pp. 175ff.
119. Cited in Desmond Christy, 'Gazzetta', London *Guardian*, 7 January 1993, G2, p. 5.
120. Falk, 'Letters from Prison – American Style: the political vision and practice of Noam Chomsky', in CA, p. 579.
121. Parini, 'Noam is an Island', p. 41.

Bibliography

Political Books by Noam Chomsky

American Power and the New Mandarins, Harmondsworth: Penguin Books 1971, originally published 1969.

At War With Asia, London: Fontana/Collins 1971.

Problems of Knowledge and Freedom, London: Barrie and Jenkins 1972.

For Reasons of State, London: Fontana/Collins 1973.

The Backroom Boys, London: Fontana/Collins 1973.

Peace in the Middle East? Reflections on Justice and Nationhood, New York: Pantheon 1974.

'Human Rights' and American Foreign Policy, Nottingham: Spokesman 1978.

Language and Responsibility, Based on Conversations with Mitsou Ronat, translated by John Viertel, Hassocks: Harvester Press 1979.

Radical Priorities, ed. C.P. Otero, Montreal: Black Rose Books 1981.

Towards a New Cold War: Essays on the Current Crisis and How We Got There, London: Sinclair Browne 1982.

The Fateful Triangle: The United States, Israel and the Palestinians, London: Pluto 1983.

Réponses inédites à mes détracteurs parisiens, Paris: Spartacus nd [1983?].

Turning the Tide: US Intervention in Central America and the Struggle for Peace, London: Pluto 1985.

Pirates and Emperors: International Terrorism in the Real World, Montreal: Black Rose Books 1987.

On Power and Ideology: The Managua Lectures, Boston: South End Press 1987.

The Chomsky Reader, ed. James Peck, London: Serpent's Tail 1987.

The Culture of Terrorism, London: Pluto 1988.

Language and Politics, ed. C.P. Otero, Montreal: Black Rose Books 1988.

Necessary Illusions: Thought Control in Democratic Societies, London: Pluto 1989.

Deterring Democracy, London: Verso 1991.

Chronicles of Dissent, ed. David Barsamian, Monroe: Common Courage Press/Edinburgh: AK Press 1992 (incorporates Chomsky interviews in Barsamian's *Stenographers to Power*, Common Courage 1992).

What Uncle Sam Really Wants, eds. Arthur Naiman and Sandy Nieman, Berkeley: Odonian Press 1992.
Rethinking Camelot: JFK, the Vietnam War, and US Political Culture, Boston: South End Press 1993.
Letters from Lexington: Reflections on Propaganda, Monroe: Common Courage Press/Edinburgh: AK Press 1993.
Year 501: The Conquest Continues, Boston: South End Press 1993.
The Prosperous Few and the Restless Many, ed. David Barsamian, Berkeley: Odonian Press 1993.
World Order and Its Rules: Variations on Some Themes, Belfast: West Belfast Economic Forum and the Centre for Research and Documentation 1993.
Manufacturing Consent: Noam Chomsky and the Media, The Companion Book to the Award-winning Film by Peter Wintonick and Mark Achbar, ed. Mark Achbar, Montreal: Black Rose Books 1994.
Keeping the Rabble in Line, ed. David Barsamian, Monroe: Common Courage Press 1994.
World Orders, Old and New, London: Pluto 1994.

I have listed the editions that I have referred to in the text rather than the original US editions. Note that the original edition of *For Reasons of State* in the United States contained the material released separately in Britain as *The Backroom Boys*. Note also that there are important revised editions of *Radical Priorities* (Black Rose 1984), *Turning the Tide* (Black Rose 1987) and *Deterring Democracy* (Vintage 1992). Two of Chomsky's *Open Magazine* pamphlets on the Gulf War are collected in Greg Ruggiero and Stuart Sahuka, *Open Fire: The Open Magazine Pamphlet Series Anthology*, New York: New Press 1993. There is also a curious book, mainly written by Michael Albert and Robin Hahnel, entitled *Liberating Theory* (Boston: South End Press 1986). Chomsky is listed as one of the seven co-authors of the book, but his influence is clearly muted.

With Edward Herman

Noam Chomsky and Edward Herman, *The Washington Connection and Third World Fascism (The Political Economy of Human Rights: Volume 1)*, Montreal: Black Rose Books 1979.
Noam Chomsky and Edward Herman, *After the Cataclysm: Postwar Indochina & the Reconstruction of Imperial Ideology (The Political Economy of Human Rights: Volume II)*, Nottingham: Spokesman 1979.
Edward Herman and Noam Chomsky, *Manufacturing Consent: The Political Economy of the Mass Media*, New York: Pantheon 1988.

Works by Others

Daniel Brooks and Guillermo Verdecchia, *The Noam Chomsky Lectures: A Play*, Toronto: Coach House Press 1991.

BIBLIOGRAPHY

Werner Cohn, *The Hidden Alliances of Noam Chomsky*, New York: Americans for a Safe Israel 1988.

Konrad Koerner and Matsuji Tajima, with Carlos P. Otero, *Noam Chomsky: A Personal Bibliography 1951–1986*, Amsterdam: John Benjamins 1986.

Carlos P. Otero, ed., *Noam Chomsky: Critical Assessments*, Vol. III: *Anthropology*, two tomes, London: Routledge 1994.

Raphael Salkie, *The Chomsky Update*, London: Unwin Hyman 1990.

Geoffrey Sampson, *Liberty and Language*, Oxford: Oxford University Press 1979.

Peter Wintonick and Mark Achbar, *Manufacturing Consent: Noam Chomsky and the Media* (film and video), Montreal: Necessary Illusions 1993, available in Britain from Connoisseur Video, 10a Stephen Mews, London W1P OAX.

Audio-tapes and transcripts of Chomsky interviews and talks can be obtained from David Barsamian of Alternative Radio, 2129 Mapleton, Boulder, CO 80304, USA. According to Achbar, transcripts, audio-tapes and video-tapes can also be obtained from Roger Leisner of Radio Free Maine, PO Box 2705, Augusta, ME 04338, USA; and Turning the Tide, 35 Prospect Street, Bloomfield, CT 06001, USA.

Index

INDEX

Energetic
BODYWORK